THE SLOW RISE TO A GLOBAL WORLD

THE SLOW RISE TO A GLOBAL WORLD

First Edition

Steven Harris-Scott

George Mason University

Bassim Hamadeh, CEO and Publisher
Mazin Hassan, Acquisitions Editor
Tony Paese, Project Editor
Berenice Quirino, Associate Production Editor
Jess Estrella, Senior Graphic Designer
Danielle Gradisher, Licensing Associate
Natalie Piccotti, Director of Marketing
Kassie Graves, Vice President of Editorial
Jamie Giganti, Director of Academic Publishing

Copyright © 2019 by Cognella, Inc. All rights reserved. No part of this publication may be reprinted, reproduced, transmitted, or utilized in any form or by any electronic, mechanical, or other means, now known or hereafter invented, including photocopying, microfilming, and recording, or in any information retrieval system without the written permission of Cognella, Inc. For inquiries regarding permissions, translations, foreign rights, audio rights, and any other forms of reproduction, please contact the Cognella Licensing Department at rights@cognella.com.

Trademark Notice: Product or corporate names may be trademarks or registered trademarks, and are used only for identification and explanation without intent to infringe.

Cover image copyright© 2012 Depositphotos/javarman.

Printed in the United States of America.

ISBN: 978-1-5165-3815-7 (pbk) / 978-1-5165-3816-4 (br)

CONTENTS

INTRODUCTION   VII

UNIT I THE BEGINNINGS OF A TRULY GLOBAL WORLD, 1200–1500   1

Reading 1 The Mediterranean Basing Competition and Galley Warfare   3
   Robert E. Harkavy

Reading 2 The Ottoman Empire   16
   Daniel Goffman

Reading 3 The Globalization of Disease After 1450   33
   Sheldon Watts

Reading 4 African Traditional Religion, Nature, and Belief Systems   48
   Ibigbolade Simon Aderibigbe

Discussion Questions   63

UNIT II THE EMERGENCE OF A MODERN GLOBAL WORLD, 1500–1900   67

Reading 5 The Scientific Revolution   70
   Claudia Stein

Reading 6 From Pen to Print—A Revolution in Communications?   79
   Mark Knights and Angela McShane

Reading 7 Peter the Great and Westernization, 1689–1725   91
   John M. Thompson

Reading 8 New Causes   106
Peter N. Stearns

Reading 9 European Interests and Imperialism   116
Arthur Goldschmidt Jr. and Lawrence Davidson

Reading 10 The Rise of Nationalism   126
Arthur Goldschmidt Jr. and Lawrence Davidson

Reading 11 The Industrial Revolution Outside the West   141
Peter N. Stearns

Discussion Questions   154

UNIT III THE FIGHT FOR A MODERN GLOBAL WORLD, 1900–PRESENT   159

Reading 12 Recovery Through Nationalism   162
John E. Moser

Reading 13 The Chinese Civil War and European Cold War, 1945–9   176
Mark Chi-Kwan

Reading 14 The Cold War and Nationalism   185
Malcolm Anderson

Reading 15 Africa, Europe, and Asia in the Making of the 20th-Century Caribbean   196
Aisha Khan

Reading 16 Africa   209
Antony Best, Jussi M. Hanhimäki, and Joseph A. Maiolo

Reading 17 Cold War and Globalization   234
Bruce Mazlish

Discussion Questions   244

CONCLUSION   249

INTRODUCTION

Modern world history—encompassing both the early-modern period from around 1450 through 1750 and the modern period from 1750 onward—can be explained as a slow and steady march to a more globalized world, and this textbook certainly charts it that way. However, that is not the only way to describe the last six centuries of world history, and this textbook touches on other complex topics as well. For example, competition between states, nations, kingdoms, and empires over political, economic, and social forces occupies a lot of the story told within these pages. On the other hand, much of this textbook also charts the many destructive events that helped forge our modern, global world.

One important aspect of this textbook, using as it does the scholarship of other experts in a variety of historical subfields, is to cover some of the less-told parts of the story of world history that usually do not receive top billing in an introductory global history text. This certainly does not mean some of the old ground is not tread upon, but it is often covered in slightly different ways that are, I argue, somewhat novel. For instance, Venice, Genoa, and the Ottoman Empire are still competing in the early-modern Mediterranean world, but in this text we discuss their competition from a naval perspective, not a (purely) economic one. Early-modern Africa is also discussed, but from a religious point of view with slavery going unmentioned.

Modernity begins to slowly grip the world via the Scientific Revolution (not, the Scientific "Renaissance") and the European Enlightenment—both of which are, of course, still important, but discussed in unique ways in this text. Industrialization is crucial but interrogated critically. The Global Great Depression is broached but from the perspective of the future Axis powers—not the Allies. Nationalism plays a big part in this textbook, but the focus is on twentieth-century superpowers, not nineteenth-century European powers. China's Civil War has important Cold War ramifications in this textbook and is simultaneously affected by that budding global struggle. Modern Africa and the Caribbean still have many recognizable issues, but their dynamism is also included. Finally, when modern globalization is achieved, it is for myriad reasons—cold wars and hot wars, economic instabilities and expansions, rivalries and collapses, diversity and nationalism—and it is treated with appropriate complexity. If this book does anything, it is hopefully to exemplify the modern world's complexity by offering that complexity in digestible portions designed with an introductory global history course in mind.

As such, this book is divided into three units corresponding to three chronologically significant components of the early-modern and modern world. The first covers the first half or so of the early-modern period, namely from the 1200s through the 1500s. This unit touches on Venice, Genoa, the Ottoman Empire, the immediate post-Contact Americas, and early-modern Africa. The second unit begins around 1500 with the Scientific Revolution and ends around 1900 with the uneven spread of industrialization and the growth of nationalism in the Middle East. Also dealt with in the second section are the technological advances that made the European Enlightenment and Industrial Revolution possible. Finally, the third unit charts the twentieth (and into the twenty-first) century, from economic downturns to superpower nationalism, the Chinese Civil War to the modern Caribbean and Africa, concluding with the full emergence of modern globalization itself.

UNIT I

THE BEGINNINGS OF A TRULY GLOBAL WORLD, 1200–1500

Introduction

Although much of world history can be explained through competition between states, nations, kingdoms, and empires, the period of the fourteenth, fifteenth, and sixteenth centuries following the Black Death pandemic in Eurasia were especially notable for that competition. This unit explores that competition through the following lenses: Venice, Genoa, and the Ottoman Empire in the Mediterranean; the Ottomans in Europe and Europeans in the Ottoman Empire; the Spanish and other Europeans, Africans, their diseases, and the Native Americans; and finally, competition between religions in Africa.

First, on the main western edge of the massive Afro-Eurasian trading network of the early-modern period lay the Italian city-states of Venice and Genoa, who engaged in a maritime rivalry that rarely but occasionally broke out into open warfare. The ultimate goal was supremacy over the Mediterranean portion of the vast trading network connecting southern Europe to India and China. As Robert E. Harkavy explains in "The Mediterranean Basing Competition and Galley Warfare," neither Venice nor Genoa was able to gain dominance for long before the Ottoman Empire rose to prominence. By 1500, the Ottomans were the top naval power in the Mediterranean, although Spain soon challenged them. Regardless, the focus of major power naval competition had moved out of the Mediterranean by then in favor of the Atlantic and Indian Oceans.

More crucially, the Ottoman Empire had a dramatic impact on the development of Europe during the 1400s and 1500s, as Daniel Goffman charts in his chapter, "The Ottoman Empire." Lately, historians have mostly deemphasized the importance of the "European Renaissance" by correctly noting that many places experienced a rebirth such as the Ottomans in Turkey and the Middle East and the Ming in China. Goffman argues that Renaissance Europeans viewed the Turks with both foreboding and fascination—foreboding because of the Muslim powers' expansionism and fascination because the Ottomans were able to create the large, successful empire of which many European rulers of that day dreamed. In particular, Goffman desires to bring the Ottoman Empire into European and Mediterranean history on an equal or even greater footing, as opposed to being purely an antagonist to European growth.

When Western Europeans did venture out beyond their known world—due in large part to the strength of the Ottoman Empire—they brought with them a powerful, albeit largely unknown, ally: Eurasian diseases. In "The Globalization of Disease after 1450," Sheldon Watts describes most of Eurasia and North Africa as a single, unified disease zone by the mid-fifteenth century. Therefore, when Europeans and Africans arrived in the Americas, malaria, smallpox, typhus, influenza, and measles had already been endemic in the Eastern Hemisphere for centuries. This fact proved disastrous for the Native American populations that experienced "first Contacts" with Europeans and Africans during the 1500s, 1600s, and 1700s. Due to a lack of domesticated animals in the Americas, the American disease environment had not equipped the indigenous peoples to fight off these new diseases, and as such, indigenous populations declined by up to 90% within only a few generations. Arguably, no single event has had more of an effect on the course of world history than that.

Finally, Ibigbolade Simon Aderibigbe provides a short overview of the indigenous religions of the African people in "African Traditional Religion, Nature, and Belief Systems," in part due to how often it is parodied by Western audiences. This is particularly important in the context of world history because the religious beliefs of African captives were brought to the Americas as part of the Atlantic Slave Trade before Christianity or Islam had made significant incursions into the continent. Especially notable is how many elements of the African Traditional Beliefs mirror those of other world religions, such as the belief in a supreme being with multiple minor divinities below that supreme being—akin to bodhisattvas in Buddhism and saints in Catholicism.

The Mediterranean Basing Competition and Galley Warfare

Venice, Genoa, Ottoman Empire, Spain, c.1200–1600

Robert E. Harkavy

Telescoping both the Mongol/Ming China maritime expansion and basing acquisitions between about 1270 and 1410 in Southeast Asia and the Indian Ocean and Portugal's elaboration of a closer-to-global basing network in the sixteenth century, was the some four-century long (1200–1600) battle for colonies, bases, commercial access and maritime supremacy in the Mediterranean involving first Venice and Genoa, then the Ottoman Empire and Spain, amounting at times to a complex quadripolar struggle over access and influence which, to a lesser degree, involved France as well. Venice, indeed, largely dominated the Mediterranean for more than two centuries to the extent it is sometimes mentioned in "long cycle"[1] treatises as an early prototype maritime hegemon, an early example of the interplay between commercial and maritime dominance, albeit its small size and incapacity to field large armies and to dominate more than a small corner of Europe.

And, surely, neither Venice, Genoa nor the Ottoman Empire was a global maritime power, rather, regional ones (Spain's ventures in the Mediterranean were somewhat of a sideshow to its vast expansion of colonies and bases in the western hemisphere and Asia). But, Venice's reach did go beyond the Mediterranean Sea, what with navy bases around the Black Sea, and a reach for its galley fleets extending to England and the Spanish Netherlands in Bruges and Antwerp (Belgium).[2] The Ottoman Empire, while extending its basing access network westward in the Mediterranean almost to the Straits of Gibraltar, also had maritime outlets in the Red Sea/Persian Gulf area, making it a double-window maritime power analogous to later France with its windows on the Atlantic and Mediterranean coasts.[3]

Robert E. Harkavy, "The Mediterranean Basing Competition and Galley Warfare: Venice, Genoa, Ottoman Empire, Spain, c. 1200-1600," *Strategic Basing & Great Powers, 1200-2000*, pp. 32-43, 256-257. Copyright © 2007 by Taylor & Francis Group. Reprinted with permission.

The competition for access in the Mediterranean involved a shifting of tides between rival states. Their basing access often overlapped, geographically speaking. Aside perhaps from the early period of Venetian ascendance, there was no fully unipolar maritime dominance. Nor was there an analogy to the separate and coexisting Portuguese and Spanish empires, which were clearly demarcated. There was incessant warfare and changing of control over basing points, hence, no analogy to the Cold War, with its slowly shifting tides of influence and access, but without actual fighting. The best analogy would be to the later British–French–Dutch–Spanish competition over naval access in the Caribbean, Africa and in South and Southeast Asia, albeit on a much smaller geographical scale. This was the period of galley fleets and warfare; hence, short radii of naval operations, longer times for naval movements, more challenging logistical problems in provisioning fleets and sustaining external garrisons.[4] In a way, it was a microcosm of future European maritime rivalries.

The expansion of the Venetian maritime and commercial empire, held together by an elaborate string of naval bases, *points d'appui* and control of commercial quarters of major entrepôts, began at the outset of the thirteenth century (note this was about 70 or 80 years before Mongol maritime expansion in the Far East). The expansion took place rather rapidly, beginning early on in the first decade of the thirteenth century in Corfu, Candia (Crete), Rhodes, Modon, Coron and Negroponte in Greece, Famagusta in Cyprus and Constantinople (well more than two centuries before its capture by the Ottomans).

Later in the thirteenth century, Venice's reach would be extended to Soldaia (Romania), Tana (Ukraine) and Trebizond (Turkey) on the Black Sea; a bit later to Ragusa (Yugoslavia) on the Adriatic Sea,[5] to Lajazzo (Turkey) in the eastern Mediterranean, Acre (Israel), Tyre (Lebanon), Moron (Greece); still later in the fourteenth century to Tenedos (Greece), Scutari (Yugoslavia), Beirut (Lebanon), Treviso (Yugoslavia), Smyrna (Turkey), Pola (Yugoslavia), Ibiza (Spain), and others. In the first-named group were major bases for galley fleets used to intimidate other navies and to protect commerce.

Genoa's basing network, smaller than that of Venice, was elaborated almost 50 years later, beginning around 1250. Its major points of access, entrepôts and commercial control (also often small colonies devoted to commerce) were in Acre and Tyre, Chios (Greece), Cyprus, Trebizond (Turkey), Tana (Ukraine), Porto Longo (Greece), Dalmatia, Rhodes and Famagusta.[6]

Constantinople's harbor was shared with Venice; so too access to Pera, Trebizond and Tana, at least during periods of peace between the two Italian city-state maritime powers. The Mediterranean was mostly a Venetian and Genoese lake for 200 years or more in the thirteenth, fourteenth and part of the fifteenth centuries.

Also noteworthy during the period of Venetian, and then Genoese, maritime expansion was the close relationship between naval power and competition, and commercial rivalry. The latter was what it was all about: trade routes, entrepôts, carrying trade, etc. This maritime and commercial competition was also related to a degree of colonization, hence, portending the later Portuguese, Spanish, Dutch and British empires, but on a much small scale. In Constantinople, Acre, Tyre, Lajazzo, etc., the main Venetian and Genoese bases and entrepôts, small commercial colonies, really foreign enclaves, were set up on a long-term basis. In some of these ports around the eastern Mediterranean, Aegean and Black seas, Venetian and Genoese colonies, at least during peaceful interludes, coexisted side-by-side in a kind of peaceful competition. Both assisted the Crusaders (Pisa was also involved in this commercial and maritime competition, for instance, in Romania).

However well before the Ottoman Empire and Spain became major factors in the Mediterranean competition for bases, territories and commercial access, Venice and Genoa periodically went to war, so that their competition was a deadly one. There were, actually, five major wars between the two city-state maritime powers: 1258–1270, 1295–1299, 1350–1355, 1378–1381 and in 1431.[7] This maritime rivalry extended over some 175 years, and as such, might be viewed as similar to the equally very lengthy maritime competition between England and France in the eighteenth and nineteenth centuries. The situation in which Venice and Genoa, in between fighting, often shared basing points and entrepôts was repeated by England, the Netherlands, and France in India a few centuries later. The latter colonial powers, with mixed commercial and territorial motives, also had a long history of wars "beyond the line," but with colonies and bases cheek by jowl, and with intermittent fighting. There is a marked contrast here with the Cold War pattern of rival basing networks, few if any colonies, minimal commercial rivalry and no warfare.

Trade routes to China and India were also bound up in the competition for bases in the eastern Mediterranean and Black Sea areas between Venice and Genoa. One route to China went through Constantinople and across the Black Sea to the Crimea (Soldaia, Kaffa),[8] on to Tana in the north Caucasus, and then on through territories controlled by the Mongols towards China. Another went from Constantinople to Trebizond on Turkey's Black Sea coast[9] then to Tabriz in Persia, and then either to Ormuz and on to India or to China via Bukhara. Still another route went to Cyprus and then to Lajazzo (near modern-day Alexandretta) and hence to Tabriz and on to India or China. More southerly routes went through Alexandria, Cairo, on to Jidda, and to Aden, and then India. Maritime competition between Venice and Genoa in the Mediterranean and Black Sea concerned all of these alternative trade routes.

To begin with, Venice had to establish control of its own bailiwick in the Adriatic Sea. Hence, according to Lane:

> In medieval Europe, no navy exercised a cut-and-dried command over any extended body of water, but the Venetians very nearly did so in the Adriatic. Their patrols on the rivers and off the mouths of the rivers were reinforced as need be by fleets of galleys strong enough and fast enough to suppress all opposition. The boost given Venetian naval power by the conquest of Constantinople made the Venetians feel more responsible for the suppression of piracy, especially in the Adriatic. Every year, not only in time of war but as a routine measure, they outfitted a fleet of galleys devoted to making the seas safe. Naturally it accompanied the merchant ships going to Apulia and Romania and used the Dalmatian cities, especially Ragusa, as

subordinate bases. A separate squadron for the protection of commerce in the Gulf was felt necessary in 1330. Frequently thereafter it was patrolled by a Captain of the Gulf, while the main war fleet was operating in the Aegean or Beyond-the-Sea.[10]

Control over the Mediterranean was, however, not possible. There was not a possibility of establishing what later would be recognized as a "Mahanian" command of the sea, requiring the naval hegemon to have the ability to sweep the enemy from the seas, as later Portugal, the Netherlands, Great Britain and the U.S. were able for the most part to do. Further, according to Lane:

> Neither Venice nor any of her rivals was able to sweep the enemy from the seas. They lacked the technical means of setting up effective blockades. Trade moved, or could move, by short hops through many alternative routes. Vessels were not built and rigged so that they could patrol off a port indefinitely in variable weather to the extent that the British did at the end of the eighteenth century. War fleets had even more difficulty finding an enemy who wished to avoid battle than Lord Nelson had when he crossed the Atlantic twice in search of Napoleon's fleet. And even after an overwhelming victory, the winner was unable to blockade effectively the enemy city. He could not prevent the defeated from sending out a new fleet, even if only a very small one, for a quick raid on an exposed point or an attack on merchant shipping.[11]

The Venetian basing system outside the Adriatic was gradually developed beginning in the early thirteenth century. The most important bases were those related to two streams of trade; one to "Romania" (the Greek Peninsula, Aegean Islands, neighboring land that had been part of the Byzantine Empire); the other referred to as "Beyond-the-Sea" (Cyprus, Syria and Palestine). The main base for at least the first of these streams was Constantinople, where a large Venetian colony developed in the thirteenth century. There were other important colonies/bases related to trade: Corinth, which was a center of trade for the Pelo ponnesus;[12] and Solaia, on the eastern coast of the Crimea from which grain, salt, fish, furs and slaves were exported to Constantinople.

On the critical route between Venice and Constantinople, the main subsidiary bases were Ragusa (Yugoslavia) on the Adriatic, Modon and Coron in southern Greece, and Negroponte on the Greek Aegean coast. Negroponte was the main base in the Aegean between Crete and Constantinople. Modon and Coron, near the southern tip of Morea, became known as the "two eyes of the Republic," where all ships returning from the Levant were ordered to stop and give news of convoys and pirates.[13] Ragusa on the Adriatic was a loyal dependency and a base for fleets operating out of the end of the Adriatic.

In the second main trade route, after rounding the southernmost part of Greece, convoys went to Candia on Crete, perhaps to Rhodes, and on to Cyprus and then to St. Jean d'Acre north of Haifa, where a road then led to Safed and Damascus (here was the remnant of the Crusader Kingdom of Jerusalem after the fall of Jerusalem itself). Both Acre and nearby Tyre, as with the cases of Constantinople and Corinth, had large Venetian colonies with a considerable industrial and commercial infrastructure.

One reason, however, that it was difficult for a galley-based fleet then to achieve complete control of the sea was the slow speed of power projection. For example, it took almost two months for a galley fleet to move from Venice to Constantinople.[14] And there was a seasonal nature to this; as winter storms had to be avoided. Typically, Venetian "caravans" (commercial fleets accompanied by galley warships) left in the spring and returned in the fall, or left in August, wintered in the eastern Mediterranean, and returned in the spring. Hence, there was a very slow reaction time for military actions in an era of slow long-distance communications.

Almost all of the main base areas were also important producers of commodities that Venice developed as part of its carrying trade. Crete was an important producer of grain, wine, oil and fruits. From Romania came raw silk, alum, wax, honey, cotton and wine. As would still later be the case for the Portuguese and Dutch empires, bases and entrepôts were nearly inseparable and naval power was closely related to commercial competition (and colonization) in an era when commerce raiding was a normal part of conflict between nations and empires. For the first half of the thirteenth century, Venice maintained a near unipolar maritime dominance in the Mediterranean and the Black Sea, in the period of the Crusaders, the faded Byzantine Empire, Arab might in the core Middle East, and a bit before the zenith of the burgeoning Mongol Empire. Europe itself was in its Dark Age, politically fragmented, before the development of more centralized monarchies in France and Spain, much less Germany.

In the middle of the thirteenth century, Genoa became a rival naval power to Venice, and for more than a century, in a context of complex diplomacy among multiple political centers, there was a form of maritime bipolarity in the Mediterranean/Black Sea region. Central to this struggle, highlighted by five wars punctuating long periods of peace, was the contest over basing access and colonies. This was despite the fact that both Venice and Genoa were Guelf (as opposed to Ghibelline), that is, siding with the Pope rather than the Holy Roman Emperor.

By the mid-thirteenth century, the Genoese were as well entrenched as the Venetians in Acre and Tyre, and more active in Syria, all due to their assistance to the Crusaders. The first war between Venice and Genoa was caused by a series of incidents in Acre. It was won by Venice, which made good use of Crete as a forward base of operation. Genoa made extensive use of Salonika as a base during this war,[15] which saw Venetian victories in main fleet engagements at Acre in 1258, at Sittepozzi in 1263 and at Trapani in 1266. It also made use of Malta for attacking Venetian convoys in the lower Adriatic and Aegean seas.

Despite losing the first naval war to Venice, Genoa greatly increased its power in the latter part of the thirteenth century. It decisively defeated Pisa in 1284, leading to complete naval dominance of the Tyrrhenian Sea. Genoa maintained a large presence at Pena in the Constantinople harbor. Its base at Kaffa on the northern shore of the Black Sea enabled penetration into the Crimea and up the rivers of southern Russia, i.e., the Don and Dnieper. Other Genoese bases and commercial centers were at Chios (famed for mastic) and Focea (near modern Izmir), known for its aluminum mines.

Around 1291, the Mamluks wiped out the last remnants of the Kingdom of Jerusalem, as Acre, Tyre and Tripoli fell to the Muslims. After that, Lajazzo became the main Venetian base and entrepôt in Asia Minor.[16]

In the second Venice–Genoa war in the 1290s, Venice first captured and destroyed Genoese possessions in Cyprus. But Genoa, operating out of Pena, completely defeated the Venetians off Lajazzo. Venetian fleets attacked Genoese strongholds at Pera, Focea and Kaffa. Genoa also won a large naval battle in the Adriatic off the coast of Dalmatia, near the island of Curzola. Later, Venice attacked Genoa itself, utilizing a nearby base in Monaco. The war ended in 1299, essentially as a stalemate, further enmeshed in Guelph vs. Ghibelline rivalries juxtaposed to those between city-states, particularly involving internecine fighting among the Genoans.[17]

A third war between Venice and Genoa occurred in the 1320s. This war started over disagreements over the use of Tana by both sides, which were driven out by the Golden Horde. In 1328, Venice sent a big fleet into the Black Sea, interrupting trade between Kaffa and Pera. Otherwise, there were extensive naval battles and commerce raiding throughout the eastern Mediterranean, Aegean and Black seas. Venice (allied with the Catalans) suffered a big defeat at Porto Longo, Genoa a defeat at Alghero. Venice made extensive use of its base on Crete for operations toward Constantinople. This was an example of a war between rival major naval powers whose bases were interspersed within the same general area (what might have been if the U.S. and USSR had ever engaged in a naval war).

Venice suffered some defeats in the mid-fourteenth century that whittled away at its basing structure. It was pushed out of Dalmatia by the King of Hungary, though its fleet still ruled the Adriatic. Genoa took over the Cyprus port of Famagusta.

Venice's naval reach also extended to Europe's Atlantic coast. Galley fleets went back and forth to Bruges.[18] Despite the loss of Famagusta to Genoa, Venetian fleets still went directly to Beirut and Alexandria; and hence, Venice controlled the spice route to India via Egypt and Syria, but Genoa also competed vigorously for trade in the Levant.

Venice and Genoa bitterly contested trade and maritime dominance to and in and around the Black Sea. They shared access to Constantinople. They contested over the island of Tenedos south of the Turkish Straits; Venetian occupation and fortification of Tenedos led to war.

In the 1420s and 1430s, there was further conflict between Venice and Genoa, in the context of a then growing threat from the Ottoman Empire. In 1424, Venice sent a fleet to Salonika, but it was later lost.[19] (At this juncture, Venice was bogged down in wars on the Italian Peninsula, mostly versus Milan.) In 1431, Venice unsuccessfully attacked Chios, Genoa's main base in the Aegean. In 1453, the Turks captured Constantinople and then, feeling a Turkish threat to Italy, in the Peace of Lodi in 1454, an alliance was formed of Venice, Genoa, Naples, the Papal State and Milan. Venice was then still the strongest state in Italy and still a formidable naval power in the Adriatic, Aegean and eastern Mediterranean. But now, a larger and more formidable foe loomed. And so ended what was a some 200-year contest for basing access, naval supremacy and commercial dominance between Venice and Genoa. Perhaps only the later hegemonic naval rivalry between Britain and France lasted so long.

In the late fifteenth century, and encouraged by the Pope, the Italian city-states were mostly allied together against the Ottomans, though some at various times were allied with them, so there were continuing tensions among the Italian states. And gradually, the Turks expanded, first by land in Albania. In 1470, the Ottomans took Negroponte, long a Venetian main base. And, Turkish cavalry raided Dalmatia and Frioli, not far from Venice. In 1479, Venice admitted defeat in a 16-year war, conceding Negroponte and some other Aegean islands, and also the Albanian fortress of Scutari. Shortly thereafter, the Turks took Otranto on the Italian heel. On the other hand, Venice was able to establish greater control over Cyprus. But by this juncture, Venetian naval power had passed its zenith, even as the city-state's influence in Italy itself was maintained.

This zenith of Venetian power coincided with the onset of a whole new era of power politics in Europe. In 1494, France invaded Italy to back up its claim on the Kingdom of Naples. Venice organized a counter-coalition involving some Italian states, the German emperor and the King of Spain. England, meanwhile, was a counterbalance to France. Amidst all this, Venice tried to keep a dominant position in Italy and to maintain naval dominance in the Mediterranean. In a complicated set of maneuvers, Venice occupied key cities in Apulia in 1495, helped to drive the French out of Naples, persuaded cities such as Otranto and Brindisi to help man Venetian fleets, supported Pisa against Florence, then allied with the new French king.

But, Venice was overstretched in trying to be both a land- and sea-power. And at this point, the Ottoman Empire launched a sustained offensive against the Venetian maritime empire.[20] In 1479, a big Ottoman fleet went into the Ionian Sea, capturing the main Venetian strongholds in Greece, including Modon and Coron, the "two eyes of the Republic," which Venice had controlled since 1204, for almost 300 years. Dalmatia and Frioli were raided. In 1503, Venice made peace by surrendering numerous strongpoints in Greece and Albania, adding to those lost in 1479 (Samothrace, Imbros, Lembros). But at this time, closer to home, it acquired Trieste. But in 1509, the League of Cambrai (France, the German emperor, the Pope, the King of Hungary, the Duke of Savoy, the King of Spain), wanting to repel the Turks, also threatened to dismember the Venetian empire. Venice, via alliance diplomacy, eventually regained all of its mainland territories after a seven-year war, after the Pope and the King of Spain changed sides and then later Venice allied with France.

But Venice was losing its long-held maritime predominance. The Ottomans conquered Syria and Egypt in 1517, then Rhodes in 1522.[21] Then, under the leadership of the red-bearded Khaireddin, the Ottomans took over the Barbary coast including Algiers by 1529. By that time, the Ottoman Empire had acquired strongholds all around the Mediterranean, from Greece and Albania, to Egypt (Suez) and Syria, and to Algeria. Cyprus would be added much later in 1591. So, in the period between the capture of Constantinople in 1453 and the important base at Negroponte in 1470, up to 1529, the Turks became a dominant naval power in the

Mediterranean, reducing Venice to a second class seapower after a 300-year plus reign as maritime hegemon.

The Ottoman Empire was actually a "two-sea" naval power, as France later would be in the Atlantic and the Mediterranean. It had major bases at Jidda on the Red Sea and at Aden, from around 1516, and another sometime later at Basra at the head of the Persian Gulf. From these bases it was to contest, however unsuccessfully, Portuguese naval expansion in the Indian Ocean.

During the time the Ottoman Empire was expanding its basing network in the Mediterranean in the late fifteenth and sixteenth centuries (mostly at the expense of Venice, and with Genoa's naval power and its bases by then nearly having evaporated), Spain, from the other end of the Mediterranean, was beginning to expand its basing network in the "Middle Sea." Indeed, this occurred simultaneously with Spain's development of an empire in the western hemisphere centered on the Caribbean and the South American littoral on the Pacific Coast (Havana and Kingston, for instance, became Spanish outposts in 1511 and 1509, respectively), and also at the same time as Portuguese expansion into the Indian Ocean region. Spain was, of course, approaching the apogee of its hegemonic power which, arguably, was reached later in the sixteenth century up to the defeat of the Armada by Britain in 1588. Referring to Spain in the Mediterranean during the early sixteenth century, Lane states that (relative to the Ottoman Empire) "only through Spanish and Habsburg leadership was a naval power of possibly countervailing strength developed in those same decades."

Spain during this period actually used a lot of Italian ships and seamen, particularly after it acquired Sicily. It captured Naples in 1501–1503 and took the Apulian ports from Venice. In 1505 too, Spain's campaign along the North African coast netted the important strongholds of Mers El Kebir (much later a French base), Oran, Mostaganem, Tenes, Bougie and Algiers. In 1519, the Hapsburg who was to become Emperor Charles V inherited the Spanish throne, so he combined the power of Spain, the Holy Roman Empire, and a claim on Milan and other resources in Germany and the Netherlands. In 1535 his forces attacked Tunis (Galeta) with a huge fleet and also took Malta, which was given to the Knights of St. John, whom the Turks had driven out of Rhodes.[22]

Venice, in the early sixteenth century, a declining power in the Mediterranean, was forced to steer a tortuous course between burgeoning Ottoman and Spanish power. In the sixteenth century, it twice aligned with Spain and the Hapsburgs against the Turks. In the first of those wars the Christian coalition suffered a humiliating defeat at Prevesa. In the second in 1570–1573, the Christian coalition led by Spain's Philip II, won a major victory (albeit with inconclusive political ramifications) against the Ottomans at Lepanto. Due to fear of Spain, Venice made a separate peace with the Turks in 1540 after Prevesa.[23] At that time, Venice lost the last of its possessions in the Aegean north of Crete.

In 1571, as noted, the Christian coalition led by the Hapsburg prince, Don John of Austria, won a famous victory that halted the expansion of Ottoman naval power. Venice was able to retain, as a result, its position at Zante, Corfu and the Dalmatian coast, but it had to give up Cyprus. Venice's naval power had declined dramatically since the period in the 1420s of the Milanese wars and the demise of rival Genoa. Indeed, by the time of Lepanto, what had been—as measured by fleet naval power and basing structure—a naval rivalry over Mediterranean hegemony between Venice and Genoa, had slowly transitioned into a rivalry between the two major powers, Spain and the Ottoman Empire, both of whose domains spread way beyond the Mediterranean. The former controlled most of the western Mediterranean and the latter the eastern Mediterranean, with the North African coast becoming a focus of military rivalry along with Malta, Sicily and the lower Italian coast.

There was an additional factor here. France, rival to the Habsburgs, and despite its Christian identity, allied for a while with the Ottomans. During the period 1570–1573, France was granted some of the trade in the Levant. In turn, France allowed the Ottomans to use Marseille as a base (earlier, the Ottomans had had access to Toulon), somewhat outflanking the Venetians.[24]

But after the 1470s, the focus of major power naval competition moved out of the Mediterranean to the oceanic waters of the Atlantic and Indian oceans.

Summary

The basing competition in the Mediterranean in the four centuries between 1204 and the 1570s has some obvious characteristics that bear noting, particularly in comparison to the later imperial-colonial era and that of the Cold War. Those characteristics include polarity (as applied to basing structures if not overall power rankings); the degree to which basing structures are separate or, alternatively, interspersed, the degree to which bases serve commercial as well as security functions; the basis for base acquisitions in conquest and colonization versus merely via diplomacy; the extent to which actual warfare resulted in the altering of the basing access equation i.e., the matter of "pick-off," and the roots of the location, uses and number of bases in extant technologies, in this case overwhelmingly involving traditional galley warfare.

As noted, the some 400-year-long competition for bases (and associated garrisons, colonies, entrepôts) in the Mediterranean from Venice's initial expansion to the era of Lepanto first involved a lengthy bipolar naval competition between Venice and Genoa, then as the latter faded, a competition between the former and the Ottoman Empire, and then what slowly evolved into a bipolar competition between the latter and Spain, with Venice a remnant fading factor. This was a regional form of bipolarity in an era well before the development of a global system, and where at the time of the rivalry between the two Italian city-states, the much larger Mongol Empire (and later the Golden Horde of Tamerlane) dominated the Eurasian landmass. At the end of this period, the bipolar competition between Spain and the Ottoman Empire more closely resembled a more broadly based bipolarity, also at a time when France and Austria (the latter linked by dynastic ties to Spain) were also major powers.

The maritime empires of Venice and Genoa were interspersed, cheek by jowl, wherein periods of cooperation and co-location of colonies and commercial zones gave rise to periodic bouts of warfare which involved a zero-sum competition for bases in the eastern Mediterranean, Aegean and Black seas. Later, the basing networks of the Ottoman Empire and Spain would mostly be concentrated at the opposite ends of the Mediterranean, with a zone of conflict roughly in the middle. In both of these telescoped competitions, there was frequent warfare resulting in base "pick-offs" for the winners, usually subject to diplomatic negotiations at the close of hostilities.

This was certainly an era throughout which saw the coexistence of security and economic entrepôts functions for distant bases. Both the fleets of Genoa and Venice combined commerce and naval firepower—much of the work of both navies consisted of protection of convoys all over the Mediterranean and Black seas and (in the case of Venice) to England and Flanders. Commercial colonies were co-located with naval bases in the Levant, Cyprus, Crete, Constantinople and in several Black Sea ports such as Tana, which abutted onto the territory of the Golden Horde. Indeed, it was commercial advantage which was what the naval competition was largely about (later, in the Cold War, perhaps only Marxists would so interpret the U.S.–Soviet competition for basing access). The entrepôt function of bases would, of course, also be a prominent feature of the subsequent Portuguese, French, Dutch and British empires. However, the competition between Spain and the Ottoman Empire seems much less subject to an economic interpretation; rather, religious ideology and more purely security concerns were involved. Hence, there was somewhat of a model for the much later Cold War.

The galley warfare in the Mediterranean up to Lepanto, and its relation to bases, involves a number of characteristics that set it apart from the later age of oceanic empires, even aside from the small scale involved, though that is a major point. Guillmartin in his excellent treatise, *Gunpowder and Galleys*, makes the point about what he refers to as "the Mahanian Fallacy," claiming that Mahan's dicta were not relevant to the earlier Mediterranean system.[25] Mahan's emphasis was on sea control, on destroying the enemy's fleet in battle, after which destruction of the enemy's seaborne commerce would follow automatically. His two major emphases, hence, were seapower and control of the sea. What the French called "guerre de course," somewhat the weapon of the weak ("asymmetric war" in modern parlance) was seen as a waste of resources and effort, at best a sideline. But as Guillmartin points out, Mahan's dogmas were not valid in the Mediterranean system of the sixteenth century, the climax of the era of galley warfare. According to him, galleys, by their very nature, could not effect control of the sea. Particularly, galleys could not conduct year-round blockades.

Galleys were very much dependent on fortified ports, on bases. Hence, as Guillmartin says, "it would be no exaggeration to characterize the nature of sixteenth century, Mediterranean warfare at seas as a symbiotic relationship between the seaside fortress, more particularly the fortified port, and the war galley."[26] But, radii of action of the galley and galley fleets were very restricted relative to sailing ships because of their large required manpower and their needs for space and provisions. Hence, "the size of the galley's crew, the crucial military importance of their health and vigor and the severe limitations on storage space aboard specialized rowing vessels limit severely the galley's radius of action and ... tie it tightly to its bases."[27] Oarsmen, water and provisions were available only in limited quantities. The main point: the radius of action of galley fleets was restricted by logistics factors and was an inverse function of the size of the fleet or squadron involved. Hence, all sides engaged in "little wars" of economic attrition, *guerre de course*, and the seizing of strategic bases for what was constant raiding. As noted, Spain developed a chain of bases along the northern Mediterranean coast from Gibraltar to Messina, and in the Balearics and Sardinia. The Venetians in their heyday, had numerous fortified ports down the eastern coast of the Adriatic, around the Morea, in Crete, Cyprus and around the Black Sea. The Ottomans created similar chains of bases both on the north and south coasts of the Mediterranean.

All the major contending powers based small galley fleets forward from their homelands. Venice had small galley fleets at Canea on Crete, and in Cyprus and Constantinople; Spain had a considerable galley fleet in Messina.

One other point bears mention. Sustaining a large galley fleet, particularly for a major expedition, required logistical support, manpower reserves, and critical specialized facilities such as shipyards, arsenals, powder mills, and ovens for baking ships' biscuits in requisite quantities. The latter was a major logistical consideration. These requirements for a logistical base capable of supporting a major operation could only be satisfied by a major port city with a first-rate harbor and a rich hinterland and a well-developed trading network to support it. According to Guillmartin, only three cities on the Mediterranean fully accommodated these criteria;[28] Barcelona, Venice and Constantinople, not coincidentally representing the three major naval powers of the period. Alexandria and Salonika were said not quite to qualify. Others said to be backed by lesser economic resources or less government interest were Seville, Malaga, Marseilles, Genoa, Toulon, Algiers, Naples, Messina and Smyrna, though they could all act as forward bases for major expeditions. Genoa, of course, had earlier rivaled Venice.

Seasonal factors also played a role. The Mediterranean campaigning season was short, from mid-March to mid-October. Galley fleets could only go limited distances before needing to get home to beat the advent of winter, and this was particularly problematic if a lengthy siege to reduce an opponent's seaside fortress was desired.[29] As noted by Guillmartin, "the Ottoman fleet which recaptured Tunis in 1574 left Istanbul on 15 May and returned in November," with about five weeks' journey in both directions, leaving just over three months for effective military action. He sees this as indicating the limits on long-range power projection of a sixteenth century galley fleet for an operation conducted about 1000 miles away from the home base.

The contest for forward bases closer to the foe's center of gravity for purposes of power projection was fought back and forth by Spain and the Ottomans. Spain, on the defensive at the height of Ottoman power, had to worry about a range of possibilities, including capture of a port in Spain itself. Malta was particularly critical—"close enough to the Ottoman sources of naval power to permit a strong and sustained attack upon it, yet close enough to the Spanish sphere of influence to be a serious threat to Spain in Turkish hands." La Goleta, the island fortress in Tunis harbor, was also a concern, and Spanish naval forces there were enhanced. Port Mahon on Minorca in the Balearics was also a concern, but for Spain, less worrisome because of its nearness to the homeland (allowing for a relief operation), and so far from the Ottomans' home base that a siege could only be a short one. Likewise, for the same reason, there was less of a concern about the Spaniards' bases at Oran and Mazarquimir on the North African coast. Meanwhile, for economic as well as security reasons, Spain based as many galleys as possible in its Italian possessions such as Messina in Sicily.

Venice also forward-based galleys, is this case forward in the eastern Mediterranean to protect a shrinking colonial empire, to protect its wheat supplies from the Aegean islands, and to counter-threaten Ottoman bases. In the big battle at Lepanto, Venice itself contributed 61 galleys and eight galleases, Candia 18 galleys, Canea eight (both in Crete), Retino three, Corfu three, Cefalonia two, Zente two, and one each from Lesina, Quero, Veglia Capo de Istria, Cataro, Padua, Bergamo, Arbe and Brescia. Hence, by 1570, Crete, Corfu and a couple of smaller Greek bases were all that was left of a once more formidable forward presence.

Notes

1. See George Modelski and William R. Thompson, *Leading Sectors and World Powers: The Coevolution of Global Politics and Economics* (Columbia: University of South Carolina Press, 1996), Table 8.5, p. 137.

2. Frederick C. Lane, *Venice* (Baltimore: Johns Hopkins Press, 1973), p. 126.

3. G.V. Scammell, *The First Imperial Age: European Overseas Expansion c.1400–1715* (London: Unwin Hyman, 1989), p. 15.

4. A good general work on Mediterranean galley warfare is John F. Guilmartin, *Gunpowder and Galleys* (Cambridge: Cambridge University Press, 1974).

5. Frederick C. Lane, op. cit., pp. 128–132; and Peter Padfield, *Tides of Empires*, Vol. 1 (London: Routledge and Kegan Paul, 1979), Chapter 3 under "Mediterranean Centre."

6. Lane, op. cit., pp. 13–80, 174–179; and Padfield, Vol. 1, Chapter 3.

7. Lane, op. cit., especially Chapter 7 and 14.

8. See the map in Lane, *Venice*, op. cit., p. 71 and also pp. 128–129, 174–175. 9 Ibid.

9. Ibid.

10. Ibid., pp. 68–69.

11. Ibid., p. 68.

12. Ibid., p. 177.

13. Ibid., p. 43.

14 Ibid., p. 70.

15 Ibid., pp. 73–75.

16 Ibid., pp. 82–85.

17 Ibid., pp. 174–179.

18 Ibid., pp. 126–128.

19 Ibid., pp. 228–231.

20 Ibid., chapter 16, pp. 288, 349.

21 Padfield, *Tide of Empire*, Vol. 1, op. cit., pp. 88–95.

22 Padfield, op. cit., pp. 88–89, for discussion of the battle of Goleta.

23 Ibid., pp. 91–95, for discussion of the battle of Prevesa.

24 Ibid., p. 89.

25 Guilmartin, *Gunpowder and Galleys*, op. cit., Chapter 1.

26 Ibid., p. 96.

27 Ibid., p. 98.

28 Ibid., pp. 101–102.

29 Ibid., p. 105.

The Ottoman Empire

Daniel Goffman

The "Renaissance" has long been imagined as a western European phenomenon, even a doggedly Eurocentric one. It was born in Italy on the eve of the European "age of discovery," and carried from there to the rest of Europe. It has been intimately coupled to, and in important ways fused with, the colonialism, imperialism, and sense of superiority associated with early modern and modern western Europe. The concept, though, is slippery. It has been used to refer to an artistic movement, to an intellectual movement, and to a cultural transformation. It also has been said to mark the beginning of modernity and the critical moment in European history when the past became historicized. Recently, some scholars have tried to broaden the meaning of the Renaissance by arguing that other Renaissances occurred in other parts of the world, and especially in the Islamic Middle East. Others have attempted to modify the significance of the Renaissance (as well as the definition of early modern) by redirecting our focus from artist to patron, from art to commerce and produce, and from regional to global. This latter reinterpretation pays particular notice to the role of the Ottoman Empire in the creation of a Renaissance in Italy and the rest of Europe. Scholars have noted a Renaissance consciousness of the Ottoman East and the movement of diverse commodities from the Ottoman world into the European one. They have paid less attention, however, to the fact that thousands of Italians, Frenchmen, and Englishmen lived in Ottoman lands and had to negotiate with Ottoman authorities and communities. How did their accommodations with and adjustments to that world influence their own art, literature, and world-views? What might they have learned from that encounter about dealing with others and constructing empires? In other words, how deeply

Daniel Goffman, "The Ottoman Empire," *The Renaissance World*, pp. 347-363. Copyright © 2004 by Taylor & Francis Group. Reprinted with permission.

and in what ways did the Ottomans (and others) participate in the creation of Renaissance and early modern Europe?

In the past decade or so, scholars have broadened their definition of "Renaissance" in an attempt to break away from the word's Eurocentric derivation. There are several catalysts for this endeavor. The field certainly has responded to more general critiques of historians' views of Europe's relationship with the rest of the world. For example, while postcolonial scholarship originally focused its withering attack upon historiography on the "age of imperialism," in recent years it has turned its attention to the "age of discovery." In this context, scholars have observed that early European encounters with Americans and Asians are better characterized as negotiations rather than conquests. In most cases, European success was far from certain; in some cases, Europeans suffered setbacks that suggested to contemporaries that western Europe was as likely to be conquered as to conquer others.

This postcolonial venture into the early modern, then, also has problematized postcolonial studies. A fundamental premise of the field has concerned power relationships; that is, the ability of Europe to impose its military, economic, political, and intellectual will upon the rest of the world. Scholars, though, have questioned the appropriateness of this framework to the early modern era. After all, Europeans ventured into the west, east, and south Asian worlds only when the Ottoman, Chinese, or Mogul rulers allowed them to do so. Furthermore, they remained very much on the defensive in the Mediterranean seas until well into the seventeenth century. Consequently, scholars have coined new phrases, such as "Ottomanism" and "imperial envy," to convey the sense of fear, awe, inferiority, and jealousy that first Italians, and then other Europeans, often felt toward the worlds they encountered and with which they attempted to negotiate.

Using this framework, literary scholars have begun to recognize how non-European civilizations influenced the writers of the day. Those who study Elizabethan drama, for example, have found profound traces of the Ottomans in the plays of Christopher Marlowe and William Shakespeare and have uncovered the genre of "Turk plays." Those who study early English expansion have discovered an early modern obsession with the Islamic Mediterranean in the many narratives of Englishmen captured by and living in that world. It is not surprising, then, that Renaissance scholars also have begun to extend their gaze beyond the European subcontinent in their search for new ways to conceptualize the caldron that we call the Italian Renaissance.

Of all the polities that Italians and other Europeans living through the Renaissance contacted, they found the Ottoman Empire both the most threatening and the most fascinating. The empire was threatening both because it was emphatically not Christian, and because of its aggressive expansion into southeast Europe and the eastern Mediterranean during the very years of the Italian Renaissance, the same areas into which Italian city-states such as Genoa and Venice had expanded in earlier centuries. It was fascinating because of its ability (or so it seemed) to construct a large, successful, and relatively centralized state during the very years that Italian and other Christian European states were struggling (and failing) to construct such entities.

Until recently, scholars by and large failed to note this contemporary fascination with the Ottoman world. Instead, they concentrated almost exclusively upon the Ottoman Empire as an outside threat to a Europe just emerging from a dark age and about to embark upon an unprecedented domination of non-European worlds and civilizations.[1] This concern reflected not only an early modern European fear of the Ottomans—that "terror of Europe"—but also the sense of European superiority that accompanied the nineteenth-century "age of imperialism." In other words, we have remained largely oblivious to a long, elaborate, and in some ways fruitful relationship between the Ottoman and Italian (and other European) worlds, and have regarded this expanding neighbor to the east, if at all, as an external menace, a Terrible Turk.

One consequence of this perception has been that, outside of the sphere of international relations, scholars have considered the Ottoman Empire hardly at all in their examinations of fifteenth- and sixteenth-century Italy. A key condition for the Italian Renaissance, in the scholarship of Jacob Burckhardt, Garrett Mattingly, and others, has been the existence of a political vacuum—broken only with the French invasion of the peninsula in 1494—within which the Italian states and elites could act as patrons, struggle among themselves, and autonomously develop new artistic, intellectual, and diplomatic apparatuses. This sense of distance between the Italian and eastern worlds long persisted in our scholarship despite the Byzantine loss of Constantinople in 1453, the slow yet inexorable Genoese and Venetian loss of their empires in the Black Sea and eastern Mediterranean in the latter half of the fifteenth century, and the shocking Ottoman landing at the Italian port town of Otranto in 1480.

In reality, if there was a vacuum at all in Italy during the Renaissance, its dealings with eastern states and economies chronically punctured it. By focusing on the Christian world exclusively, and consequently imagining that the Ottoman conquest of Constantinople severed Italy from the east even as French and Spanish distractions and the Alps severed Italy from the north, we have washed out a rich and essential relationship between these worlds that we too narrowly divide as Christian and Islamic. An Italian physical retreat from the eastern Mediterranean certainly occurred. The change of rule in Istanbul represented only the most spectacular of a series of withdrawals. Equally dismaying for the Genoese was the loss of easy access to the Black Sea; equally disastrous for the Venetians was the loss of islands and ports in the Aegean and eastern Mediterranean seas. Nevertheless, the tangible need of the Italian states for their empires was more commercial than political, and the Genoese and the Venetians—as well as other Italian states—found ingenious ways to sustain and even expand their commercial and other links with the Ottomans and other Islamic polities.

In short, even though historians and literary critics have succeeded in constructing a portrayal of the early modern European and Mediterranean worlds that integrates the idea of the Ottoman Empire, they have not given us much sense of what that empire looked like, or precisely how Venetians, French, and English men and women, and other Christian Europeans familiarized themselves with it and applied knowledge gained in that encounter to their own lives and societies. Two examples, one considering Renaissance diplomacy and the second examining how individual Englishmen navigated the Ottoman world, may suggest ways to make more sense of this encounter and to understand more concretely how Ottoman civilization might have contributed to the transformations that ushered in early modern Europe.

The argument that a new diplomacy arose in fifteenth-century Italy is one of the many fruitful explorations that derived from the Burckhardtian concept of a Renaissance genius arising out of a political vacuum. This line of reasoning presents a self-contained Italian world, in which the increasingly secular squabbles between the rulers of Rome, Venice, Florence, Mantua, Genoa, and other city-states demanded a more sophisticated and permanent system of diplomacy than the often *ad hoc* structure that existed in the medieval Catholic world. The French invasion of 1494, the argument continues, initiated the movement of this new diplomacy, characterized by the legal fiction of extraterritoriality, the placement of permanent emissaries in foreign capitals, and regular reports about the politics, society, and ambitions of rival rulers to states north and west of the Alps. By the end of the early modern period, a version of the system of diplomacy that still exists today was in place throughout western Europe.

This is a tidy and persuasive hypothesis that has held historiographical sway for half a century. Furthermore, the general outline of its story is accurate; a new diplomacy did emerge in Italy during this period, and the new structures did travel northwestward into Europe. Nevertheless, the argument's most fundamental premise—that the independent, politically fragmented, and self-sufficient nature of the Italian peninsula in the fifteenth century was the creative spark that motivated this new diplomacy—is only partially true. Italy remained an integral part of the eastern Mediterranean world in the fourteenth, fifteenth, and sixteenth centuries, and a chief stimulant toward innovation in methods of diplomacy was an urgent need of Italian states to adapt themselves first to a Seljuk and Turcoman, and then to an Ottoman world in the making. Furthermore, these adaptations depended upon the ambiguities, flexibilities, and porosity of eastern Mediterranean frontiers.

The vocabulary through which Ottoman documents describe foreigners suggests this ambiguity and flexibility. For example, although each of these terms later came to connote different types of foreigners or subjects, a fifteenth-or sixteenth-century Ottoman statesman might have referred to an outlander as *ecnebi*, *firenk*, *yabanci*, *misafir*, *muste'min*, *gavur*, or even *zimmi*—terms that refer, with varied and shifting connotations, to foreigners, visitors, or non-Muslims. Such an official might have described this outlander's community as a *taife* or a *millet*. Today, we might understand that, in the Ottoman world, a *muste'min* referred to a temporary visitor to the empire, a *gavur* to an enemy infidel, and a *zimmi* to a non-Muslim inhabitant of the empire. We might think of a *taife* as a group, and a *millet* as a religious community of non-Muslim Ottoman subjects (Armenian Christians, Greek Orthodox Christians, and Jews). During the formative years of the empire, however, these clear distinctions seem not to have existed. The term *zimmi* is a case in point. In a rapidly expanding realm in which identity was in persistent flux, there was confusion over the question of who constituted a subject, who did not, and at what point a person who had not been a subject became a subject.[2]

The attempt to integrate the Christian community of Chios into Ottoman society after the conquest of that island in 1566 serves as an example. Even before the conquest, the Ottoman government had demanded a *harac* (a head tax) upon the islanders, a surcharge that by that year had fallen some 30,000 gold coins into arrears. A year and a half after the conquest of the island, the government ordered an official to go there and personally examine each household in order to impose the *harac* upon them.[3] These and other sources testify not only to the Ottomans' attempts to integrate a newly conquered non-Muslim population into their society but also to that people's resistance to such incorporation. Over time, the loyalties of Chians to previous Genoese rulers (who also had not shared their religion, being Catholic rather than Greek Orthodox) dissipated, and they came to accept their integration into the Ottoman world.

The agreements through which the Ottoman state attempted to normalize its relationship with newly conquered peoples and foreign entities reflect the ambiguity with which this government dealt with its diverse populations. Today, we refer to such agreements—when they pertain to foreign states—as "capitulations." Nineteenth-century Ottomans referred to them as *imtiyazat-i ecnebiye*. These terms are virtually synonymous. Nevertheless, neither accurately reflects the meaning of these documents for the early modern period. In its formative years, the usual term was *ahidname-i humayun*, or imperial pledge. Furthermore, the Ottomans did not limit the use of this term to guarantees that the state made in reference to foreign governments. Instead, the term covered many sorts of pledges made with many types of communities. The state often (but not exclusively) employed another term, *taife*, to refer to the group to whom such pledges were made. For example, Mehmed II, after conquering Constantinople in 1453, granted to the patriarch of the Greek Orthodox *taife* an *ahidname* that pledged a particular relationship (considerable religious and juridical autonomy) between the sultan and that subject population of the empire; two decades later, this same sultan had an *ahidname* written up that granted considerable economic and political autonomy to the Genoese *taife* of the island of Chios. As late as the 1620s, the Ottoman government granted an *ahidname* to Catholic monks (that protected them principally from Greek Orthodox Christian rivals) who traveled across the southeastern European parts of the empire to minister to and gather revenue from the Catholic Ottoman *taife*.[4] Using exactly the same terminology, Mehmed II granted *ahidnames* (predominantly commercial in nature) to the Florentine, Genoese, and Venetian *taifes* in the 1450s, and his successors wrote up such an *ahidname* with the French *taife* in the 1530s (probably not ratified until decades later), with the English *taife* in the 1580s, and with other states (that is, *taifes*) thereafter.

In short, in its formative centuries, the Ottoman government consistently used the same terminology and the same form in pledges to subject communities, foreign communities, and independent states. This refusal to differentiate between types of communities probably derived in large part from the rapidity with which the polity expanded. The Ottomans swiftly integrated into their society the remnant of the Byzantine Empire, a variety of other Christian states in southeastern Europe, rival Turkic states, large portions of the Genoese and Venetian empires, and much of the Arab world. Why acknowledge the independence of states when they soon would be absorbed into Ottoman society? Furthermore, the Ottomans found, in Islam, legal justification for granting considerable autonomy to conquered peoples. Thus, the *harbi*—that is, the foreign, non-Muslim enemy—received an *aman*, or safe conduct, upon taking up residency in the empire, and was transformed into a *muste'min*, or foreign inhabitant. After a period of time, this foreign inhabitant often became a *zimmi*—that is, an Ottoman subject. In other words, Ottoman experience with non-Ottoman groups combined with an Islamic world-view to envision the foreigner not as an "other," a member of a community that was, perhaps innately, different from the Ottomans, but as a wayfarer on her or his way toward incorporation into Ottoman society.

Italians and other Europeans, of course, sought to resist such absorption, and we see a "middle-grounds" struggle between competing notions of pledges and contracts in their challenge to Ottoman attitudes. They did so by attempting to adjust the terms of their *ahidnames*. Over time, such manipulations helped transform the very meaning of the word, as these certificates more and more resembled treaties rather than Ottoman assurances of fair treatment. For example, envoys began negotiating the right for certain foreigners to reside in the empire indefinitely without sliding from the class of *muste'min* into that of *zimmi*. Thus, a Venetian merchant could reside in Aleppo, for example, for decades, even a lifetime, and remain a member of the Venetian "nation" in that city.

Even though European states began routinely insisting on this codicil in their *ahidnames*, on the ground and in relations with local officials, such legal protection did not always suffice, because the terms of the agreements embodied a developing disparity between Islamic law and Ottoman customs on the one hand, and the historically concrete on the other. As, first, Italian settlements, and subsequently those of French, English, and Dutch, progressed, differing interpretations of the rights and obligations of alien sojourners led to frequent clashes between officials and foreigners in Istanbul and elsewhere. The roots of the tension lay in the fact that these alien traders and diplomats, of whom many spent decades in Ottoman port towns and cities, established their own enclaves (often referred to as "nations" or "factories") and more and more expected to retain capitulatory advantage over their Ottoman and non-Ottoman rivals. Many Ottoman officials, operating within an Islamic world-view and striving not to lose their competitive edge in the marketplace, saw things differently and continued to seek to collect allegedly exorbitant duties and other surcharges, and to convert such habitués into Ottoman subjects.

Almost 60 years after the Ottoman conquest of Chios in 1566, for example, a Jewish tax collector on that island insisted on treating the community of Venetian merchants residing there, as well as those who visited from Crete and other islands, as Ottoman subjects, seeking from them that same *harac* and other taxes that the government collected from non-Muslim subjects. Whereas earlier the policy of the Ottoman government had been to encourage the integration of Chian subjects into the polity, now it ordered local officials to desist from imposing these surcharges upon the Venetians. In the words of the decree (and in seeming contradiction to

Islamic law): if Venetian subjects "dwell on Chios for a long or short time, I do not give consent for the *harac* and other taxes to be imposed on them."[5]

Such Ottoman representatives attempted to bend the terms of pledges in a variety of ways. Capitulatory guarantees more and more granted a type of "most-favored-nation" status to their recipients. Such terms tended to increase tensions between Ottomans and non-Ottomans. For example, they meant that duties on goods for the English, the French, and other foreigners tended to be lower than those imposed on Ottoman subjects. Ottoman merchants fought such inequities, often through local officials. In 1624, for example, the consul of Venice in the port town of Izmir complained that the collector of customs there persisted in artificially raising the value of cotton yarn in order to collect a higher export duty.[6] Such measures were largely futile, however, and the competitiveness of local merchants was gradually eroded.

The rearguard actions of Ottoman subjects continued in a number of spheres. For example, even though the capitulatory agreements more and more covered not only aliens themselves but also their dependants (such as janissary guards, doormen, and translators), in the early seventeenth century Ottoman administrators who were responsible for administering the community of foreigners at Galata, just across the Golden Horn from Istanbul, persistently ventured to collect the head tax from them as if they were unprotected Ottoman subjects (Figure 2.1). Also in Galata, janissary watchmen, candlemakers, and customs collectors tried to collect taxes on meat and suet bought and butchered for the Venetian community as if it were a non-Muslim subject community. Finally, these same officials repeatedly attempted to categorize as non-Muslim subjects (that is, *zimmis*) Venetian and French merchants who leased shops in the bazaars of Istanbul.[7] Such behavior certainly threatened the self-rule of these communities of foreigners. Nevertheless, the Ottoman officials were behaving in neither venal nor deviant ways. They intended neither to extort, nor to exclude, nor to convert. Rather, without subverting either religious or civil autonomy, their methods were designed to integrate these long-term sojourners into Ottoman society in accordance with Islamic law.

Discrepancies between *ahidnames* and Islamic and local laws created even more confusion in the Ottoman provinces than in the capital city. In the first decade of the seventeenth century, for example, a certain cavalryman named Ali seized a Venetian merchant, Yakmo, on a Bosnian byroad, dragged him off to his home, slit his throat, tossed his "rotting carcass" into a sack, and buried it in his garden.[8] No one doubted that Ali had committed murder, and the local magistrate had him brought to justice. The difficulty was that a municipal judge in the small Bosnian village near which Ali had abducted the merchant ordered Yakmo's goods sold and his money and documents confiscated, in accordance with his reading of Islamic laws governing inheritance but contrary to the Venetian *ahidname*. In two other cases, Ottoman tax collectors on the island of Chios and in the port town of Izmir attempted to collect head taxes from Venetian merchants.[9]

Figure 2.1 Nicolay. *Le navigationi et viaggi nella Turchia*. The Bodleian Library, Oxford.

Nor was it only Muslim Ottomans who felt confused by (or perhaps took advantage of) the legal discrepancies between the various legal traditions current in the early modern Ottoman world. Christians and Jews were prominent in the collection of taxes in Ottoman domains, and such agents doggedly sought the head tax and other dues from foreigners, as we have seen with the Jewish tax collector on Chios. Such conflicts also intruded into the lawcourts, as when in 1613 Christian Ottoman subjects living in Izmir refused to accept foreign legal testimony against them, arguing that such "witnesses must be from the *zimmis* of this place." The state disagreed, ruling that "all misbelievers are alike" in such matters.[10]

The opportunity to worship constituted an essential part of foreign settlement in the Ottoman world. Even though Islamic law precluded the construction of new churches and synagogues, the myriad non-Muslim places of worship erected in Istanbul, Izmir, Salonika, and elsewhere suggests frequent evasion of this law. Furthermore, Christian and Jewish communities could maintain and repair existing structures, as is apparent in the many Byzantine churches that survived the conquest of Constantinople in 1453.[11] In the capital city and elsewhere in the empire, Italians and members of other foreign communities repaired churches and other places of worship. In 1622, for example, the Venetian community repaired an ancient structure, over the protests of "some people" who argued that it was a new church. The government responded that the church "is an old one. It has not been recently built." Two years later, Venetians in the town of Gallipoli petitioned to repair the grounds, gardens, and walls attached to their church. The government again consented, as long as the church had not been built "since the conquest." In a similar fashion, it protected a Venetian monk and the monastery in which he lived in Jerusalem when some "rebellious people" tried to seize the property with the excuse that the monk had converted to Islam.[12] In well-established cities such as Jerusalem as well as in rebuilt cities such as Izmir (the ancient Smyrna), Christian and Jewish communities, both indigenous and foreign, had little trouble finding abandoned or ruined pre-Ottoman churches and synagogues to rebuild. In short, the Ottoman government routinely defended the right of non-Muslim inhabitants as well as foreign communities to worship, and made it possible to build the structures necessary for them to do so.

In a state system based upon monotheistic belief but lacking religious uniformity, such a policy became an essential element in communications between states and societies. Western Europe, divided after 1517 between Protestantism and Catholicism and committed to the idea that a society must embrace its monarch's religion (*cuius regio eius religio*), eventually had to adopt the practice, long followed in the Ottoman world, of allowing foreign diplomatic communities the freedom of worship. Without such a right, no ambassador, consul, or other representative could accept long-term residency. Indeed, such a policy constitutes an essential element in extraterritoriality. The English government, for example, could never expect a Spanish ambassador to worship in an Anglican church any more than could the Ottoman government expect an English ambassador to worship in a mosque. In each case, the state learned to accept the idea of immunity from the religious (and legal) obligations of the host country and recognize the concept of diplomatic extraterritoriality.

These examples reflect the relative openness of the Ottoman world as well as the inescapable misunderstandings of a frontier zone between civilizations. Some foreigners simply melted into this almost aggressively malleable land. Many, however, insisted upon the legal and cultural security that their political and social autonomy afforded and strove to preserve and even augment collective self-rule. In doing so, they merely emulated the practices of countless other Ottoman communities and associations. Unlike Ottoman subjects, though, the innovations that their activities produced were transferable to their home countries. In short, these sojourners developed methods and procedures that became templates for many of the institutions that we associate with the new diplomacy of the Italian Renaissance.

In order to protect foreigners from Ottoman law (upon which Ottoman officials based their demands), for example, European governments began negotiating the right to govern their subjects living in Ottoman cities according to their own laws rather than Ottoman laws. This innovation was then exported, first to Italy during the Renaissance and subsequently to the rest of Europe. In the religiously homogeneous societies of western Europe, such extraterritoriality became an essential mechanism in communications between governments, and especially across the Catholic/Protestant divide.

Europeans also began posting permanent representatives in Istanbul; their job was not only to represent expatriate communities with the central government but also to find out as much as possible about Ottoman policy and the workings of Ottoman society. Such an ambassadorial system, with its resident envoys and cultural and political attachés, also became an essential element in early modern and modern diplomacy. Furthermore, the Italians and other Europeans realized that it was not enough to have official representatives in the Ottoman capital city. They also had expatriate communities in other Ottoman cities and began appointing official representatives in each. There was considerable variation in the relationship between such consuls and compatriot ambassadors and home governments. Nevertheless, in each case a fundamental mission was to protect and communicate. This network became the basis for the consular system that is also a feature of modern diplomacy. All of these innovations represented attempts to protect their subjects from a culture and society that western Europeans considered strange and arbitrary, and from the local authorities who represented it.

Recent studies of the Italian Renaissance have examined the influence of the East, especially on consumer culture and the widening possibilities for goods and ideas. They have found evidence for this influence in paintings, woodcuts, and essays produced by Renaissance artists and writers. There has been little acknowledgement, however, that two parties were involved in such transmissions. This was not just a period of expanding global commerce; it also saw a consequent growing presence of western Europeans in the Ottoman and other worlds. As we have seen, Renaissance Italian states learned a great deal about negotiating with others through their experiences in the middle grounds between the retreating Genoese and Venetian empires and the expanding Ottoman one. Comprehending what these Europeans learned on the frontier, and how they went about acquiring this knowledge, demands an intimate understanding of the world in which they lived.

If Italians had dominated such encounters during the fifteenth and much of the sixteenth centuries, by 1550 the states of the Atlantic seaboard had begun to dislodge their Mediterranean rivals. It is no coincidence that this displacement coincided with the transalpine migration of the Renaissance. Just as France, the Netherlands, and England explored and adopted many of the artistic and intellectual innovations of the Italian Renaissance, so did they uncover a parallel world of exotic goods and begin to probe the lands from which they came. They did so first in Ottoman realms.

By the 1580s, for example, the English government (working through and with the newly formed English Levant Company) had assigned a resident envoy to Istanbul, through whom it negotiated its own *ahidname* with the Ottoman government. Soon Englishmen had established communities, and English authorities had appointed consuls in Aleppo, Izmir, and the Morea as well as in the Ottoman capital. By the 1620s, an English commercial and political network, which emulated Italian ones even as it enhanced them, stretched across the Islamic Empire. The English, even more than the Genoese and Venetians a century earlier, were unable to impose their will upon the Ottomans because the structure of English trade left so much to the English Levant Company, and the Company in turn left so much to its representatives and factors resident in the Ottoman Empire. These men had to compete with a swarm of rival traders, both compatriot and non-English; they did so by developing a keen sense of the world in which they worked. The most effective English merchants learned Ottoman languages, Ottoman personalities, and Ottoman culture. Rather than colonize or impose their own administrative and commercial behavior on the Ottomans, these Englishmen learned how to adapt themselves to this unfamiliar world.

The most dramatic and significant example of English adaptation to (and attempt to exploit) the Ottoman world occurred between 1645 and 1647. It involved both the sitting English ambassador, Sir Sackvile Crow, and the envoy sent to replace him, Sir Thomas Bendysh. The first of these men was a loyal supporter of Charles I. The loyalties of the second were more ambiguous. The principal catalyst for the crisis occurred in 1645, when Charles, low on funds, supplies, and manpower, and bottled up in Oxford, ordered his ambassador in Istanbul, Crow, to seize the monies and goods of the English nations residing in the Ottoman cities of Istanbul, Izmir, and Aleppo. The instructions link London traders to parliamentarians, asserting that "diverse Merchants inhabitants of our City of London, ... now or lately trading at Constantinople or elsewhere in Turkey, are actually in arms against us or aiding assisting or abetting to the present Rebellion." It consequently accuses them of "high treason," declares their "Goods, Merchandizes, & Estates ... forfeited & confiscated unto us," and orders Crow to ask the Ottoman sultan "to give you authority to seize & take into your custody, the merchandizes, goods, specialties, & estates of all such merchants in Rebellion against us & trading in his Dominions." Charles, finally, asks Crow to request from the sultan the authority "to apprehend and imprison the persons of such Merchants in Rebellion against us."[13] With this action, the English Civil War spilled over into the Levant.

For personal reasons as well as a sense of loyalty to his king, Crow purposefully set about confiscating the wealth of English merchants and imprisoning the most refractory of them. As the king himself realized, without a police force or an army of his own Crow could act only with the support of Ottoman authorities, from whom he secured imperial rescripts.[14] Among other actions, the ambassador convinced the Ottoman central government to send a *çavuş* (imperial representative) to Izmir with an order to the *kadi* (municipal judge) of the town to seize the goods of all English merchants there. In this undertaking, Crow had behind him the king of England, the government of the Ottoman sultan, and a bevy of Englishmen loyal to Charles. Those who rallied against his plan, however, included all of the principal men in Izmir—including the French and Venetian consuls, the heads of the Armenian and Jewish communities, the collector of customs, and various English ship captains—as well as the English consul in Izmir and many English merchants there and in other Ottoman cities who either opposed Crow or were sympathetic to those forces arrayed against Charles in England.

Crow's agent in Izmir reported to the ambassador the immediate consequences of the intra-communal quarrel:

> This morning [June 16, 1646], the Caddies son, with his Neipe and principall Officers came ... but before wee began [to seize the goods] 'twas spoken in the caddies own hous, & all over the Town, our design to seiz what we could finde; about 7 a clock his son came & entred the Consul hous, & opened all the Warehouses. ... Before we had entred at this house, the whole Town was in an uprore, being fomented by Jews, and som of the young frie left behinde, and proclaimed in the Streets, that the Town would bee undone, the Trade lost and go to wrack, if this was suffered; so that before the Consulls door were so many of the scum of the Town, the Streets were packed thick of them. On the other side, a more unruly enemy threatned worse things. The Master of the Golden Lyon [renamed the Hopewell] ... lands 40 men at Barnardistons house, and vowed hee would have his money or goods, or swore he would beat down the Town.[15]

This passage suggests a complicated world, in which lines of authority were blurred and local authorities could undermine the will of central authorities, whether Ottoman or foreign. The Ottoman municipal judge (*kadi*) seems to have tried to act on his government's orders. Local foreigner and Ottoman communities and men from vessels riding in the harbor, however, combined to overwhelm his efforts. Neither Sir Sackvile Crow nor the king of England, nor even the Ottoman sultan could dominate encounters in this realm. Those foreigners who succeeded in this environment learned to adapt themselves to it.

Crow's actions in the summer of 1646 threw the English community in the Levant into confusion and fright. His assault also had consequences in England. Most dramatically, the Parliament and the English Levant Company (with the probably compelled blessing of the king) dispatched Sir Thomas Bendysh to replace Crow. Bendysh arrived in Istanbul, after a layover in Izmir, in late September 1647. His appearance triggered a protracted quarrel between these two pretenders to the ambassadorship. In an audience with the Ottoman sultan, Ibrahim, on October 3, Bendysh ostensibly declared that Crow was a rebel against his king who carried forged credentials.[16] During the next couple of weeks, Bendysh continued his campaign to convince Ottoman officials of Crow's illegitimacy. Eventually, he succeeded. On October 23, a group of Ottoman soldiers arrested Crow at his garden in the Istanbul suburb of Galata, marched him through the streets of the city, and shipped him off in a small Ottoman vessel to Izmir. Here, he was spirited aboard an English ship and, several months later, the ex-ambassador was in London, where he spent the next 13 years in the Tower.

This account of how Sackvile Crow sought to seize the assets of his compatriots in Ottoman domains, and how English nations residing in Ottoman cities defeated him, exposes more than just an intriguing element in the English Civil War. It also reveals a great deal about the middle grounds within which this community operated, for those who triumphed did so not because of their connections in England but because of their understanding of the particular Ottoman city in which they worked, as well as their ability to maneuver through the many layers of Ottoman law, power, and authority. English diplomats, traders, and clerics could not colonize this world (although some certainly dreamed of doing so); instead, they had to adapt themselves to it and learn how to work within it.

Curiously, their own political and social worlds may have eased these journeys into Ottoman civilization, because this supple and surprisingly haphazard Ottoman political organization mirrors, in important ways, the organization of the Renaissance Italian peninsula (as well as the early modern European state) as we currently understand it. Scholars of the Italian Renaissance have shifted their interpretation of that world's political history from an emphasis upon relationships between a strong center and the periphery in states such as the Duchy of Milan, the Republic of Venice, and the Kingdom of Naples to a more subtle and complicated representation. In the words of one scholar, these polities constituted "territorial systems in which local communities were connected not only to the centre but also to one another through a variety of economic and political networks that continued, in many cases, to guarantee them a degree of autonomy in relation to the growing power of the prince."[17] This vision of the Italian territorial state as decentralized, dominated by local interests, and diverse is removed from the formerly depicted strong central authority or even despotic prince of the Italian Renaissance. Our current understanding of the Ottoman world is equally remote from the more familiar representations of a firmly centralized and increasingly despotic Ottoman realm.

For many Renaissance Italian political philosophers and Italian statesmen, the Ottoman Empire constituted a vital illustration of, as well as a model for, the princely state. Niccolò Machiavelli's celebrated statement is representative of early sixteenth-century views: "The entire monarchy of the Turk is governed by one lord, the others are his servants; and, dividing his kingdom into sanjaks, he sends there different administrators, and shifts and changes them as he chooses." For Machiavelli, then, the Ottoman state, while a monarchy, resembled a paper tiger—strong and fierce as an icon but essentially unstable and liable to collapse once its leader is detached. Giovanni Botero, often referred to as the "anti-Machiavelli," certainly disputes his predecessor's admiration for the Ottoman state. Writing in the 1580s, some 70 years after Machiavelli, he declares that "the government of the Ottomans is completely despotic." The inhabitants, he continues, "account themselves [the sultan's] slaves, not his subjects; ... and there is no personage so great that he stands secure in his life or in his estate unless it so pleases the Grand Signor."[18] Even though Machiavelli and Botero express differing views of the Ottoman state (with the first describing a legitimate, if brittle, monarchy and the second an illegitimate despotism), in their agreement that the polity depended upon a strong, feared, and controlling ruler they seem to contradict the Venetian and English experiences of an Ottoman world diverse and dominated by local interests.

Botero, Machiavelli, and other humanists had a strong understanding of the Ottomans; they based their descriptions of that world on attitude and expectation—framed largely in terms of humanistic knowledge of the ancient world—rather than anecdote and legend. Whereas these writers had gained their understanding of the ancient world from recovered classics, they almost certainly obtained their knowledge about the Ottomans from compatriots who had visited and lived in the empire. The conclusions of political commentators such as Machiavelli and Botero, for example, mirror the reports (*relazioni*) of Venetian *baili* (ambassadors), many of whom had spent years in Istanbul representing the Venetian state. These reports consistently praise the "Grand Turk" for his magnificence, power, fabulous wealth, and the legal edifice upon which his authority rests, even though they remain wedded to the anomalous idea that the sultan's power was rooted in Christian genius and energy. As the *bailo*, Marcantonio Barbaro typically remarked in 1573, "the wealth, the power, the government, in short, ... the entire state of the Ottoman Empire is founded on and entrusted to people who were all born into the Christian faith and who, by various means, were enslaved and borne off into the Mohammedan sect."[19]

This understanding of the Ottoman state as centralized, potent, and even despotic seems distant from the experiences of Venetian and English visitors. For them, it never was sufficient to possess a capitulation granting reduced customs or autonomy. Even an imperial decree focusing upon a particular issue was often ineffective. Instead, the diplomat or merchant had to navigate through an array of interests, authorities, and personalities. Whether it was a Venetian consul protesting the integration of his compatriots into the Ottoman world or an English merchant contesting imprisonment and the seizure of goods, successful resistance depended upon the individual's familiarity with a varied and multifaceted civilization.

The image of an inordinately forceful central Ottoman state, effectively organizing society around itself, clashes with current views of the structure of that empire no less than it contradicts the experiences of contemporary visitors. The Ottoman sultan seems to have been in continual negotiation with members of his household as well as with other powerful patricians, and factionalism better than despotism represents this early modern state. Ottoman society reflected this complicated political core. Even in Istanbul, visitors such as Sackvile Crow and Thomas

Bendysh worked and clashed with municipal judges, customs officials, and various religious and communal leaders as well as the Sublime Porte. Outside of the capital city, the lines of authority were even more convoluted, and they varied according to location and situation. The visitor to the Ottoman Empire, then, found a political system that in essential ways resembled contemporaneous states in Italy and elsewhere in Europe. This was a world to which visiting Englishmen and Venetians had to accommodate themselves, one from which they could learn a great deal, and one that must have seemed considerably less foreign than we have previously supposed.

The Ottoman Empire was an integral part of the early modern Mediterranean and European worlds, and first Italians, and then other Europeans, had to engage with that civilization at many levels in addition to the military and the intellectual. As a consequence, the Ottomans constituted a significant factor in the Italian, English, and other Renaissances. Renaissance diplomacy, for example, emerged principally out of the experiences of the Italian trading states with, first, the Byzantines—and then even more so with the Turkish emirates and the Ottomans in the fourteenth, fifteenth, and sixteenth centuries. The urgent need for the Florentines, Genoese, and Venetians to find ways to retain a commercial presence in that expanding empire—more than an Italian political vacuum or the French invasion of 1494 or the political ambitions of the Papal States or some other Christian European political structure—stimulated the formation of extraterritoriality, resident embassies, and routine reports on foreign and often hostile states. In short, the ideas of the "Renaissance" and "Europe" did not emerge only in contrast or opposition to other people, places, and ideas, or by the conquest of distant territories and dominion over different people. Equally important was accommodation with states and societies that the Italians, the French, the Dutch, and the English could not dominate or control. During those very years when Europe was in formation, foreigners—and especially the Ottomans—impressed fear, admiration, and envy upon the inhabitants of western European states. Italian understanding of this reality appears in the rather desperate construction of a new diplomacy along its borderlands with the Ottoman world; English comprehension of this reality appears in the inability of that state's agents to control their compatriots, as well as in the deep and thick ambivalence of the many "Turk" plays produced in sixteenth- and seventeenth-century England, including Marlowe's *The Jew of Malta* and Shakespeare's *Othello*. Finally, even the state structures of the Ottoman Islamic and Christian European worlds may have had far more in common than contemporary and more recent observers would lead us to believe.

Why have we been so slow to acknowledge how much these worlds shared? The fault may lie in part with the humanists themselves, who learned how to historicize the past and consequently profoundly to separate themselves from it. With this growing conviction of the past as a foreign land came a growing belief that traveling in foreign lands was like traveling in the past. Thus, just as Renaissance Europe began separating itself from the past and considering itself superior to it, so did Renaissance Europe begin to detach itself from other parts of the world and consider itself superior to them. In this situation, it became easy for even the accomplishments of others to seem imitative or inauthentic. Such seems to be the case with the Ottomans. Humanists and other western Europeans certainly admired many of their accomplishments, such as their ability to integrate diverse religions and peoples into their body politic. Nevertheless, Europeans effectively learned how to draw on the idea of historicity to wash out such achievements, and the Renaissance, in its inspiration as well as its accomplishment, became conceived as a uniquely European phenomenon.

Ottoman civilization was an equal partner in Mediterranean and European history, rather than an antagonistic backdrop as it generally has been considered up to now. This is not to deny difference. In fact, Ottoman relevance to western Europe probably lies in its role in creating a middle-ground tension and profound sense of difference. This tension, precipitated through contact with an intimidating civilization, forced institutional and individual creativity, as we have seen in both the Italian and English cases. Struggles to make sense of and assimilate this great power (literary critics refer to it as "imperial envy") on the part of Italian city-states, the English, and others led to new attitudes toward relationships between states and society and the development of a new diplomacy, as well as other innovations. Such legacies, unfortunately, have been largely forgotten. Instead, we remember only the negatives of this relationship: that Europeans feared the "Turk," that the "Turk" thrust himself into the heart of Europe, that Europe reduced the "Turk" to nothing more than a barbarian, and that if the European learned anything at all from the "Turk" it was how to conquer and colonize.

Notes

1 This attitude is shared by nineteenth-century masterpieces such as Jacob Burckhardt's *The Civilization of the Renaissance in Italy* (Modern Library, 2002) (first published in 1860), more recent classics such as Garrett Mattingly's *Renaissance Diplomacy* (New York: Dover Publications, 1988) (first published in 1955), and current scholarship such as Daniela Frigo (ed.), *Politics and Diplomacy in Early Modern Italy: The Structure of Diplomatic Practice, 1450–1800*, trans. Adrian Belton (Cambridge: Cambridge University Press, 2000).

2 The term "subject" may not accurately describe an inhabitant of the empire, but I do not know a better word.

3 See Başbakanlık Osmanlı Arşivi, Mühimme Defteri 5, p. 492, n. 1329; and 7, p. 174, n. 464.

4 See Başbakanlık Osmanlı Arşivi, Ecnebi Defteri 14/2, p. 62, no. 2.

5 See Başbakanlık Osmanlı Arşivi, Maliyeden Müdevver 6004, p. 51, doc. 1.

6 See Başbakanlık Osmanlı Arşivi, Maliyeden Müdevver 6004, p. 34, doc. 1.

7 See Başbakanlık Osmanlı Arşivi, Ecnebi Defteri 13/1, p. 28, no. 6; Ecnebi Defteri 13/1, p. 29, no. 4; Ecnebi Defteri 13/1, p. 35, no. 5; and Ecnebi Defteri 26, p. 144, no. 3 and p. 54, no. 3.

8 Başbakanlık Osmanlı Arşivi, Ecnebi Defteri 13/1, p. 52, no. 3.

9. Başbakanlık Osmanlı Arşivi, Ecnebi Defteri 13/1, p. 70, no. 7 and 16/4, p. 65. This was a chronic problem, on which see also 13/1, p. 120, no. 1; 13/1, p. 150, no. 1; and 16/4, p. 56, no. 1.

10. Başbakanlık Osmanlı Arşivi, Ecnebi Defteri 13/1, p. 101.

11. Debate over the destructiveness of the Ottoman conquest is ongoing (on which, see Nancy Besara, *Creating East and West: Renaissance Humanists and the Ottoman Turks* [Pittsburgh: University of Pennsylvania Press, 2004], pp. 60–2). However many Greeks died and however many Byzantine structures were razed, the survival of these churches rules out a policy of demolition.

12. Başbakanlık Osmanlı Arşivi, Maliyeden Müdevver 6004, p. 33, doc. 2, p. 102, doc. 3, and p. 20, doc. 1.

13. British Library, Egerton MS 2533, fos. 438 and 439.

14. Rescripts on this topic are preserved as Başbakanlık Osmanlı Arşivi, Mühimme Defteri 90, p. 43, n. 130 and 90, p. 44, n. 139.

15. *Subtilty and Cruelty: or a true Relation of Sr Sackvile Crow, His Designe of seizing and possessing himselfe of all the Estates of the English in Turkey. With the Progresse he made, and the Meanes he used in the execution thereof, with such other papers as are since discovered related thereto*, 2nd edn (London, 1657), pp. 60–1.

16. *Calendar of State Papers, Venice*, vol. 28, p. 21, no. 43.

17. Elena Fasano Guarini, "Geographies of Power: The Territorial State in Early Modern Italy," in John Jeffries Martin (ed.), *The Renaissance: Italy and Abroad* (London: Routledge, 2002), pp. 90–1.

18. Giovanni Botero, *Relationi universali*, pt. 2, bk. 4 (Venice, 1591), as quoted in Lucette Valensi, *The Birth of the Despot: Venice and the Sublime Porte*, trans. Arthur Denner (Ithaca: Cornell University Press, 1993), pp. 95–6.

19. As quoted in Valensi, *Birth of the Despot*, p. 24.

The Globalization of Disease After 1450

Sheldon Watts

The American Continents: A Special Case

As late as the early months of 1492, the two American continents (North America and South America) contained perhaps a fifth or a sixth of all humankind. Then, in mid-October of that year, disaster struck. From that time onwards, within 20 or 30 years of a "first contact" experience with Europeans in any given setting, the Native Americans left remaining at that setting seldom numbered more than one-tenth of those who had been there before.

Given the vastness of the two continents, "first contact" was not a once-only affair. In the case of South America, "first contact" incidents began in the late 1490s when Spaniards began to trickle over to the mainland from their bases on the Caribbean Islands. Yet, in some parts of the rain forests of Brazil, "first contact" incidents were still taking place 500 years later. For indigenous peoples in the 1990s, these incidents had the same dire consequences as did all those dating from the years immediately after 12 October 1492. With respect to the earlier history of North America, as far as can be determined, the Norse settlers and explorers who were in Newfoundland and the Great Lakes region in the 1360s did not leave behind any long-term contagious diseases.

But in North America, *after* 1492, "first contact" incidents became part of an ongoing process which, on that huge continent, took nearly 300 years to work their way through. Thus, in remote areas such as present-day Oregon, Washington State and the Dakotas, first contact and accompanying population collapse did not happen until

Sheldon Watts, "The Globalization of Disease after 1450," *Disease and Medicine in World History,* pp. 85-99, 150-151. Copyright © 2003 by Taylor & Francis Group. Reprinted with permission.

after the end of the American Revolutionary War against Britain (1783). This was 300 years after the initial first contact experience in Hispaniola.

That famous/infamous series of incidents began with the landing of Christopher Columbus on the island on 12 October 1492. Within a few decades, the ethnic group he and his crew had first encountered—the Taino—thought to have once been more than one million strong, had almost completely disappeared. Much of what happened during those terrible years remains shrouded in mystery, yet it seems quite certain that most Taino were victims of newly imported diseases and of a policy which purposefully destroyed an entire people and its cultural artifacts. Some aspects of this policy were graphically described by Bartholomé de Las Casas, a Dominican friar who came to Hispaniola in 1502. In his reports back to Spain, Las Casas created what was called the "Black Legend."

Similarly, in coastal North America, beginning in 1622 in the Virginia Colony (founded in 1607) and in 1637 in Massachusetts (founded in 1620), English settlers began to systematically destroy indigenous peoples. Though at times they regarded Native Americans as necessary allies against the French, as soon as the latter were defeated and expelled (with the fall of Quebec City in 1759 and then with the Peace of Paris in 1763), English and other European immigrant settlers had no qualms about killing off all Native Americans who stood in their way. Similarly, in Australia and the Island Pacific, a half century after first contact with whites (effectively beginning in the time of Captain James Cook in the 1780s), indigenous populations had been brought to the brink of extinction.

It is now understood that the massive reduction in the number of Native American and Island Pacific peoples—one-tenth what it had been before contact—was caused by a combination of three factors: (1) the actual diseases the invaders brought with them; (2) the settlers' genocidal practices—of the sort described by Las Casas—and, in the face of these horrible happenings; (3) the collapse of indigenous societies themselves. Their life-worlds shattered, and their triangles of curing wrecked, Native Americans and Pacific islanders failed to reproduce or to keep their newborn infants alive.

Explanations: Old World Disease Patterns and Mind-Sets

By 1450 almost the whole of the Old World (EurAsia and coastal North Africa) was well along in the process of becoming a unified disease zone. Long before that date, sophisticated Arab and Indian and Chinese businessmen and traders were crossing and re-crossing the Arabian Sea, the Indian Ocean and the South China Sea in large well-manned ships to visit focal points of progressive enterprise. In terms of global trade, western Europe was marginal. However, local peddlers, touring scholars, missionaries, mercenary soldiers and other agents did manage to maintain enough links with the Middle East to keep western Europe within the larger EurAsian disease zone.

Then, beginning around 1450, breaking out of the impoverished homeland that jutted out into the Atlantic, the Portuguese began to force their way into the Asians' and Arabs' trading networks. They first attacked coastal North Africa, then sailed around to the West African bulge, then round the Cape and northward along the coast to East Africa. From there, working their way further eastward on heavily armored ships with which they shelled and destroyed everybody else's shipping, the Portuguese proceeded to India (Goa) and finally on to China (Macao). Not to be outdone by their tiny neighbor, in 1492, the Catholic monarch of Castile (Isabella) with the support of her husband, Ferdinand, King of Aragon, invested in the expedition (headed by Columbus) which attempted to reach China and its fabled treasures by sailing west, rather than east as the Portuguese were doing.

Recent detailed studies have shown that most of the western European laymen who joined the fleets going out to the New World in and after 1492 were men-on-the-make. (In saying this I have purposefully excluded priests, monks and women: in early years, the latter were few in number). At home in Europe, none of these men-on-the-make had managed to achieve what Old World societies regarded as high status, either because of accidents of birth (aristocrats and gentlemen were "born" not made), or because they had failed to contract an advantageous marriage, or because they had failed in business dealing, or because of general bad luck. Leaving European ports with the expectation that their future lay in their own hands, these rugged men-on-the-make assumed that if they managed to survive the rigors of the unknown places beyond the seas and became wealthy, they would return to their natal lands and buy their way (or at least their children's way) into high status.

In short, these western Europeans were opportunists who—after escaping the moral bonds imposed by their home communities—were prepared to do *anything* to further their personal goals. Added to these characteristics, were the special traits of the Iberians (denizens of the Spanish kingdoms and of Portugal) who claimed to be descended from the Gothic peoples who had come into the land in the late Roman period. With the exiling of the Jews from the Spanish lands in 1492, and the fall of Granada and the murder of all remaining Muslims in the same year, employment opportunities at home for mercenary soldiers and for hireling thugs melted away. Accepting this reality, many of them made their way to the New World to seek their fortune.

Development and Disease

The literate few Iberians and Italians who sailed to America in the fifteenth, sixteenth and seventeenth centuries had a rough idea about what Hippocrates (in "Airs, Waters, Places") and later medico-philosophical synthesizers had said about disease causation. These approved writers held that someone might come down sick with a serious illness if he or she had recently undergone a "change" of climate or other dramatic alterations in life-style.

If the Hippocratic paradigm were correct, it should have been Columbus and later European adventurers who came down sick with fatal diseases after they left their home environment. Yet, in the event, it was the pagan New World peoples they met and mixed with who, in very large numbers, fell sick and died of diseases that seemed to leave the Europeans untouched.

As is well known, within a few years of their first arrival, Iberian Europeans began to realize that, in addition to mining silver, gold and other precious minerals for export back to the Catholic Kings in Spain, it was necessary to plant and harvest crops and to raise cattle and the like in order to supplement the foodstuffs brought in so irregularly from the Old World. They also finally realized that indigenous New World peoples tended to die off if made to work as slaves on European enterprises. Accordingly, in order to further their projects, the Europeans cast around for an alternative labor supply.

As it happened, by the early 1500s the Portuguese, the Iberian neighbors of the Spanish, were in the process of establishing large slave depots on the central west African coast (now Angola). Despite initial protests from their respective home governments, out in the colonies, Portuguese slave ship agents and Spanish slave purchasers very soon established a *modus vivendi*. With it, the infamous transatlantic slave trade came into existence. A few decades later, with the eclipse of Portuguese enterprise, first Dutch, and then English and Scottish slave ship owners provided the transport needed to bring more than 15,000,000 African slaves to the New World. Funding was provided by venture capitalists in Antwerp, London, Amsterdam, Augsburg and (between 1557 and 1627) Genoa.

With this, a working prototype of all later development projects came into being. At the center of the world-encompassing web of enterprise were venture capitalists, based in a handful of great European cities, who funded enterprises intended to bring in a huge return on investment. The enterprises were usually of the sort that collected or grew Non-western raw materials which would then be shipped to western Europe.

In the case of the Americas, by the early sixteenth century Europe's venture capitalists were funding the ships which brought fine manufactured cotton cloth from India to coastal Africa where it was handed over to local African leaders in exchange for slaves abducted from neighboring African societies. These slaves were then shipped across the Atlantic to provide the labor force needed on New World development projects.

One of the early types of development consisted of the sugar cane plantations of coastal Brazil and the Caribbean Islands. Grown and initially processed in the New World, when shipped across the Atlantic and further refined, cane sugar created an entirely new form of consumer demand. Because of its novelty and its popularity among ordinary people who had never before spent money on such trivialities, cane sugar did much to establish the pattern for our modern consumer society.

Setting the tone for later consumer societies, sixteenth-century European venture capitalists at the center of the worldwide web did not allow themselves to be swayed by moral concerns. They themselves were gentlemen. This meant that they could regard everyone else in the enterprise—ship crews, slaves, factors (merchants' traders) and plantation managers in the New World or in the far Pacific—as low status people who could be used for any purpose, whatever the consequences. In short, gentleman venture capitalists regarded the lives of their "factors" and servants as expendable.

Exemplifying this attitude, in the case of fellow white men in the far Pacific, were the practices of the Netherlands' East India Company (established in 1602). With its headquarters in Amsterdam and its "factories" (trading bases) in Indonesia, the Company could not fail to be aware of the short life-expectancies of its "factors" and servants out in the far Pacific. Indeed, in the 200 years after 1602, early death from fevers, dysentery and other water-related diseases found in the Archipelago drained away the lives of huge numbers of young men who otherwise would have remained at home and contributed to population growth in the Netherlands. As it was, between 1662 and 1795, Dutch population size remained static. Here then, by tending to "business" and not worrying about moral issues, the great merchant families of Amsterdam were able to build up and retain hegemonic control over Dutch society.

Disease Imports to the Non-West

In the first decades of exchange between the Old World and the Americas, the principal lethal diseases appear to have been influenza, smallpox, measles, typhus and malaria. With the establishment of the slave trade directly between west African ports and Brazil and the West Indies, and the return trade from the Americas to western Europe and thence south along the West African coast, the creation of a unified transatlantic disease zone was finally complete. Now, in addition to the diseases of western Europe and Asia, the New World was also subjected to a full range of African illnesses. Some of these, for example *falciparum* malaria, were far more lethal than the earlier malarial form (*vivax* malaria) which some scholars hold had been brought in to coastal North America from marshlands in western Europe.

Complicating matters, each killer disease actually consisted of two or more variant types. In the case of smallpox, there were three main variants, *Variola major*, *Variola minor*, *Variola intermedius*. When examined in sophisticated laboratories in the early 1970s, there were found to be a total of 450 sub-strains of smallpox, eight of them *Variola major*.

Each disease had its own specific causal agent (pathogen) and its own specific means of transmission. Some, as in the case of smallpox, needed no non-human intermediary. That virus was transmitted directly from one human to another, either through breathing air exhaled by a victim, or by coming into contact with the scabs or flesh which had dropped off the victim's body, or by coming into contact with a victim's clothing or blankets even weeks after the person had died. Measles, in its variant forms, was also transmitted directly from one infected individual to another.

Another early disease import to the New World was malaria (caused by a *plasmodia*) which was transmitted through an intermediary host, one or another type of mosquito. The malaria *plasmodia* (in one of its three forms) reached its full maturity within the human host, and infected this host's bloodstream, from whence it was transferred to another human, by way of a female mosquito of the appropriate sort (in which the *plasmodia* egg first hatched). Thus, even though the appropriate mosquito types might have been in the New World before the arrival of Columbus, they would only become bearers of malaria when females of their type bit and ingested some of the blood of a malaria-bearing migrant from the Old World. In a somewhat similar way, typhus (its causal agent is the *Rickettsia prowazeki*) was also transmitted to humans via an intermediary host, a human body louse, or to be more precise, the fecal matter deposited on human skin by a body louse.

As of the late fifteenth century, influenza (one of the five principal infectious disease killers newly introduced into the New World) was directly tied to the presence of domesticated animals of the sort not found in the Americas before. Indeed, within weeks of the landing on Hispaniola of Christopher Columbus and his henchmen, with their swine, cattle and other fresh meat on the hoof, local Taino people (until then a million in number) were struck down by swine fever, a form of influenza. Not until December 1518 were the Taino who had survived this epidemic attacked by virulent smallpox.

Thereafter, smallpox seems to have replaced influenza as the New World's principal killing disease. In a parallel development in the far Pacific, beginning in the 1750s, smallpox left by fishermen, indigenous to the island of Timor, who had dried their nets and gear on the north-eastern coast of Australia, became the principal killing disease of that continent's Aboriginal population.

Though only one of the five principal killer diseases brought to the western hemisphere around 1500 was directly linked with mammals (influenza, from swine), it would appear that in the distant past, three of the others (malaria, smallpox and measles) had also been linked in one way or another with EurAsian and African humankind's animal companions. [...] in the era between *c.* 13,000 BCE and early October 1492 CE there were no large mammals in the New World that could be domesticated and brought to live in close proximity to humans. Without close contact with friendly, cuddly animals of this sort, the processes of disease evolution which had occurred in the Old World in pre-historic times after sizeable cities had been established could not take place in the New.

In the case of smallpox (in the forms in which it was last known to ordinary scientists in 1977), the protective material originally used for vaccination against the illness, by Jenner in 1796, was derived from the udder of a cow suffering from cowpox. It would thus seem that through the mutative processes of natural selection, the causal agents of cowpox and smallpox had at some past time hived off from one another, to become two distinct diseases. As of 1977 (when it was abolished in the natural world), smallpox had no non-human host.

Turning again to malaria, African and Asian farmers have recently reminded visiting medical scientists that mosquitoes much prefer the blood of cattle to that of humans; if the two mammal types are in the same barn, the mosquitoes will light on the cattle every time. Thus it is likely that ancestral malaria, probably as found along the banks of the Indus River in India, began as a disease associated with cattle and only later became associated with humans.

Posited as happening at some time on the Indian subcontinent, a similar transference may also have taken place in West Africa where, after 1000 BCE, the cattle-keeping ancestors of today's Fulani mingled on a seasonal basis with agriculturalists. However, among adult Africans who in their lifetime did not travel far from their natal village, malaria would not be much of a problem, given that they had acquired immunity to the local variant while they were young children. Difficulties only began when large numbers of Africans were enslaved and taken far from their natal villages into new malaria zones where the immunity they had acquired to their local variant was not effective against the strange new types to which they were being exposed.

In Europe, by the early 1500s, when black African slavery had already become common in Portuguese ports and elsewhere in that mosquito-pestered little country, virulent malaria had become well established, brought in by the slaves and by their Portuguese captors. Virulent malaria was also well established in the mosquito-pestered flat lands south of Rome where absentee-owner estates held black Africans in bondage. In time, some of these estates became unfit for human habitation and fell derelict.

Acquired Immunity

In the half century after 1521 (when smallpox first struck the Aztec metropolis, Tenochtitlán), one reason why first generation white immigrants were convinced that they were chosen by God to inherit the western hemisphere was that they seemed to be immune to the sickness which was causing such havoc among indigenous populations. Medical historians now realize that early sixteenth-century white immunity existed not through the intervention of a supernatural force, but because very mild forms of smallpox were endemic in Europe at the time.

As I hinted earlier, endemic viral infectious diseases, such as smallpox (and yellow fever), tended to light on babies and young children, and rather than killing them all off (thus, in the long term, obliterating the virus's necessary hosts) caused only mild discomfort. In exchange for hosting it, the virus then provided recipients with life-long immunity to all further attacks. In the random logic of natural selection this meant that the infant human host (having served its purpose) would then reach maturity and produce infants, who in turn would host the smallpox virus (or the yellow fever virus) and thus enable it to perpetuate itself.

Like smallpox, a case of measles in one or another of its forms (also caused by a virus), similarly provided life-long immunity or near immunity. From the thirteenth century onwards measles was endemic in Europe, the Middle East and China, though in forms that were slightly different from those known today. Given what we know about its behavior in the 1530s, in EurAsia measles could sustain itself in mild form in interacting village communities numbering only a few thousand people.

Thus it happened that most of the Spanish and other Europeans who happened to be in the once heavily populated Valley of Mexico when measles struck in virulent epidemic form in 1531, found that they personally were immune (or suffered only light cases from which they easily recovered), even though indigenous people all around them were dying in great numbers. This confirmed the Europeans in their belief that Native Americans were cursed by God and that He intended that they should disappear.

In common with measles and smallpox, a mild attack of typhus also conferred life-time near-immunity to the disease. At a time when Spaniards abhorred bathing or changing their underclothes, it is likely that most of them were infested with body lice and that since infancy they had had experience with mild forms of typhus. By way of contrast, Native Americans abhorred body filth and bathed as frequently as circumstances permitted. Unfortunately, in prejudiced Spanish minds, this custom linked the peoples of the New World (none of whom had ever heard of the Prophet Muhammad or of Christ) with the ritually-well-washed Muslims who—until they had been killed off or sent into exile by Queen Isabella in 1492—had inhabited Andalusia in southern Spain.

Disease and the Destruction of New World Populations

Within 30 or 40 years of "first contact" (beginning in October 1492) in any particular "disease region" in the New World indigenous population numbers dropped precipitously, generally leaving only one person alive where there had been ten before. In defining a "disease region" one must take into account the special characteristics of the disease involved.

In the case of measles (which ravaged the Valley of Mexico in 1531–32) the "disease region" would be relatively small and self-contained, since the disease is highly contagious, usually acquired through direct contact with a sick person or with virus-laden droplets in the air which had been expelled from the lungs of the sick one. Here, the time between infection and the appearance of symptoms (the incubation period) was brief, limiting the geographic scope of disease transmission.

But the situation was quite different in the case of smallpox. Here, the virus causal agent was present in a bearer for a week or more before the person came down sick. During that time a Native American who happened to be in the business of carrying news and trade-goods between distant places might be able to travel 50 or 60 kilometers a day. This meant he might have traveled three or four hundred kilometers from the epicenter of a smallpox epidemic before falling sick and becoming an infective agent. For this reason, the "disease region" of smallpox might well include whole territories that had not yet been visited by whites.

The most famous example is that of the Incas of Peru, until the mid-1520s, rulers of a mighty empire that stretched for hundreds of kilometers along the Andes and the west coast of South America. Smallpox, probably brought in by Native American runners from the north, ravaged the heart of the empire in 1524–25. This was six years before the arrival of man-on-the-make

Francisco Pizarro in 1531. In its early stages the epidemic killed the Inca king and many of the royal family, leading to a disputed succession and civil war. In the midst of this, Conquistador Pizarro (himself immune to smallpox) had no difficulty in coming in and taking charge.

We have already answered *part* of the rhetorical question, "Why did they die?". As we have pointed out, until 1492 no New World person had ever come into contact with smallpox or any other of Europe's cornucopia of infectious diseases. Not having acquired any immunity to these diseases, when they struck, New World peoples died in terrifyingly large numbers.

Yet, there may well be more to it than that. As every veterinarian (animal doctor) knows, no matter what disease hits a herd of cattle, some beasts survive, exemplifying the principle of "herd immunity." Of course, when dealing with domesticated animals it is assumed that a human owner is on hand to feed and water the sick animals until they recover. In the case of human beings, similar requirements have to be met.

Thus, wherever in the Old World smallpox broke out in lethal form, there would always be some responsible older people around (who had acquired immunity as children) to serve as carers during the ten to 12 days a smallpox patient was semi-delirious and unable to manage for her- or himself. But in the Americas, when an epidemic of smallpox first broke out as in the Valley of Mexico in 1520 or in the Pequot lands of New England in 1634, there would be no indigenous people around who had acquired immunity. Any family member brave enough to bring water and food to a sick person would soon fall sick herself. This sort of happening didn't have to repeat itself very often before all sane persons took to their heels and fled, spreading contagion into the countryside as they ran along. A famous example was the epidemic crisis that hit the Andean city of Arequipa and its densely populated hinterland in 1589, leaving more than a million dead.

Living as we do more than four hundred years after these terrible events, and in the absence of specimens of the disease casual agents that wrought such havoc (which could be analyzed using modern laboratory techniques), we can do no more than speculate about what happened and why.

This brings us to contentious topics. The first involves assessing the genetic make up of (long dead) individuals in particular population groups. The second is to assess the degree of disease-resistance *diversity* that might have been found in any given (long dead) population, say, "Population A" compared to some other (long dead) population, "Population B."

Let me begin with "Population A," the inhabitants of western Europe around 1200 CE. It is now known that the ancestors of the people who had come to settle in western Europe before 1200 CE had moved there from many far off regions. Some of these ancestors (or ancestral groupings) had come from central and western Asia, some from the Middle East and North Africa, some from eastern Europe and so on. Each of these ancestral groupings had their own distinctive genetic inheritance and, with it, their own distinctive clustering of chromosomes. At the level of the individual, each chromosome carried disease resistance units known as *alleles*.

After each of these various ancestors (ancestral groupings) settled down in western Europe, they and their progeny intermarried with women and men descended from other ancestral groupings. Happening over the course of several thousand years, emerging out of this mixing process were late-medieval Europeans. They were very much a mongrel people.

Because of this complex genetic situation in western Europe, there were a large number of possible combinations of alleles (disease resistance units) in the late medieval population. Indeed, given that alleles are attached to chromosomes, and that brothers and sisters do not share the same chromosomes, even siblings had slightly different immune systems. Next door neighbors also carried combinations that differed one from the other.

Thus, a disease pathogen attacking any member of the allele-rich population that was western Europe in the years after 1450 (the date after which most immigrants to the New World were born) would, in assaulting each individual person, confront a slightly different immune system. Sorting out these differences in defense systems and overcoming them one by one presumably had the potential to slow down the movement of the disease. It might even encourage it to remain in mild endemic form, rather than breaking out as a virulent epidemic. This then (in simplified form) was the situation in western Europe.

But in the New World, the accidents of settlement history were entirely different. Though much of this remains conjectural, it would seem that as of 11 October 1492 (the eve of Columbus' landing) the entire population of the Americas was descended from only four or five small Asian groupings (each perhaps under a dominant Patriarch). At various times 12 or 13 thousand years ago these small groups (two or three hundred strong) had made their way across dry land between present day Siberia and Alaska. Some of the descendants of these groups gradually made their way southwards, eventually to southern Chile.

Because the number of founding ancestors was very small (perhaps only a few dominant Patriarchs had initially been involved in the migration), the number of alleles possessed by their millions of descendants several thousand years later was also small when compared to mixed-breed European populations (with their far-flung and varied ancestral roots). It can be argued that as a result, in the whole of New World there was not much diversity in alleles. This meant that an epidemic disease, such as measles or smallpox, at work in that population, had far fewer immune system differences to overcome than would have been the case in western Europe. This would perhaps explain why, in the Valley of Mexico, measles went berserk every 20 or 30 years. Measles hit the Valley in epidemic form in 1531–32, in 1563–64, in 1592–93, and in 1595–97, leaving tens of thousands of people dead, many of them children.

Records kept in New Spain by Catholic priests suggest that later epidemics were marginally less severe. Perhaps this was because Spanish settler males (in the absence of Spanish females) tended to sleep around with Native American women and, in the process, gradually enriched the local gene bank and, with it, the diversity of alleles found in the population. Yet the lessening severity of epidemics in places that had been repeatedly ravished early on—such as the Valley of Mexico—may also be related to gradual mutations in the viral disease agents themselves.

Using the slippery technique, "argument by analogy" we can remind ourselves that a disease not before known in mainland Europe—venereal syphilis—had also been highly virulent when it first appeared in 1494 among military men and prostitutes in Italy and France. According to alarmists' reports at the time, heralding their early death, within a few weeks of contracting the disease the noses and penises of syphilis victims dropped off. However, 50 years later, medical authorities claimed that venereal syphilis had lost some of its most alarming symptoms and now took many years to complete its lethal work. If this were true, it would suggest that the disease had adjusted itself to a new environment, taking care not to kill off victims before they had time to breed children who could later serve as disease hosts.

A somewhat similar mutation in disease behavior (at first highly virulent, then much less so) *may* have happened to the viral agents of smallpox and measles in New Spain after 1650. However, without samples of actual disease causal agents from before and after 1650 that can be tested using modern laboratory techniques, suppositions about such changes remain only that.

Solid arguments, derived from biology, supplement, and may ultimately supersede, earlier "cultural" arguments. One "cultural" argument, most often applied to North America (based on two or three observations by bemused whites), held that according to native custom, whenever a community member fell sick, it was the duty of the whole community to visit, frequently. If the sick person had come down with an air-borne communicable disease—measles or smallpox—the visiting process would obviously put the entire community at risk.

A much less valid, but frequently repeated "cultural" argument, holds that Native Americans, when confronted with smallpox and its sores and pustules commonly resorted to steam baths in search of cleansing and cure. Modern historians who claim that this was the worst thing they could have done, are, unknown to themselves, simply reiterating sixteenth-century Spanish claims that bathing was "evil"—because it was a Muslim custom.

As we have seen throughout this book, "disease" is a reality (synonymous with disease agent/pathogen), but "illness" is—at least in part—a perceptual state. "Illness" (as perceived by "self") can be caused by *individual* misfortune and circumstances. But a state of mind conducive to serious illness would also be found among an entire ethnic group (or, as in the Aztec Empire, a collection of ethnic groups) whose lived-world had totally collapsed.

In the Spanish-ruled lands of America after 1492/1521, native people found themselves in a situation where their heads of government had been killed off by disease or murdered, where all their religious and cultural writings had been burnt, where their cities, temples and aqueducts had been dismantled and destroyed, where their lands had been stolen and their livelihoods destroyed, and where they had all been reduced to the dank equal status of serfs.

Here then, life-worlds of the sort known before the Conquest (not that these had been Gardens of Eden) were replaced by a new life-world in which control of "self" and over-all control of the ethnic group were in the hands of an "Other." This "Other" consisted of Spanish landowners, Spanish entrepreneurs, Spanish priests (who insisted in collecting scattered rural communities into tight-packed, disease-ridden "congregations") and—at the center of the development web in Genoa and in northern European cities—gentleman venture capitalists.

In North America, the cast of characters in the "Other" was slightly different (in the English colonies there were no priests to speak of) but the end result was much the same. After the arrival of local whites as land-thieves, individual natives' sense of self-worth and personal identity was shattered.

Within the Americas—North and South—each ethnic group responded to this situation in their own way. In the Valley of Mexico, according to a survey taken in the 1580s, it would seem that survivors married at a younger age than had been the case before 1521, and had more live births. However, it would also seem that parents—demoralized by the Spanish regime—did little to keep their babies alive; the result was population stagnation, or continued decline. Further to the south, in the Andes, it would seem that a high proportion of married young people did not bother to have children at all. Given that very few Native American migrants were coming in, this too resulted in population decline.

A similar situation seems to have prevailed in much of North America. Here, demoralized Native American males often felt that since there would be no future worth living for, there was no point in marrying. Indeed many of them decided that there was no point in doing anything at all other than drink the whiskey and cheap rum which the white folks made available. In the late eighteenth and nineteenth centuries, drunken tribal chieftains readily agreed to treaties which handed over all tribal lands to white occupation, in perpetuity.

But in earlier centuries, some groups of Native Americans had clearly demonstrated that they would not easily accept being made into landless slaves. For example, in the spring of 1519 Aztec warriors had had no trouble in killing off most of the soldiers brought in by Cortés before they themselves were brought low by something other than western armaments. Two years later, when most Aztec warriors were in the process of dying from smallpox, Cortés had no difficulty in defeating them in battle; but then this was not exactly a fair fight.

Turning to the situation in North America, it is known that during the early years, Native Americans fought long and hard against land-grabbing settlers before they too were brought low by something else. In the absence of that "something else" (lethal European-borne diseases) it can be argued that had the full complement of New World people still been around in 1800 or 1850, they would have outnumbered European settlers by a factor of 50 to one. In the days before Gatling guns, man for man, Native American warriors were fully the equal of warriors of European stock.

The supposition that killing diseases (rather than just superior armaments and leadership) made possible the conquest of the Americas by Europe can, in part, be supported by evidence drawn from another part of the world, New Zealand. When, in the late eighteenth century, land-hungry British settlers came to North Island and South Island they found them occupied by the Maori. These people may well have been beneficiaries of a richer inheritance of alleles than were the indigenous people of Australia or the New World.

The Maori themselves had only come to New Zealand as conquerors around 1200 CE. As a peripatetic Polynesian people, it is possible that they had already had experience with some of the disease types found in East Asia. In any case, it would seem that they were not blitzed by European-borne diseases at first contact to the extent that most other Non-western people were. As a result, the Maori were able to retain their societal cohesion and their ability to defend themselves against European aggressors, sometimes using guns purchased from whites. Beneficiaries of a humanitarian governor, in 1840 the status of the Maori as a permanent element in the New Zealand population was recognized by the Waitangi treaty arrangement (this, at any rate is the reading in the Maori-language version of the treaty). Though they lost considerable ground in the next 90 years, by 1935 they were still very much present and were undergoing a major cultural revival. Their integrity and separate identity still intact, the Maori currently account for 15 percent of the population.

World Historical Consequences

In the New World, the processes of globalization (which were entirely dependent on development and development agents) could not have worked their way to fruition had not key regions in the two continents first been denuded of their Native American population. This denuding process, as we have seen, was achieved through the interaction of three factors: European-imported diseases, European sadistic behaviors and the collapse of Native Americans' lived-worlds.

In world historical terms, in the long run, the denuded region of most consequence was that lying inland from the Gulf of Mexico. Stretching from West Florida to beyond the Mississippi, in the years after 1815 this vast region became the home of *King Cotton*. Without this African slave-grown cotton (and England's own newly discovered reserves of coal), England's fledgling "industrial revolution" would probably have petered out and Britain would have joined Venice and Flanders/Netherlands as the home of yet another failed attempt at modernization.

But as Kenneth Pomeranz nicely demonstrates in his *The Great Divergence: China, Europe and the making of the modern world* (2000), Britain (rather than China—as late as 1750 China still had many things going for it) *did* achieve full modernization. Building on breakthrough achievements first in cotton, then in steam, after 1850 England's gentleman capitalists created the British world economic system. A century later, this world economic system was inherited by America.

Bibliography

Alchon, Suzanne Austin (1991) *Native Society and Disease in Colonial Ecuador*, Cambridge: Cambridge University Press.

Baker, Brenda J. and George J. Armelagos (1988) "The Origin and Antiquity of Syphilis: paleopathologic diagnosis and interpretation," *Current Anthropology* 29 (5): 732–7.

Bastien, Joseph W. (ed.) (1985) *Health in the Andes*, New York: American Anthropological Association.

Black, F. L. (1994) "An Explanation of High Death Rates among New World Peoples When in Contact with Old World Diseases," *Perspectives in Biology and Medicine* 37 (2), 292–307.

Blackburn, Robin (1997) *The Making of New World Slavery: from the Baroque to the modern 1492–1800*, London: Verso.

Braudel, Fernand (1985) *Civilization & Capitalism, 15th–18th Century*, Vol. 3, *The Perspective of the World*, London: Collins/Fontana Press.

Cook, Noble David and W. George Lovell (eds) (1991) *"Secret Judgments of God": Old World disease in colonial Spanish America*, Norman, OK: University of Oklahoma Press.

Cook, Noble David (1998) *Born to Die: disease and New World conquest, 1492–1650*, Cambridge: Cambridge University Press.

Crosby, Alfred W. (1972) *The Columbian Exchange: biological consequences of 1492*, Westport, CT: Greenwood Press. A pioneering work: some of its core concepts are now museum pieces.

Geary, Patrick (2002) *The Myth of Nations: the medieval origins of Europe*, Princeton, NJ: Princeton University Press. On the diverse origins of the settler/inhabitants of post-Roman Empire Europe.

Gruzinski, Serge (1993) *The Conquest of Mexico: the incorporation of Indian societies in the Western world, 16th–18th centuries*, Cambridge: Cambridge University Press.

Hall, Richard (1998) *Empires of the Monsoon: a history of the Indian Ocean and its invaders*, London: HarperCollins.

Henige, David (1986) "When did Smallpox reach the New World (and why does it matter)?" in Paul Lovejoy (ed.) *Africans in Bondage: studies in slavery and the slave trade*, Madison: University of Wisconsin Press: 11–26.

Inikori, Joseph and Stanley L. Engerman (eds) (1992) *The Atlantic Slave Trade: effects on economies, societies, and peoples in Africa, the Americas and Europe*, Durham, NC: University of North Carolina Press.

Joralemon, Donald (1982) "New World Depopulation and the Case of Disease," *Journal of Anthropological Research* 38: 109–27.

McCaa, Robert (1995) "Spanish and Nahuatl Views on Smallpox and Demographic Catastrophe in Mexico," *Journal of Interdisciplinary History* 25: 397–431.

MacLeod, D. Peter (1992) "Microbes and Muskets: smallpox and the participation of the Amerindian allies of New France in the Seven Years War," *Ethnohistory* 30 (1): 42–64.

MacLeod, Roy and Milton Lewis (eds) (1988) *Disease, Medicine, and Empire: perspectives on western medicine and the experience of European expansion*, London: Routledge.

Miller, Joseph (1988) *Way of Death: merchant capitalism and the Angolan slave trade, 1730–1830*, London: James Currey.

Pomeranz, Kenneth (2000) *The Great Divergence: China, Europe and the making of the modern world economy*, Princeton, NJ: Princeton University Press.

Porter, H. C. (1979) *The Inconstant Savage: England and the North American Indian 1500–1660*, London: Duckworth.

Stannard, David E. (1992) *American Holocaust: Columbus and the conquest of the New World*, Oxford: Oxford University Press.

Thomas, Hugh (1993) *Conquest: Montezuma, Cortés, and the fall of Old Mexico*, New York, Simon & Schuster.

Thomas, Hugh (1998) *The Slave Trade: the history of the Atlantic slave trade 1440–1870*, London: Papermac.

Thornton, John (1992) *Africa and Africans in the Making of the Atlantic World*, Cambridge: Cambridge University Press.

Ubelaker, Douglas H. (1992) "Patterns of Demographic Change in the Americas," *Human Biology* 64 (3): 361–79.

Verano, John W. and Douglas H. Ubelaker (eds) (1992) *Disease and Demography in the Americas*, Washington, DC: Smithsonian Institution Press.

Watts, Sheldon (1997) "Smallpox in the New World and in the Old: from holocaust to eradication, 1518–1977," in *Epidemics and History: disease, power and imperialism*, London: Yale University Press.

Wong, R. Bin (2002) "The Search for European Differences and Domination in the Early Modern World: a view from Asia," *The American Historical Review* 107 (2) April: 447–69.

Wright, Richard (1993) *Stolen Continents: the Indian story*, London: Pimlico.

African Traditional Religion, Nature, and Belief Systems

Ibigbolade Simon Aderibigbe

Introduction

Religion is found in all established human societies in the world. It is one of the most important institutional structures that make up the total social system. There is hardly a known race in the world, regardless of how primitive it might be, without a form of religion to which the people try to communicate the divine. This religion becomes inseparable with the total life experience of the people. It thereby permeates into every sphere of the people's lives, encompassing their culture, the social, the political, and the ethical, as well as the individual and societal expectations in their ups and downs. As is the case of nearly every other people in the world, religion is one of the keystones of African culture and is completely entwined in the people's lifestyle. A basic understanding of African religion will provide an awareness of African customs and belief systems.

Perhaps no religion has been so confused in the minds of Western audiences as the African Traditional Religion. The images of this religion have been presented as hopelessly savage and full of ugly superstition. This is solely because the earliest investigators and writers about the religion were mostly European and American anthropologists, some missionaries, and colonial administrators who had no knowledge of the true African spiritual situation. Their works portrayed a distorted image of a religion drawn from half-truths and fertile imaginations. However, an increasing number of African theologians are conducting valuable studies in the African Religion. They have been able to unveil the position that the tenets, spiritual values, and satisfaction which are found in the other world religions—namely, Christianity, Islam, and

Ibigbolade Simon Aderibigbe, "African Traditional Religion, Nature, and Belief Systems," *Religious Thoughts in Perspective: An Introduction to Concepts, Approaches, and Traditions*, pp. 123-136. Copyright © 2012 by Cognella, Inc. Reprinted with permission.

Buddhism, to mention a few—could also be found in African Traditional Religion. Furthermore, it is imperative to say that these researches have left a positive impact, in the sense that they have helped highlight the general truths, concepts, and trends about the religion, thereby dispelling most of the popular misconceptions about the religion.

The emphasis of this chapter will be on the basic concepts of African Traditional Religion. These are its nature, characteristic features, and its conceptual framework.

The Nature of African Traditional Religion

The African Religion is the religion of the Africans and strictly for the Africans. It is not a religion preached to them, but rather a part of their heritage that evolved with them over the years. They were born and not converted into it. It has no founder, but rather a product of the thinking and experiences of their forefathers who formed religious ideas and beliefs. Therefore, its existence cannot be attributed to any individual as in other world religions, such as Christianity, Islam, Confucianism, Buddhism, Hinduism, and so on.

Through the ages, the Africans have worshipped without being preoccupied with finding names for their religions. It was the investigators of religion who first supplied labels such as paganism, idolatry, and fetishism, to mention a few. In order to correct the misconception of such derogatory terms, it became important to designate the religion with a name that describes its true and real nature.

The name African Traditional Religion has been used by scholars to describe the religion. The name was not coined in order to brandish the religion as primitive, local, or unprogressive—rather, it is employed to reflect its location in geographical space and to underscore its evolution from the African personal experience (Aderibigbe, 1995). Furthermore, it is used to distinguish the religion from any other type of religion, since there are other religions in Africa that did not grow out of the African soil but were brought from outside. This shows that the religion is particular to the people, and it would be meaningless and useless to try and transplant this religion to an entirely different society outside of Africa (Mbiti, 1975).

To the African, religion is a hidden treasure secretly given by the Supreme Being solely to the African as a vehicle of communicating and for expressing himself before the sacred entity. In order for a non-African to see and appreciate the wealth of spiritual resources embedded within the religion, he needs to actively participate in order to unveil the nature of the religion, which cannot be understood by mere casual observation. This is why the true nature of the African Religion has been wrongly described and expressed by many, particularly foreign writers and scholars who were outsiders and had no deep knowledge of the experience of the true African spiritual dynamics. These unfortunate misconceptions have been variously demonstrated in derogatory terms for the religion, the denial of African concepts of God (Aderibigbe, 1995), and as ugly superstition that is demon-oriented. It therefore lacks the spiritual fulfillment necessary for the salvation of the soul. Consequently, their works are full of fabrications, exaggerations, half-truths, and biases against the religion and its adherents.

Nevertheless, their works have left a significant impression on most Westerners. Most people remember the African Religion with the image of a missionary in a cannibal's pot about to be cooked and eaten or an evil witch doctor trying to cast a voodoo spell upon a victim. However, with the increase of scholars in the field of African theology such as E. B. Idowu (1962) and Mbiti (1975), there have been some successful attempts to correct some erroneous ideas about African Religion and its belief systems, thought patterns, rituals, and culture generally. The true nature of African Religion cannot be based on erroneous claims of the Europeans concerning the Religion, but rather on what the Africans think and feel about their religion. The true nature of African religion is hinged on the embodiment of the religion in a belief system and functionalism that are actualized in the everyday life of the indigenous African.

A basic understanding of the religion will provide an awareness of African customs, belief systems, concept of God, relationship with the divinities, spirits, ancestors, and the view of death and life beyond death.

Characteristic Features

The fact that African Traditional Religion has no sacred scriptures like other world religions does not necessarily mean that it is devoid of organized religious beliefs and practices. The religion is characterized by a belief system which consists of the totality of the African beliefs, thought patterns, and ritual practices. The religious beliefs of African Religion are in two inclusive categories: the major beliefs and the minor beliefs. The major beliefs are in a fivefold classification. The major beliefs in their hierarchical order have significant relevance on the totality of African religious belief systems.

The above diagram represents an overview of the belief system in a hierarchical order.

Belief in the Supreme Being

In the religious belief system, the belief in the Supreme Being is fundamental to all other beliefs and is firmly entrenched in African belief and thought. This is contrary to the Western view that the primitive African is not capable of having any conception of a single Supreme Deity. As Idowu points out:

> Those who take one look at other people's religion and assert glibly that such people have no clear concept of God or no concept of God at all should first look within themselves and face honestly the question, "How clear is the concept of God to me ..." (Idowu, 1973).

The Africans believe in the Supreme Being and recognize Him as the ultimate object of worship. He is not an abstract power or entity, neither is He an idle Negro king in a sleep of idleness occupying Himself only with His own happiness (Baudin, 1885). Rather He is actively involved in the day-to-day affairs of the people. The people strongly attest to the fact that He is the creator and author of all things in heaven and on earth. The names and attributes of God clearly connote the people's belief in Him. He is regarded as omnipotent, holy, the creator and source of all other beings that originate from Him and are in turn responsible to Him. The exalted place of the Supreme Being as above other creatures gives rise to His worship in various African societies, either fully as is the case of the Ashanti of Ghana and the Kikuyu tribe of Kenya, or with partial worship as the Ewe and Abomey peoples of Togo do. Among the Yoruba and Igbo of Nigeria, the lack of an organized cult such as temples, shrines, altars, or priests for Him does not in any way diminish His presence and significance. He is believed to be present everywhere. At the same time, this is why He is not limited to a local shrine or represented in images or symbols. God is real to the Africans—His name is constantly on their lips. Each people have a local name which uniquely belongs to Him. The names by which the Deity is called in Africa are descriptive of His character and emphatic of the fact that He is a reality and that He is not an abstract concept (Idowu, 1973). As Westermann (1937) observes:

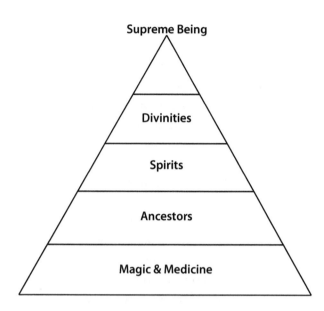

> The figure of God assumes features of a truly personal and purely divine Supreme Being ... it cannot be overlooked that he is a reality to the African who will admit that what he knows about God is the purest expression of his religious experience.

The Yoruba people refer to Him as Olodumare—Almighty God; Olorun—owner or Lord of Heaven; Aterere Kari aye—Omnipresent God. The Igbo refer to Him as Chukwu—the Great Source Being or Spirit; Chineke—the Source Being who created all things. The Akan of Ghana refer to Him as Onyame—the Supreme Being, the Deity. The Memde of Sierra Leone refer to Him as Ngewo—the Eternal One who rules from above. These various names and their meanings give us a vivid understanding of the African concept of the Supreme Being. To Africans, God is real, the Giver of Life and the All-Sufficient One.

Belief in Divinities

The belief in divinities form an integral part of the African belief system. The divinities were created for specific functions and do not exist of their volition. The relationship of the divinities to the Supreme Being is born of African sociological patterns. Most African countries have a king or chief as the head of the society, and he is always approached by other chiefs who are lesser in rank to the king. This is due to the belief that the king is sacred and must not be approached directly. The role of the divinities like the lesser chiefs as intermediaries between the Supreme Being and man is that of serving as a conventional channel of communication, through which man believes he should normally approach the Supreme Being. This distinctive role of the divinities led to the erroneous conclusion of the Europeans that the Supreme Being is never approached directly by Africans.

To the African, divinities are real, each with its own definite function in the theocratic government of the universe. The divinities are halfway as a means to an end and can never be ends in themselves. The real and final authority comes from the Supreme Being. This is why after each prayer and supplication before the divinities the Yoruba end the devotions with -*ase*, meaning "may it be sanctioned by the Supreme Being." The divinities have different names in different African societies. The Yoruba call them Orisa. To the Igbos, they are known as Alusindiminuo. The Akan address them as Abosom. There are numerous divinities in Africa, and their number varies from one community to another or from one locality to another. Their number ranges between 201 and 1,700 in various Yoruba localities. The names of divinities depict their nature or natural phenomenon through which they are manifested. For example, the divinity first associated with the wrath of God among the Yoruba was Jakuta, meaning "he who fights with stones." The same god among the Igbos is known as Amadioha. Among the Nupe the same divinity is called Sokogba—Soxo's ax.

The divinities in African concept can be classified into three categories. First are the primordial divinities. These are believed to have been in existence with the Supreme Being before and during the creation of the world. They are believed to have partaken in the creative works of God. Their origins are not known and are beyond man's probing. One of such divinities is Obatala, a Yoruba divinity believed to have been entrusted with the creation work of the physical part of men. Consequently, he is popularly referred to as Alamorere (the fine molder). He is also called Orisa-nla and designated as an arch-divinity; he is believed to be the deputy of Olodumare, deriving his attributes from those of the Supreme Being.

The second are the deified ancestors—those who were heroes during their lifetime by living extraordinary and mysterious lives are deified after their death. They are no longer mere ancestors, but absorb the characteristics of an earlier divinity. A vivid example is Sango, the deified Alaafin of Oyo, who assumed the attributes of Jakuta, the erstwhile thunder divinity in Yoruba land.

There are also divinities that found expression in natural phenomena. Such divinities are spirits associated with natural forces such as rivers, lakes, trees, mountains, forests, etc. Their habitations are considered sacred, and there are usually priests who are custodians of such places and through whom the spirit may be consulted. An example of this is the Olokun (water divinity), which is common among the Yoruba and Edo people.

Finally, divinities are believed to be ambidextrous. With this nature, they are capable of being good and bad simultaneously. Positively, they help in solving people's various problems by helping in procreation, fertility, increasing man's prosperity, and so on. On the other hand, when denied veneration, they could inflict misfortunes on a community.

Belief in Spirit

Africans believe in and recognize the existence of spirits referred to as apparitional beings who inhabit material objects as temporary residence. According to African belief, spirits are ubiquitous and can inhabit any area of the earth because they are immaterial and incorporeal beings. Though divinities and ancestors are sometimes classified as spirits, they are, however, different from the kinds of spirits being discussed here, in the sense that they are more positively associated with the people. They are, in fact, described as "domesticated" spirits. While men venerate, respect, and communicate positively with the divinities, he associates with the spirit out of fear and awe. Spirits are normally synonymous with inimical activities detrimental to man's prosperity, so the people try to placate them so that their progress may not be hindered. Spirits inhabit such places as rivers, hills, water, bushes, and trees. Such places are naturally sacred. For instance, among the Yoruba, the Akoko (known by the Igbo as Ogilisi) is reputed to be an abode for spirits.

Spirits have been classified into groups. Among the Yoruba, there are spirits known as Abiku or Ogbange. The Igbo refer to them as born-to-die children. These are considered sadistic spirits that specialize in entering into the womb of women in order to die at a specific period, thereby causing their victims pain and anguish. Such spirits could plague a particular woman several times if treatment is not applied. This is why in Yoruba land pregnant women are not allowed to walk about at noontime, because it is believed that this is the time the spirits roam about and they are capable of ejecting the original fetus of the pregnant woman and implant themselves as substitutes for the ejected fetus.

The second category of spirits is believed to be spirits of the dead whose souls have not been reposed. These are spirits the dead whose bodies have not been buried with due and correct rites. It is believed that their spirits will not be admitted to the abode of the departed. Thus, until they are properly buried, they will continue to wander about. Such spirits could also belong to those who engaged in wicked works while alive and also died wicked. Such spirits could haunt the community, wreaking havoc if not continually appeased.

The spirit of witchcraft belongs to the third category of spirits. It is a human spirit, and it is believed it can be sent out of the body on errands of havoc to other persons or the community in body, mind, or estate. Such spirits may cause diseases, miscarriages in women, insanity, or deformity in human beings.

Finally, Africans recognize spirits in anthropomorphic terms since they are believed to possess the same human characteristics such as tastes, emotions, and passions.

Belief in Ancestors

This belief is based on the concept that the world is dual: it is comprised of the physical world and the spiritual world. The spiritual world is recognized as an extension of the physical, thereby controlling it. Africans have a strong belief in the continued existence of their dead. The communal and family bonds are held to continue even in the next world. They are usually referred to as ancestors or the living dead. They are closely related to this world, but are no longer ordinary mortals. The Africans believe they can come to abide with their folks on earth invisibly to aid or hinder them to promote prosperity or cause adversity. This is why belief in them is not only taken seriously, but is also one of the most important features of the African Religion. The ancestors are factors of cohesion in the African society. This is because of the respect and honor given to them as predecessors who have experienced the life the living are now treading.

However not all the dead are ancestors. There are conditions laid down that must be fulfilled before assuming the exalted status of an ancestor. The first condition is that the dead person must have lived a good and full life. Second, he must have died a good death and not an abominable death caused by accident, suicide, or a violent or unusual death such as from chronic diseases. Finally he must have died in old age and be survived by children and grandchildren. When these conditions are fulfilled, he automatically becomes an ancestor and receives veneration so intense as to be erroneously regarded as worship. Idowu has this to say of the African belief in ancestors:

> To some extent, they are believed to be intermediaries between the Deity or the divinities and their own children; this is a continuation of their earthly function of ensuring domestic peace and the well-being of their community, to distribute favors, to exercise discipline or enforce penalties, to be guardians of community ethics and prevent anything that might cause disruption (Idowu, 1973).

Based on this belief, the Africans bury their dead in the family compound in the hope that they will continue to influence their lives. In the African societies, there are various ways of venerating the ancestors. It may be by pouring a libation of food and drinks and/or by prayers. It may be carried out by individuals or on a communal basis. Furthermore, there are also religious festivals which are usually carried out in the ancestral cult. In Yoruba land, the Oro and Egungun festivals are the symbolical representations of the ancestral cult.

Almost all the tribes in Africa have one form of ancestral cult with festivals associated with it for the veneration of the ancestors. An example is the Ashanti of Ghana, where we have the sacred Golden Stool, which is the ancestral symbol of the Ashanti. Other tribes in Africa with ancestral cults are the Mende of Sierra Leone, the Lugbara of Central Africa, and the Ovambo of Southern Africa.

Belief in Magic and Medicine

Magic and medicine form a significant part of the traditional beliefs of Africans. By definition, magic is an attempt on the part of man to tap and control the supernatural resources of the universe for his own benefit (Idowu, 1973). Through the use of supernatural powers, he tried to achieve his own desires through self-effort. Man's use of this power could either be positive or negative, depending on his conception of the power. Medicine, however, is the science or art of the prevention, treatment, and cure of disease. The art of medicine is important because man recognizes that health can be lost and medicine helps the body return to its normal state.

Basically, the difference between magic and medicine is that in the use of magic, man tries to enforce his will by using supernatural powers at his disposal; while through the use of medicine, man tries to utilize the powers at his disposal to prevent or cure any form of misfortune which might befall his body or estate. This is clearly seen in the words of R. S. Rattray, concerning the Akan belief about medicine:

> If God gave you sickness, he also gave you medicine (Rattray, 1923).

This is why medicine men, known as traditional doctors, abound in Africa. They regard their powers as a gift from God through the divinities. They claim they are given the art of medicine by divinities through dreams or through spirit possession. Among the Yoruba, the tutelary divinity of medicine is Osanyin. The divinity is believed to be the custodian of the art of medicine. Though magic is negatively viewed, when it is associated with medicine, the two become so interlinked that it becomes difficult to know where one ends and the other begins. This is because both employ supernatural powers and can be employed for both evil and good, depending upon the individual involved.

Another common trait about magic and medicine highlighted by Awolalu and Dopamu in writing about the religion of West Africa is that some tribes in Africa have a common name for magic and medicine. For example, the Yoruba call oogun, *egbogi*, and *isegun*. The Igbo call them *ogwu*, while the Akans of Ghana call them *suman*.

Finally, it is essential to point out that both magic and medicine constitute a part of the mysteriousness of the African Religion. This is because they derive their supernaturalness, efficacy, taboos, and custodians from the religion. This is why incantations and rituals are common features of magic and medicine in the African Religion.

Other Beliefs in African Religion

There are some other beliefs within the African Religion that are basically derived from the five major beliefs discussed above. They complement the major beliefs, and together they form the totality of the African Religious Belief. They are referred to as minor beliefs.

Belief in the Hereafter

Like all other world religions, the concept of a life after death is firmly entrenched in the people's belief: African Religion also holds the view that life exists beyond this physical world, which is considered the temporary abode of men while heaven is the spiritual and real home of man. Africans believe that man is made up of both body and soul. The soul does not die like the physical body, but rather it returns to the Supreme Being, who is believed to reside in heaven. The Supreme Being is the final destination of man to whom he belongs and must return. This belief is clearly illustrated in the Yoruba adage *Aye loja orun nile*—that is, the world is a marketplace and heaven is home. No one sleeps in the marketplace. After each day's transactions he or she returns home to rest.

However, not everyone is qualified to enter into heaven. Only those who have engaged in good works while on earth would be granted eternal rest with the Supreme Being, the Supreme Judge of all men. Among the Yoruba there is a saying which encourages man to do good while on earth in order to earn eternal life: *Serere to ri ojo ati sun*—do good so you can earn eternal life. It is believed that those who live an ungodly life on earth will be banished and separated from the Supreme Being.

Belief in Morality

Morality in African Religion is religiously based, since every sphere of the African life is closely associated with being religious. This is why Adewale (1988) asserts that the ethics (morality) of Africans from one to another is religious. Africans have a deep sense of right and wrong, and this moral sense has produced customs, rules, laws, traditions, and taboos which can be observed in each society (Mbiti, 1975).

Morality deals with human conduct, and this conduct has two dimensions, the personal and the social. It guides people in doing what is right and good for both their sake and that of their society. It evolved in order to keep society in harmony, which is achieved through the system of reward and punishment. African morality is centered around some basic beliefs. It is believed that morals are God given and were instituted simultaneously with creation. Therefore, its authority flows from God and must not be challenged. For his part, man is compelled to respond appropriately to these moral demands; failure to comply could incur the wrath of God. This is why certain calamities which may befall a community or person are often interpreted as a punishment from God.

Furthermore, Africans believe that some supernatural beings like the ancestors and the divinities keep watch over people to make sure they observe moral laws. They could punish or reward moral behavior. This further strengthens the authority of the morals. Human beings also play an active role in controlling the morality of the people. The individuals keep a close watch on those with bad moral attitude and often uproot them before they turn the society into an immoral one. This is based on the belief that the welfare and solidarity of the people are closely related to the moral action of individuals. Good deeds are normally encouraged, for these bring harmony, peace, and prosperity. On the other hand, misdeeds could bring calamities of all kinds.

Finally, the importance of morality to Africans cannot be overemphasized. It is evident in their myths, legends, and proverbs, which stress the need to keep the moral demands of human conduct.

Belief in Worship

The act of worship is an integral part of any religion and African Religion is not excluded. It is believed that through worship, one turns to his object of worship in adoration and supplication. Worship in African Religion is directed to the Supreme Being and veneration to the divinities. It is believed that if there is effective worship of both, there will be peace and harmony between the supernatural beings and man.

There are various forms of worship in African Religion. There is the formal and also the informal, the direct and the indirect. In parts of Africa with a direct form of worship, it is characterized by altars, priests, and sacrifices. This is especially so with the worship of the Supreme Being. In the case of indirect worship, there are no temples or priests specially designed for the Supreme Being.

The veneration of divinities could be done regularly on a communal level or individually. This is because they are frequently called upon for one favor or another. On the individual level, the informal type of veneration is carried out privately at the personal shrine normally located in the compound. At the communal level, the formal kind of veneration is carried out at the public shrine, where everyone within the community participates, including family heads, clan heads, priests, priestesses, and traditional rulers.

The main components of worship and veneration are prayers, songs, libations, invocations, and offerings. On the whole, worship or veneration in African Religion is employed to show adoration of and communication with the supernatural beings. It is believed that when these beings are adequately worshipped or venerated, they will bestow upon man the necessary blessings required for successful living on earth.

Sources of Information on African Traditional Religion

Africans have a rich cultural heritage, which has been handed down from one generation to another. The richness of their heritage reflects in all spheres of their lives, especially in the area of the Traditional Religion. Though the religion does not have a sacred scripture like other world religions, it has means by which its religious beliefs and practices can be known and appreciated. These devices are categorized into oral and non-oral. The oral devices are proverbs, myths, pithy sayings, legends, liturgy, everyday speech, songs, and Theocratic names. The non-oral devices consist of artistic expression.

Oral Traditions

This is regarded as the scriptures of African Traditional Religion. The lack of knowledge in the art of reading and writing caused the African society to employ a means of preserving and transmitting their religious beliefs and practices through oral traditions. They are testimonies of the past, which are transmitted from person to person over the ages. Some of them are records of actual historical events memorized by the people. Others are created by the people's imagination. Consequently, some are regarded to be more reliable than others. For example, proverbs, pithy sayings, and names are believed to be more reliable than legends, myths, daily speeches, and folktales, which are often distorted and cannot be regarded as authentic for grasping the people's beliefs and practices. Here are some forms of oral traditions and their functions:

Myths

In the African traditional society, storytelling at night is the most common recreation in many homes enjoyed by the children and young people. Myths attempt to explain certain things, especially the origin of man and the world. They are vehicles for conveying certain beliefs about man's experience in his encounter with the created order and with regard to man's experiences in the supersensible world. Through myths, man tries to find explanations for certain things. For example, how death came into world; why only women conceive; why they must labor before giving birth to children; why different languages in Africa came into being. Answers to such questions are conveyed in stories which help to preserve them in the memory, making it easier for retention. Myths give us an insight into some of the religious concepts of the Africans who evolve them. Myths are variable sources of information in African Religion because they serve as practical ways of preserving the nonliterate beliefs for possible transmitting without losing their theological themes, since most of these myths are popular stories that draw from beliefs and ideas familiar to the people. Some myths, especially those used during rituals, may enjoy a high degree of authenticity. Such myths could provide the basis for the scriptures of African Religion.

Proverbs

Proverbs are a major source of African wisdom and a valuable part of her heritage. They are a rich deposit of the wisdom of many generations and are held in high esteem. There are hundreds of such proverbs in different African societies which carried with them theological instructions, moral teachings, and metaphysical significance (Jacob, 1977). These proverbs reveal a lot about African religious beliefs, since they are mostly formulated from human experiences and reflections that fit into particular situations of life throughout the ages. It is no gainsaying that among Africans, proverbs are cultivated as an art form and cherished as an index of good oratory. For example, among the Yoruba, proverbs are regarded as "horses for retrieving missing words" that are used for conveying deeper meaning. From some of these proverbs one can learn the various attributes of God as creator, omnipresent, holy, merciful and upright, etc. Thus, we find many proverbs referring to God as an object of religious beliefs, such as the Akan proverb "If you want to tell God anything, tell it to the wind"; "God drives away flies for the cow with no tail" (Yoruba); "God has both the yam and the knife, only those whom he cuts a piece can eat" (Igbo). The importance of proverbs to Africans cannot be overemphasized, and this is clearly expressed in the Igbo adage, "A child who knows how to use proverbs has justified the dowry paid on his mother's head."

Names of People

Names are given immediately upon birth and considered to be very much a part of the personality of the person. In most African countries, the name of the Supreme Being is often made part of the child's name (Mbiti, 1969). This shows that they recognize the Supreme Being. Such names are used as practical demonstration of people's religious feelings, an expression of worship, and the events prevailing at the time of birth. This practically demonstrates how much the people associate the Supreme Being with the continuation of life and the birth of children. There are many names which signify a particular attribute of the Supreme Being. This would mostly depend on the circumstances surrounding the child's birth. Among the Yoruba, we have such names as Oluwatobi (God is great), Oluwaseun (God is victorious). The Burundi name their children Bizimana, meaning "God knows everything." A careful study of various names by researchers of African Traditional Religion could give a deeper insight into the people's religious beliefs, especially their belief in the Supreme Being.

Prayers

Prayers are an essential part of religion. They constitute the act of communicating with the Supreme Being, which is the essence of religion. Like other world religions, prayers are an integral part of African Traditional Religion. Africans pray to the Supreme Being for guidance, blessings in matters of daily life, good health, protection from danger, etc. These prayers are directed to Him, the deities, and the ancestors requesting for one favor or another. The prayers may be made privately by an individual or communally at public meetings and for public needs. When Africans pray, their prayers are always short and straight to the point. They do not "beat about the bush." There are different modes by which the people pray to the supernatural beings. There is the direct form of prayer, where people communicate with the Supreme Being without the help of intermediaries. However, the indirect form of prayer is when people pray on behalf of others. These include priests (both men and women), rainmakers, chiefs, kings, and sometimes medicine men (Mbiti, 1975). Africans pray because they believe the Supreme Being listens to them and accepts and answers their prayers. He is believed to be everywhere simultaneously. Here are a few examples of prayers in African Traditional Religion as illustrations.

For example, in the morning, the Yoruba have prayers like, "God, let us be successful today." Before worshipping, the Yoruba also pray, "Father, accept our offering and supplication to you."

When there is drought, Africans pray, "God, give us rain"; "Help us, O God"; "God, pity us." In times of sickness, African prayers implore the Supreme Being: "God, heal our sickness, let the sick be well again"; "Take this sickness away from our house, our town, our tribe." When a journey or other forms of a project are to be embarked on, Africans pray for God's protection and successful completion of the project. Prayers such as, "May God go with you"; "May God help you," etc., are offered. There are also general prayers of blessings, such as "God preserve you and keep you." Prayers are also offered for long life, such as "May God spare you to see your children's children."

It must be stressed that in all situations, the Africans pray to show their belief in and dependence on the Supreme Being. The prayers also provide information on the African concepts about the Supreme Being. These concepts form the center of the African Traditional Religion.

Non-Oral Sources

Apart from the oral sources, through which valuable information on African traditional religion is secured, there are some non-oral devices which provide valuable information on the beliefs and practices of Africans where their religion is concerned. These non-oral sources are identifiable in three forms: (i) artifacts; (ii) wooden masks; and (iii) the sacred institutions (Abioye, 2001). These three non-oral traditions are essentially artistic expressions that in concrete terms "showcase" the African traditional religion in all its ramifications. Here is a brief discussion of each of them.

Artifacts

All African societies are very rich in artifacts. These artifacts have become concrete reflections of African belief and devotion to the Supreme Being, the divinities, and the ancestors. The artifacts associated with the African Religion are in two categories. There are objects that are products of archeological findings. Artifacts in the second category are made up of the works of contemporary artists. Archeological excavations have, in some cases, led to more information and better understanding of certain African beliefs and practices. An example of this is the discovery of the temples and altars of Onyame, the Ashanti Supreme Deity, by R. S. Rattray. This singular discovery has gone a long way to show the inadequacy of the foreigners' usual claim that Africans had no organized worship of the Supreme Being because they did not have the idea of God. Indeed, the discovery has led to the search and successful discovery of many other different forms of organized worship among various African tribes. In addition, contemporary artifacts comprising of dance staffs, apparatuses for divination, musical instruments, votive figures, and many other forms of ritual objects provide information on African religious beliefs and practices. Many of these objects are found in shrines, while others are part of the general stocks of artistic works of many African artists attempting to recapture the rich African cultures in different forms.

Wooden Masks

These are concrete forms of covering the face in the attempt to hide the identity of the persons putting on the masks. The practice of putting on masks covers the whole of Africa and is regarded as a part of basic rituals, particularly having to do with the ancestral worship and the cult's expressions of the African people. In the first form, people who are regarded as incarnations of the spirits of the ancestors put on masks to conceal the earthly personality behind the mask and give cogency to the belief that the person wearing the mask is an ancestral spirit. In the second form, members of secret societies in Africa put on masks. Examples of mask usage are found among the Ogboni in Yoruba land and the Poro among the Mende of Sierra Leone.

In addition to the masks, there have been stools found in shrines. They are regarded as having religious implications in their artistic expression. The stools become objects of religious expression by the fact that they are not only found in shrines, but also in some other places. For example, among the Akan of Ghana, the stools have become altars upon which the head of the Akan lineage offers food and drink to their ancestors on appropriate occasions, thereby praying for the protection of the lineage. He also prays for good health and long life with an abundance of harvests.

Sacred Institutions

Beliefs of Africans in the Supreme Being and all other aspects of their religion are reflected in the several traditional institutions all over Africa. Traditionally, these institutions are regarded as sacred. An example of such institution is the traditional ruling institution. Among Africans, the traditional rulers are not mere political heads. They indeed represent the Supreme Being. Thus, the authority they have is in trust for the Supreme Being. This is why traditional rulers are not seen as ordinary persons. They are sacred. For example, the Yoruba call an *oba Igbakeji Orisa* (deputy of the Supreme Being). Among the Ashanti, the golden ornaments the king wears symbolize the belief that the Supreme Being is personified by the sun. Thus, when the Ashanti king wears the golden ornaments, he signifies the eternal fire of the sun (Abioye, 2001). In addition, among the Yoruba and the Akan, the cult of thunder has become a kind of sacred institution. In both African societies, the ax has assumed the symbol of the Supreme Being's judgment. The Supreme Being is regarded as the ultimate judge, and he can express his wrath against evildoers. The ax is the tool for this wrath. For the Yoruba, the divinity executing Olodumare's wrath is Sango. Consequently, axes are found in his shrines. Indeed, the original thunder divinity among the Yoruba was Jakuta, which literally means "one who throws stones." The stones are also found in the shrines of Sango, the new divinity of thunder. The Akan of Ghana refer to the ax as *nyame akuma* (God's ax), and the ax is found in the shrines of Onyame as a symbol of his wrath.

Review Questions

1. To what extent should African Traditional Religion be regarded as the "window" of African heritage?

2. In your opinion, what features of African Traditional Religion constitute the unique nature of the religion?

3. Examine and explain the context and significance of the words "African" and "Traditional" in constituting the name of the religion.

4. Why has it been so easy for "outsiders" to give misleading nomenclatures to African Traditional Religion?

5. Describe how the "fanatical" veneration of divinities by devotees of African Traditional Religion reflects African sociological values in the traditional society.

6 African traditional religion professes monotheism. Compare this form of monotheism to the that found in Christianity and Islam.

7 What challenges and future do you envisage for ATR in the global competition for religious space and relevance?

Bibliography and Further Reading

Abioye, S. O. 2001. "African Traditional Religion: An Introduction," in G. Aderibigbe and D. Aiyegboyin, eds. *Religion: Study & Practice*. Ibadan: Olu-Akin Press.

Abraham, W. E. 1982. *The Mind of Africa*. London: Weidenfeld & Nicolson.

Aderibigbe, G. 1995. "African Religious Beliefs," in A. O. K. Noah, ed. *Fundamentals of General Studies*. Ibadan: Rex Charles Publications.

Adewale, S. A. 1988. *The Religion of the Yoruba: A Phenomenological Analysis*. Ibadan: Daystar Press.

Awolalu, J. Omosade. 1979. *Yoruba Beliefs and Sacrificial Rites*. England: Longman.

Awolalu, J. O. and P. A. Dopamu. 1979. *West African Traditional Religion*. Ibadan: Onibonoje Press.

Bascom, William. 1969. *Ifa Divination: Communication Between Gods and Men in West Africa*. Bloomington: University of Indiana.

Courtlander, H. 1973. *Tales of Yoruba Gods and Heroes*. New York: Crown Publishers.

Ekpunobi, E. and S. Ezeaku, eds. 1990. *Socio-Philosophical Perspective of African Traditional Religion*. Enugu: New Age Publishers.

Ellis, A. B. 1894. *The Yoruba-Speaking People of the Slave Coast of West Africa*. London: Chapman & Hall.

Idowu, E. B. 1973. *African Traditional Religion: A Definition*. London: SMC Press.

———. 1962. *Olodumare: God in Yoruba Belief*. London: SMC Press.

Jacobs, A. B. 1977. *A Textbook on African Traditional Religion*. Ibadan: Aromolaran Press.

Kayode, J. O. 1979. *Understanding African Traditional Religion*. Ile-Ife: University of Ife Press.

Kierman, Jim. 1995b. "African Traditional Religion in South Africa." In Martin Prozesky and John de Gruchy, eds. *Living Faiths in South Africa*. Cape Town: David Philip.

———. 1993c. "The Impact of White Settlement on African Traditional Religions." In Martin Prozesky and John de Gruchy, eds. *Living Faiths in South Africa*. Cape Town: David Philip.

King, M. O. 1970. *Religions of Africa*. New York: Harper & Row Publishers.

Lucas, J. O. 1948. *Religions in West Africa and Ancient Egypt*. Lagos: CMS Books.

Mazrui, Ali A. 1986. *The Africans: A Triple Heritage*. London: BBC Publications.

MacVeigh, Malcolm J. 1974. *God in Africa: Conception of God in African Traditional Religion and Christianity*. Cape Coast: Claude Stark.

Mbiti, J. S. 1991. Introduction to African Religion, 2nd ed. Oxford: Heinemann.

———. 1982. *African Religion and Philosophy*. London: Heinemann Educational Press.

———. 1970. *African Concept of God*. London: SMC Press.

Merriam, A. P. 1974. *An African World*. Indiana University Press.

Discussion Questions

The Mediterranean basing competition and galley warfare: Venice, Genoa, Ottoman Empire, Spain, c. 1200–1600

1. How did the activities of Venice, Genoa, and the Ottoman Empire during the late medieval period (the 1200s and 1300s) and the early modern period (the 1400s and 1500s) in the Mediterranean Sea connect to the larger Afro-Eurasian world?

2. What was the relationship like between Venice and Genoa during the 1200s and 1300s? How did that change as the Ottoman Empire entered the region during the 1400s and 1500s?

3. What affect did Spain have on the balance of maritime power when it entered the scene in the 1500s?

4. How were maritime activities in the Mediterranean Sea affected by the seasons and by weather?

5. What happened to draw the focus of major-power naval competition out of the Mediterranean Sea during the 1500s?

The Ottoman Empire

1. Why have historians begun to downplay the European Renaissance? Do their reasons make sense to you? Why or why not?

2. Is it legitimate to think of the Ottoman Empire as the product of a *Middle East Renaissance*? Why or why not?

3. What was the European perception of the Ottoman Empire during the European Renaissance?

4. How would you characterize the relationship between the Italian city-states (in particular, Genoa and Venice) and the Ottoman Empire? Use at least two examples that support your characterization.

5. What was the Ottomans' perspective on peoples they conquered? Were you surprised by the way the Ottomans treated conquered peoples? Why or why not?

6. How did Italians and other Europeans respond to the Ottoman style of conquest?

7. In particular, how did the Muslim Ottoman Empire treat non-Muslims in their empire? Were you surprised by that element of their conquests? Why or why not?

8. When they visited the Ottoman Empire, what similarities to their homelands did Europeans discover?

9. Why does the author describe the Ottoman civilization as an "equal partner" in Mediterranean and European history, as opposed to being simply an "antagonistic backdrop"?

The globalization of disease after 1450

1. What does the author mean when he says that "disaster struck" the Americas in mid-October of 1492? Be specific.

2. Why does the author describe the first contact between Europeans (and Africans) and Native Americans as "not a once-only affair"?

3. What three factors combined to massively reduce the populations of Native American and Pacific Island peoples?

4. Why does the author say that the Old World (Eurasia and Africa) was in the process of becoming a "unified disease zone" by 1450? What does that mean? What explains it?

5. What specific diseases were transmitted from the Old World to the New starting around 1500? Why were Native Americans so susceptible to contracting and dying from those Old World diseases?

6. Why were Europeans not even remotely as susceptible to those diseases as Native Americans?

7. Why, in particular, was smallpox so deadly to Native Americans and so widespread a killer in the Americas?

8. What effects did all the epidemics have on the psyche of Native American populations? Give some examples.

9. What connections to larger world historical forces does the author make? Are they legitimate? Why or why not?

African Traditional Religion, nature, and belief systems

1. What are some differences between the *African Traditional Religion* discussed by the author and other world religions like Buddhism, Christianity, and Islam?

2 What are some similarities between the *African Traditional Religion* and other world religions like Buddhism, Christianity, and Islam?

3 How is the African Traditional Religion similar to the traditional way most African polities were organized politically and socially?

4 What role do ancestors play in the African Traditional Religion? What does this say about African families historically?

5 How do oral traditions factor into African Traditional Religion? Explain using some specific examples of how African oral tradition sustains African Traditional Religion.

UNIT II

THE EMERGENCE OF A MODERN GLOBAL WORLD, 1500–1900

Introduction

By the sixteenth century, the world was slowly—in fits and starts—becoming our modern world. Most crucially, the world was truly global by 1500, as the two hemispheres were no longer isolated from each other (notwithstanding the Viking exception). This would have terrible consequences for millions of Native Americans and Africans, and it also thrust Western Europe into a position of significance for the first time since the heyday of the Roman Empire. This unit charts some of that growth, as exemplified by the Scientific Revolution, the European Enlightenment, the Industrial Revolution, colonialism, and nationalism. However, it would take until the eighteenth century, and perhaps the early-nineteenth for nations like Britain and France to truly gain the upper hand in world politics and the global economy. Therefore, this unit also surveys the response to this budding modernity among non-European polities like Peter the Great's Russia and the still powerful but slowly declining Ottoman Empire, along with the broader Middle East, Latin America, Sub-Saharan Africa, and China.

The first two chapters of this unit cover the intellectual development Europe underwent during the sixteenth, seventeenth, and eighteenth centuries. That development was important for two reasons: it laid the philosophical and ideological foundations for European expansion, while also providing the technological and scientific progress needed for that expansion. Claudia Stein's essay on "The Scientific Revolution" makes an important distinction between the sixteenth century, a period she describes as the "Scientific Renaissance" because of the effort to revise past mistakes, and the seventeenth century, which was the true "Revolution" of scientific thought and creation. By the latter century, a true break from the past was being offered, most clearly seen through the Scientific Method, especially through a rash of experimentation.

Meanwhile, Mark Knights's and Angela McShane's chapter "From Pen to Print—A Revolution in Communications?" looks at one of the most important inventions in the early-modern world: the printing press (gunpowder and the compass being the other two commonly-cited important inventions,). In particular, Knights and McShane explain the historiographical debate over whether the printing press was, in fact, a revolution in communications or just an improvement to an existing industry. They point to the Enlightenment (and to a lesser degree, the European Renaissance and the Protestant Reformation) as the best argument for the printing press being a true revolution. On the other hand, books were fairly prevalent before the press was invented, and disinformation and authoritarianism could be spread just as easily, through books, so how revolutionary could it have been?

Regardless, it is undeniable that the Scientific Revolution and the Enlightenment were dramatically important both in Europe and globally. One ruler who desperately desired for his country to emulate Western European nations was Russia's tsar, Peter the Great. John M. Thompson in "Peter the Great and Westernization, 1689–1725" argues that Peter mostly failed at his Westernization project, however. At best, it was uneven, and even today, "Russian society still suffers from a split personality, with part of the national outlook secular, rational, and tolerant and part zealous, emotional, and xenophobic" (114–15). Peter the Great's most significant accomplishment, arguably, was actually more of an extension of the past, continuing Russian expansionism to gaining dominion or influence over Eastern Europe, a position it still maintains, to some degree, today. Thompson claims that Russia's lack of certain resources, along with its lack of institutions and pertinent attitudes, made modernizing difficult.

True modernity is seen by most historians as the advent of industrialization in Britain in the late-eighteenth century and its successive expansions to continental Europe in the early-nineteenth century and the United States by the middle of the century (followed by Russia and Japan around the turn of the century). Peter N. Stearns asks two age-old historical questions in his chapter: "New Causes: Why Did the Industrial Revolution Happen, and Why Did It Happen in Eighteenth-Century Britain?" Stearns mentions numerous factors necessary for industrialization, and essentially, Britain had all of them: plentiful resources in iron ore and coal, commercialization, consumerism, raw materials and increased capital provided by colonies, scientific development and Enlightenment thinkers, competition with other empires, a massive population boom facilitated by American crops, consolidated estates in Britain, a severely atrophied guild system, urbanization, and a relatively non-interventionist state in terms of economic development. Regardless of which of these was most important, Britain was able to enjoy about a half-century of solo industrialism before France, then Prussia, then the United States started to catch up, leading to that small little island's empire spanning the globe.

One of the areas Britain and other European powers were able to assert themselves during the nineteenth century was the Middle East. At the nexus of Afro-Eurasian and Indian Ocean trade for centuries and until the eighteenth century, the Middle East had enjoyed a much more exalted place in world history than Europe. By 1800, however, Europeans had achieved and maintained military, political and economic superiority compared to the region, which would only expand in the nineteenth century, as explained by Arthur Goldschmidt, Jr. and Lawrence Davidson in their essay, "European Interests and Imperialism." With that political and economic dominion came cultural ideas such as nationalism, which Goldschmidt and Davidson argue in the successive chapter, "The Rise of Nationalism," is the most "popular and durable ... among the ideas the Middle East has imported from the West" (157). That imported nationalism was uneven throughout the region, however, due to the differing histories of the kingdoms and empires there.

Finally, the modern world came fully into being by the late-nineteenth century with the industrialization of other parts of the globe and the reverberation of "new" Western imperialism throughout it. As Peter N. Stearns points out in "The Industrial Revolution outside the West," this advent of global modernity was due in large part to the Western monopoly over industrialization for over a century. That monopoly, however, tended to incentivize many places against industrialization, as new demands were made on raw materials from colonized regions. Still, the seeds of industrialization were planted in places as far-flung as Russia, India, Japan, and Brazil by the late-nineteenth century due to this budding globalization. And, while Russia and Japan would industrialize by around the turn of the century, India and Brazil—much less the rest of Latin America, China, the Middle East, and most of sub-Saharan Africa—would take much longer to do so. This uneven spread of industrialization and modernity did lead to the end of slavery and serfdom, however, so there were significant benefits to this process. Nonetheless, the age of the "haves" and "have-nots," or the developed and the developing world was upon us.

The Scientific Revolution

Claudia Stein

The term 'Scientific Revolution' refers to a period stretching roughly from 1500 to 1700. Its beginning is generally associated with the works of the astronomer Nicolaus Copernicus (1473–1543) and the anatomist Andreas Vesalius (1514–64) and its climax with the English EXPERIMENTAL PHILOSOPHER Isaac Newton (1643–1727). While the precise nature of developments is a matter of debate, all scholars agree that it is a key moment when a specific way of looking at the natural world—what we call 'modern science'—began to take shape.

Although very familiar to us today, the term was only coined in the 1940s by historians and philosophers interested in the history of the sciences (Box 5.1). With the term 'revolution', they emphasized the idea of a sudden and dramatic change in the way Europeans understood the physical world in the early modern period. But what exactly *did* change? For these scholars, most of them champions of intellectual history, the change manifested itself in the way people were *thinking* about nature. For them, the most important element of scientific endeavour was 'thought': bold, logical, objective, abstract and, of course, male. Their writings hailed the so-called Scientific Revolution as the triumph of a fearless, rational mind over the superstitious and backward reasoning of the dark Middle Ages.

Since the 1970s, however, this heroic view of the Scientific Revolution has come under attack. Scholars felt increasingly uneasy with the very idea of the Scientific Revolution as a singular and discrete event. Medieval historians, for example, have shown that their period was certainly not characterized by ignorance and scientific backwardness. On the contrary, they argued, medieval philosophers provided the foundation for the Scientific Revolution. Following these claims, John Henry

Claudia Stein, "The Scientific Revolution," *The European World 1500-1800: An Introduction to Early Modern History,* pp. 194-202. Copyright © 2009 by Taylor & Francis Group. Reprinted with permission.

argued that no single coherent cultural entity called 'science' underwent revolutionary change in the sixteenth and seventeenth centuries, simply because the modern notion of 'science' only emerged after 1800 (Henry 1997, 4). Before that date, it is now agreed, the natural world was approached with the intellectual and practical tools belonging to a scholarly tradition best described as NATURAL PHILOSOPHY (Dear 2001, 199).

> **Box 5.1**
>
> The monograph *The Origin of Modern Science* by the English philosopher of history Herbert Butterfield, first published in 1949, probably contains the most celebratory assessment of the Scientific Revolution:
>
> > 'Since that revolution overturned the authority in science not only of the middle ages but of the ancient world—since it ended not only in the eclipse of scholastic philosophy but in the destruction of Aristotelian physics—it outshines everything since the rise of Christianity and reduces the Renaissance and Reformation to the rank of mere episodes, mere internal displacements within the system of medieval Christendom.'
>
> > (Butterfield 1957, viii)

Natural philosophers were not concerned with discovering new things but aimed at *explaining* the entire existing system of the world. Their knowledge and practices covered such diverse fields as navigation, mining, medicine, botany, pharmacology, geology, alchemy, astronomy, but also philosophy, theology and law. Henry therefore warned that the Scientific Revolution must not be seen as a revolution *in* science, but as a set of dramatic transformations moving natural philosophy towards our modern concept of science. Particularly striking is the increased use of mathematics and measurements to obtain a more precise idea of how the world and its parts work. Moreover, natural philosophers began to trust observations and personal experiences more than ancient texts and, where necessary, embarked on specifically conceived experiments to gain a better understanding of nature's secrets.

Historians also reassessed the socio-cultural context in which scientific practices developed. The long-cherished image of the lonely male investigator of nature, obsessed with his work and immune to any worldly temptations, came under increasing attack. Equipped with methods from neighbouring disciplines like sociology or anthropology, scholars began to investigate the context of early modern science. They tried to see the world through the eyes of their historical actors and asked, for example, how their scientific enterprise was shaped by institutions such as the early modern patronage system or the etiquette of court culture. Feminist scholars demanded a place for women in the heroic accounts of the Scientific Revolution. Why is it, they asked, that hardly any women featured in the many histories of the Scientific Revolution? What are the socio-cultural reasons for their invisibility? As a result of subsequent investigations, we now know more about the activities of women as independent researchers (e.g. the German painter and botanist Maria Sybilla Merian, 1646–1717), as patrons (e.g. the English natural philosopher Margaret Cavendish, 1623–73) or as matrons of an early modern 'scientific' household (e.g. Jane Dee, 1555–1605, wife of the court physician John Dee, 1527–1608), and how significant they actually were for the development of modern science (Davis 1995; Schiebinger 1989; Harkness 1997).

Despite these recent debates, many historians still speak of a 'Scientific Revolution', since natural philosophers themselves, particularly those of the seventeenth century, believed that they were doing something radically new and different from their predecessors. Peter Dear has argued that the phrase should be reserved for the seventeenth century, when there is overwhelming evidence for the desire to break with previous conceptions and practices. Natural philosophers of the sixteenth century, in contrast, merely sought to 'correct' mistakes and 'renew' ancient wisdom. This phase, personified by Nicolaus Copernicus and Andreas Vesalius, may be best conceptualized as a 'Scientific Renaissance' (Dear 2001).

The Scientific Renaissance

After his university studies Nicolaus Copernicus worked as an administrator on estates belonging to the Catholic Church in Poland. His real passion, however, was mathematics and astronomy and every minute he could spare was devoted to the investigation of the cosmos. A reclusive scholar, his findings were only published in 1543, the year he died. In this famous book, *De revolutionibus orbium coelestium* [On the Revolution of the Celestial Spheres], Copernicus put forward his observation that the sun was the centre of the universe, with the earth and planets orbiting around it. This HELIOCENTRIC view turned the prevailing understanding of the cosmos—based on a stationary spherical earth at the centre and heavenly bodies in orbits around it—upside down. The GEOCENTRIC view of the cosmos was based on the 'bible' of astronomers at the time, the *Almagest*, written by the Greek astronomer Claudius Ptolemy (after 83–161). Ptolemy, whose intellectual framework derived from the writings of his compatriot Aristotle (384–322 BCE), believed in the existence of a two-sphered cosmos: the terrestrial sphere composed of the four elements, earth, water, air and fire, on the one hand; and the surrounding celestial sphere consisting of only one element, aether, on the other. According to Aristotle, the terrestrial sphere between the earth and the moon (also called the sublunar sphere) was characterized by constant change, generation and corruption; the celestial sphere above the moon (or supralunar sphere), however, by perfection and complete harmony—a place where nothing came into being or ceased to exist (Figures 5.1).

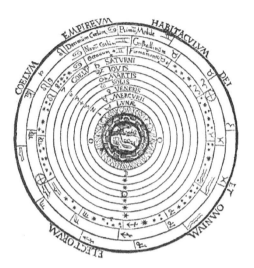 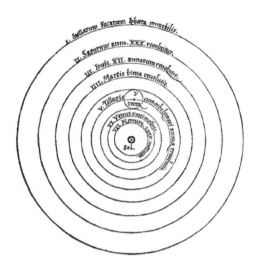

Figures 5.1 From the sixteenth century, scholars like Copernicus replaced the traditional geocentric view of the cosmos (on the left, with the earth at the centre) by a heliocentric model (right, with the sun [sol] at the centre). Diagrams in a 1660 edn of Apianus 1539 ('System of the Diverse Spheres') and Copernicus 1543, f. 9v. (Web resources).

By challenging these ancient and ultimately pagan ideas Copernicus entered dangerous territory, because over the centuries they had been assimilated into the teaching of the Church. According to the latter the earth at the centre of the universe was God's creation and anybody who questioned this view was a potential heretic. Copernicus was well aware of the controversial content of his work, although he did not consider it a 'revolutionary' break with the magical, irrational past, as many historians have argued. In the preface, which is dedicated to Pope Paul III (1534–49), he explained how he wished his findings to be understood. Copernicus first complains about the terrible state of astronomy. His explicit aim was to improve the situation by scrutinizing the views of all ancient philosophers and astronomers. From the point of view of a 'modern' scientist, this sounds distinctly odd, but for sixteenth-century university-trained academics like Copernicus it was essential to find ancient precedents for their positions. Whoever presented work as 'innovative' was unlikely to be taken seriously. Innovations—in our sense of the word—were considered trivial and insubstantial. 'Real' and 'truthful' knowledge could only be found in ancient literature and intricate philosophical debate.

By advocating a return to Antiquity, Copernicus supported the intellectual programme of HUMANISM, the great cultural movement of his time originating in fourteenth-century Italy. The principal objective of humanists (most of whom taught classical literature and rhetoric at the universities) was to reinvigorate their own society through the practices of the ancients ('The Renaissance' in Part IV). Renewal was their watchword and also the aim of Nicolaus Copernicus's study of the universe. He hoped to restore and correct ancient astronomical practice. A like-minded personality was the anatomist Andreas Vesalius, another key figure in the history of the

Scientific Renaissance. Born in Brussels in 1514 and trained as a physician at various European universities, Vesalius not only sympathized with humanist ideals but also possessed outstanding technical skills. He was widely renowned for his art of dissection, a practice effectively non-existent in universities at the time. Medical teaching there relied almost entirely on the interpretation of ancient texts. Flamboyant and happy to challenge more conservative colleagues, Vesalius propagated a return to practical anatomy to check whether the ancient medical writers, in particular the Roman physician Galen (129–c. 200), had been correct in their descriptions of the human body. The fruit of his work was a lavishly illustrated book, *De humani corporis fabrica* [On the Fabric of the Human Body], published in 1543 (the same year as Copernicus's treatise). For the first time in the history of western medicine, the human body was shown realistically ('Arts and Society' in Part IV).

Again, however, one should be careful not to project modern understanding of science onto the past and praise Vesalius as a radical liberator from the shackles of the medieval past. It is more appropriate to see *De Fabrica* as the work of an ambitious humanist (Box 5.2). Vesalius wished to contribute to the revival of Antiquity and desired to restore the kind of medicine that Galen had championed, but not by uncritical reverence of the latter as the ultimate authority. In his dissections Vesalius found many errors in Galen's work. This is not surprising, since Galen never dissected humans, only apes. Nevertheless, while acknowledging inaccuracies, Vesalius still upheld Galen as the model to be emulated. He was satisfied to correct Galen without undermining his broader physiological or pathological views. Like Copernicus, Vesalius did not seek to shake the foundations of antique knowledge, only to cleanse them of error.

Box 5.2

Vesalius's rhetoric in his introduction to *De Fabrica* (dedicated to the Holy Roman Emperor Charles V, ruled 1519–58) is very similar to that of Copernicus and reveals his true ambitions. Having deplored the decline of medicine since Antiquity, Vesalius asserts how in the present age:

> 'things have taken a turn for the better, and medicine, along with other studies, has begun so to come to life again and to raise its head from profound darkness that in several universities it has, beyond all argument, come close to recovering its former glory.'
>
> (*Vesalius 1998, f. Ii*)

However, by about 1600, the ambitions of those interested in the physical world had changed. Nothing distinguishes the 'new science' of the seventeenth century more clearly than its proponents' claim that it was 'new'. Natural philosophers increasingly aimed for a clean break with the past. Although ancient texts continued to be enormously important, they no longer served as signposts to a lost golden age, as in the sixteenth century.

Scientific Revolution

In April 1633, the papal court in Rome initiated a trial whose outcome was anxiously awaited by many involved in the investigation of nature all over Europe. The defendant was the Florentine Galileo Galilei (1564–1642), a natural philosopher, mathematician and author of *The Dialogue Concerning Two Chief World Systems* published a year earlier. In his work, Galileo discussed Copernican and Ptolemaic ideas of cosmology. A close reading of the text had convinced the papal authorities that it represented a vigorous attempt to establish the physical reality of the heliocentric Copernican system and to ridicule the Church's beliefs in the geocentric Ptolemaic cosmos. Galileo had supported his bold claims by brand-new 'discoveries' made with an improved telescope. He had observed, for example, that the ancient astronomical theory, according to which no changes occurred in the heavenly sphere, was flawed. Galileo's daily observations had revealed blemishes and irregularities on the surfaces of the sun and moon, from which he had deduced that changes *did* occur in the celestial sphere and that the Aristotelian doctrine of the heavens must be wrong. This claim was absolutely unacceptable for the Church whose entire body of teaching relied on Aristotelian premises. It thus comes as little surprise that the trial in 1633 ended in Galileo's defeat. He had to publicly refute Copernican ideas, *The Dialogue* was prohibited and its author condemned to life imprisonment in his own house, where he died in 1643. *The Dialogue* was only taken off the Church's INDEX LIBRORUM PROHIBITORUM as late as 1831.

Galileo's trial in Rome was *the* hot topic among Europe's natural philosophers. One in particular was extremely disturbed by its outcome, the Frenchmen René Descartes (1596–1650). Descartes was in fact so terrified by the verdict that he decided to leave his Catholic homeland for the Protestant Low Countries, where the intellectual climate, he felt, was less restrictive. In retrospect, he was probably right, because his aims were even bolder than those of Galileo: Descartes aimed at a radically new philosophy capable of replacing the Aristotelian paradigm. The 'Cartesian system' was part and parcel of a larger attempt to rethink the universe, a so-called 'mechanical philosophy' which became one of the most influential concepts of the seventeenth century. Indeed, by the end of the 1600s it had replaced Aristotelian ideas about the functioning of the physical world.

Descartes's ambition was to build this system on a foundation of certainty. He aimed at explanations of natural phenomena that could never be challenged. But how could absolute certainty be established? Descartes devised an ingenious intellectual strategy to test the truth value of natural knowledge. In a first instance, he doubted everything that was regarded as certain knowledge in his time and discussed the proposition from all possible angles. Nothing survived this rigorous test. Descartes then wondered whether any true and certain knowledge existed at all. He finally came to the conclusion that the only thing that could never be doubted was his own existence and his capacity for critical thought. The result of his reasoning is reflected in his famous sentence: 'Je pense, donc je suis' (or 'Cogito ergo sum', in part IV of his *Discourse on Method*: Web resources). Descartes's belief in the ability of the human mind to solve and explain anything also shaped his ideas about the functioning of the natural world. In his famous books *Discourse on Method* (1637) and *Principles of Philosophy* (1644), he tried to convince his readers that all physical phenomena could be explained by mathematical and mechanical concepts. In his view, the natural world worked like machinery, in the sense that change was brought about by (and could be explained in terms of) the intermeshing of bodies, like cogwheels in a clock. Descartes also applied his mechanical model to animals and human beings, which he imaged as complex automata or machines based on hydraulic systems, and he distinguished sharply between mind and matter, i.e. the body.

CARTESIANISM—as his mathematical view of the world soon came to be known—did not have the same sweeping success in England as it had on the Continent. This is mainly due to the development of a strong mechanistic 'experimental philosophy' in England, a type of investigation of the natural world that relied on gathering facts from experimental and observational work. One of the most important contributions to the understanding of the human body resulted from such experiments: the circulation of blood 'discovered' by the physician William Harvey. In his treatise *Anatomical Exercise on the Motion of the Heart and Blood in Animals* (1628), Harvey argued for the first time that the human heart serves to pump blood continuously around the entire body. While the ancient medical literature spoke of two independent circuits, Harvey argued that the arterial and venous systems were two components of one larger circulatory system. His hypothesis could not, of course, be demonstrated by simply opening a living animal body. To prove his claim, Harvey devised numerous experiments on a wide variety of animals and human beings over the course of a decade.

Harvey was just one of a large number of 'experiment enthusiasts' in seventeenth-century Britain and although these men faced much criticism, their methods soon prevailed. Experiments were about discovery, about finding new things, and that was exactly what many people found so fascinating about them. The greatest practitioner of experimentation was without doubt Isaac Newton. In 1703, he became president of the Royal Society, an institution—still in existence today—founded in the early 1660s as an association of like-minded individuals created to conduct experimental and natural historical inquiry on an organized basis. Newton contributed several new theorems and methods to mathematics, including differential calculus. But he also made important findings in physics. He showed, by experiment, the compound nature of white light and figured out a theory of colours. At the same time he solved the puzzle of the force of gravity. The latter theory, elaborated in Newton's celebrated *Philosophiae naturalis principia mathematica* [Mathematical Principles of Natural Philosophy, 1687], was entirely based on experimental observation and led him to the formulation of the three laws of motion, the basis of Newtonian mechanics as well as modern engineering.

Galileo, Descartes, Harvey and Newton would have been unable to pursue their interests without the support of a patron. Seventeenth-century universities offered no support to those interested in these new experimental approaches to investigate nature. A patron could be either a wealthy and noble individual such as the Grand Duke of Tuscany Cosimo II de' Medici, who sponsored Galileo's enthusiasm for astronomy, or an institution such as the Royal Society in the case of Newton ('Courts and Centres' in Part V). However, this does not make the investigation of nature in the early modern period an entirely elitist enterprise. Recent studies have identified other 'homes' where knowledge about nature was produced and exchanged such as private alchemical laboratories, museums or botanical gardens (Moran 2005; Findlen 1994; Spary 2000). An increasing research focus is also how these new ideas about nature could be disseminated and how they were adopted (and often reshaped) by people of lower social standing (Eamon 1994; Fissell 2004).

Assessment

By the time of Newton's death in 1727, educated Europeans looked at the natural world in a strikingly different way from their ancestors around 1500. While Copernicus and Vesalius had hoped to 'correct' ancient wisdom and adjust their own findings to it, French Cartesians and English experimental philosophers such as Harvey or Newton in the seventeenth century were primarily concerned with discovering new things and with the control of the natural world. Yet even though the ways Europeans thought about nature and its exploration changed beyond recognition during the period of the Scientific Revolution, one component remained the same: investigating nature always involved God ('Religious Culture' in Part III). Even Newton, the celebrated perfectionist of experimental philosophy, a cool and abstract thinker, understood his endeavour as being a service to the Almighty. There were no atheists among the natural philosophers of this period. They all saw themselves as part of God's governed universe and never doubted its creator.

Discussion Themes

1. Is 'nature' a given entity or a social construct?
2. What is the difference between 'Scientific Renaissance' and 'Scientific Revolution'?
3. What did the 'Scientific Revolution' overthrow?

Bibliography

(A) Sources

Apianus, Petrus (1539), *Cosmographia*, Antwerp

Newton, Isaac (1628), *Philosophiae Naturalis Principia Mathematica*, London

Vesalius, Andreas (1998), *On the Fabric of the Human Body* [1543], trans. William Frank Richardson, San Francisco

(B) Literature

Biagoli, Mario (1992), 'Scientific Revolution, Social Bricolage and Etiquette', in: *The Scientific Revolution in National Context*, ed. R. Porter and M. Teich, Cambridge, 11–54

Butterfield, Herbert (1957), *The Origins of Modern Science, 1300–1700*, New York

Davis, Nathalie Zemon (1995), *Women on the Margins: Three Seventeenth-Century Lives*, Cambridge, Mass.

Dear, Peter (2001), *Revolutionizing the Sciences: European Knowledge and its Ambitions, 1500–1700*, Basingstoke

Eamon, William (1994), *Science and the Secrets of Nature*, Princeton, NJ

Findlen, Paul (1994), *Possessing Nature: Museums, Collecting, and Scientific Culture*, Berkeley, Calif.

Fissell, Mary (2004), *Vernacular Bodies: The Politics of Reproduction in Early Modern England*, Oxford

Harkness, Deborah E. (1997), 'Managing an Experimental Household: The Dees of Mortlake and the Practice of Natural Philosophy', *Isis*, 88, 247–62

* Henry, John (1997), *The Scientific Revolution and the Origins of Modern Science*, London

Kuhn, Thomas (1962), *The Structure of Scientific Revolutions*, Chicago

Moran, Bruce (2005), *Distilling Knowledge: Alchemy, Chemistry and the Scientific Revolution*, Cambridge, Mass.

Schiebinger, Londa (1989), *Has Mind No Sex? Women in the Origins of Modern Science*, Cambridge, Mass.

* Shapin, Steven (1996), *The Scientific Revolution*, Chicago

Spary, Emma (2000), *Utopia's Garden: French Natural History from Old Regime to Revolution*, Chicago

(C) Web resources

Copernicus, Nicholas (1543), *De revolutionibus orbium coelestium*: <http://ads.harvard.edu/books/1543droc.book/>

Descartes, René, *Discourse on Method* (1637): <http://records.viu.ca/~johnstoi/descartes/descartes1.htm>

'Virtual Library for the History of Science, Technology & Medicine': <http://vlib.iue.it/history/topical/science.html>

From Pen to Print—A Revolution in Communications?

Mark Knights and Angela McShane

Today's digital media have transformed the lives of people living in the west. Digitized images, text and sound mean that we have new ways of accessing what we want to learn about or enjoy, and the range of things we can know about has expanded. Yet the book you are reading is testament to the long reach of another technology that had a similarly transformative effect in the early modern period: print. The printing press was one of three inventions—alongside gunpowder and the compass [...]—that seemed to revolutionize society. The politician, intellectual and essayist Francis Bacon claimed that 'these three have changed the whole face and state of things throughout the world' (Bacon 1620, Bk. I, cxxix). In this chapter we will consider Bacon's claim in relation to the invention, development and significance of printing and its role in two broader developments: first, the 'communications revolution' of the early modern period and, second, the intellectual, religious and cultural changes of the RENAISSANCE, the Reformation and Enlightenment.

Communication Media and the Coming of Print

Medieval society used a wide range of interconnected oral, written and visual media. Face-to-face exchange predominated, but many individuals and institutions kept records, while scribes produced multiple copies of old and new texts, not only theological works (although they formed the majority), but also literary classics, medical treatises, legal documents and writings related to government business. It was a visual world, too, where symbols, rituals and ceremonies pervaded religious and political interaction. Painted and sculpted images conveyed ideas and told stories, especially before the Protestant Reformation, when churches, civic buildings and homes all over Europe were highly decorated inside and out with images and objects depicting aspects of everyday life and religious belief. Printing added to this web of communicative practices, building on older technologies like the 'codex' or book form (which had largely, though not completely, replaced rolls), paper-making and fixed inks. MOVABLE TYPE in clay, wood and metal had been invented centuries before in China (between 1041 and 1234), and we know that books were printed in the east as early as 1377. But the extensive and systematic exploitation of this technology occurred first in fifteenth-century Europe, perhaps because it was a technology better suited

Figure 6.1 Beginning of Jerome's Epistleto Paulinus from the Gutenberg Bible of 1454–55 (vol. 1, f. 1r). Note how Gutenberg produced pages that replicated, as far as possible, typical scribal productions of the period: British Library, London.

to the more restricted alphabets of the west than to the hundreds of characters required for Chinese printing. The breakthrough came in the 1440s when Johannes Gutenberg combined three innovations: a way of producing movable metal type, a new kind of oil-based printer's ink and the wooden hand press. Cumulatively, these led the way to the mass reproduction of books and a myriad of other printed goods such as pamphlets, pictures, tables, maps, ballads, etc. A defining moment was the production of the 'Gutenberg Bible' at Mainz in 1454–55, the first major book printed in the west (of which forty-eight of the *c.* 180 original copies still survive; Figure 6.1 and Web resources). As Gutenberg's example suggests, printers and booksellers (the early modern equivalent of publishers) were important players in the story of the creation of a market for print (Pettegree 2002).

The expansion of the printing industry was rapid. By 1476 William Caxton had set up the first printing press in England, and by 1500 there were more than 1,000 printing shops across Europe. Their number and output also increased over time, though this was uneven throughout Europe and often depended on the degree of press freedom that governments and Churches allowed as well as on the vigour of religious, political and cultural debate. In England, some 400 titles were published by the first decade of the sixteenth century; 6,000 by the 1630s; 20,000 (after the temporary collapse of governmental control) in the 1640s; 21,000 (after pre-publication censorship was finally abolished in 1695) in the 1710s and 56,000 by the 1790s (Raven *et al.* 1996, 5; Houston 2002, 175). In Germany the Thirty Years War curbed book production: 1620 levels were not achieved again until 1765, but thereafter output became buoyant, with two-thirds of the 175,000 titles published in the eighteenth century produced in its last third. In France, where censorship was stronger, the number of titles increased less dramatically, from just 500 in 1700 to 1,000 by the Revolution of 1789; and in eighteenth-century Russia the figure only reached 250 titles a year in the 1780s (Blanning 2002, 140–2; Box 6.1).

Box 6.1
Estimates of European book production:

Before 1500	20 million copies
1500–1600	150–200 million copies
1700–1800	1,500 million copies

(*Houston 2002, chapter 8*)

The figures in Box 6.1 are necessarily imprecise, since evidence about print runs is fragmentary. Two or three hundred copies of a title may have been quite common, though larger runs were printed for controversial or best-selling items, and books were also reprinted if there was demand. Books catered for many different markets. There were expensive large (folio) editions sold in bookshops but also cheap print, such as ballads, that could be hawked around by pedlars and achieve widespread dissemination ('English Broadside Ballad Archive': Web resources). The book trade was also innovatory, developing new genres such as the periodical, which flourished in the seventeenth and eighteenth centuries. In France there were 15 periodicals in 1745 but 82 by 1785; in Germany we can trace 58 journals up to 1700 but an incredible 1,225 new ones in the 1780s alone (Blanning 2002, 158–9). Thus the printed word became widely accessible, assisting (and reflecting) an increase in literacy (Box 6.2).

> **Box 6.2**
>
> A popular German novel, set in the period of the Thirty Years War and published in 1668, explained how print itself impacted upon literacy: the hero Simplicissimus describes how he was taught to read by his hermit mentor:
>
> > 'Now when I first saw the hermit read the Bible, I could not conceive with whom he should speak so secretly ... when he laid it aside I crept thither and opened it ... and lit upon the first chapter of Job and the picture that stood at the head thereof. [When the hermit explains the nature of the image and the 'black lines' on the page Simplicissimus demands to be taught to read. He explains how the hermit wrote out for him] an alphabet on birch-bark, formed like print, and when I knew the letters, I learned to spell, and thereafter to read, and at last to write better than could the hermit himself: for I imitated print in everything.'
>
> > (Grimmelshausen 1989, 21)

Simplicissimus's story shows how both pictures and words could act to spread knowledge among all kinds of people, and how the form of printed letters began to affect how people wrote. It also reminds us that learning to read came before learning to write. In the early modern period, reading was increasingly considered an essential skill, for religious as well as social purposes. It is now thought that while the ability to read was reasonably widespread, and augmented by illustrated texts and communal reading practices, the ability to write was much less prevalent, since it took a long time to learn and was only necessary for those who needed to write for their trade.

Literacy rates were on the rise, albeit with significant social, regional and gender variations (Houston 2002). During the century between the 1680s and 1780s, literacy rates in France increased from 29 per cent to 47 per cent for men, and from 14 per cent to 27 per cent for women. In German-speaking countries, the rise was from 10 per cent of the adult male population in 1700 to 25 per cent in 1800 (Blanning 2002, 112–13). Such rates were achieved much later in Eastern and Southern Europe, but earlier in England, where male literacy ran at 30 per cent in 1640 and 45 per cent by 1715, and even higher in London, where under 10 per cent of males were illiterate by the 1720s (Cressy 1980, table 7.3). The rise in literacy, along with the rise in print, fostered the emergence of a reading public that consumed print in a variety of ways (Sharpe 2000; Raven *et al.* 1996). We can detect active and reflective readers, who scribbled notes and comments in the margins of their books; but we also know that reading was considered a sociable rather than a solitary affair (at least until notions of privacy gained sway in the eighteenth century), with material read out aloud to companions. As the amount of print available increased (particularly in metropolitan areas), so reading for some changed from an intensive experience of a few texts to an extensive one, sampling many. Above all, perhaps, print became a form of entertainment as well as a means of disseminating information.

But did all this amount to a print revolution?

The Case for A 'Printing Revolution'

In an influential text that held sway for over twenty years—and which continues to reverberate—Elizabeth L. Eisenstein argued that the development of printing marked a shift from old production methods, which had relied upon handwritten copies, and that the 'transforming powers of print', via the technology of the press, permitted a fixed and reliable mass replication of texts, images and symbols (Eisenstein 1979). Her thesis has since been challenged in several respects, so here we will consider the various arguments in some detail.

Eistenstein's key themes were that the printing press brought about:

- *Standardization*: the ability to reproduce the same text over and over again was important for the acquisition of new knowledge, e.g. in astronomy, since a 'single text might enable scattered observers to scan the heavens for the same signs on the same date'.
- *Diffusion and dissemination of knowledge*: the massive growth in the numbers of books and other forms of print led to increasing scholarly exchange, facilitated by related institutions like libraries and book fairs.
- *Preservation of texts*: print was 'the art that preserved all other arts', allowing the accumulation of texts, data and opinions with a potential to destabilize the established order. (Eisenstein in Grafton *et al.* 2002).

These features, Eisenstein argued, created a new 'print culture' in Europe, which changed the early modern world by shaping the processes we call the Renaissance, Reformation and Scientific Revolution. She pointed out that printing brought new occupational groups (such as printers, publishers and booksellers); gatherings of authors and readers in printing shops; and new marketing and manufacturing techniques. As it was easier to move books than people, these new products — she suggested — transcended geographical borders and limitations of travel. This greatly assisted the gathering and dissemination of knowledge in the 'Scientific Renaissance' [...].

Historians of the Reformation have also noted the importance of print. Scholars such as Robert Scribner see the press as intrinsic to the dissemination and contestation of the Protestant reformations [...]. Cheap print, such as ballads and primers, could be used to inculcate piety or, as in the case of visual satires, to ridicule religious opponents. Print allowed the religious debates to be played out to a wide audience and to reflect and shape its thinking (Box 6.3). Sometimes the link between print and Protestantism was clear: the decision of Sweden's new King Gustavus Vasa to bring about a Lutheran reformation led to the setting up of a Swedish publishing trade for the first time.

Box 6.3

In his *Book of Martyrs*, the English Protestant John Foxe saw printing as part of the onslaught on Catholic superstition and ignorance:

> 'hereby tongues are known, judgement increaseth, books are dispersed, the Scripture is seen ... times be compared, truth discerned, falsehood detected ... and all ... through the benefit of printing. Whereof I suppose, that either the pope must abolish printing, or ... he must seek a new world to reign over: for else as this world standeth, printing will doubtless abolish him.'

(1583 edn, 707; Web resources)

In Catholic territories, by contrast, Eisenstein argued, scientific advance was hampered by the papal INDEX LIBRORUM PROHIBITORUM (Web resources; [...]). This listed titles forbidden to be printed or read by Catholics and it came to include many scientific books, such as works by Galileo and Brahe. Yet, even in Catholic countries, print fed the imaginations of those relatively low down the social scale. Perhaps the most famous example is Menocchio, a sixteenth-century Italian miller, whose private reflections on what he read were exposed by the Inquisition and revealed a world of heretical belief (Ginzburg 1980).

Another intellectual development in which print arguably played an essential role is the Enlightenment [...]. Like the 'Scientific Revolution' and the Protestant and Catholic Reformations, the Enlightenment throve on the dissemination of ideas and challenges to existing authorities. In the mid- and later seventeenth century it played a very significant part in the intellectual ferment of two British revolutions (Zaret 2000). The massive expansion of print in the eighteenth century, which affected Catholic as well as Protestant countries, allowed the circulation of ideas and knowledge as a collective and even pan-European phenomenon. Although states increased their power and ability to clamp down upon dissidents, intellectuals could bypass state censorship and disseminate their ideas by taking advantage of improved travel and communications systems and the international print trade. The Enlightenment PHILOSOPHE Voltaire, for example, after an early spell in prison for libel in 1718, took to living near Switzerland so that he had access to publishers and printers who were free from French government censorship. In addition to the growth of communications between scholars, intellectuals and political and religious radicals across the Atlantic world, the market for pirate or cheap copies of texts became common. The multi-volume ENCYCLOPÉDIE was reproduced in unofficial editions that collectively ensured a far greater and wider impact than the 'officially' produced original would ever have done alone. Thus the French Revolutionaries looked back to the *philosophes* and their popularizers as precursors who had helped lift the veil of ignorance and tyranny. Robert Darnton argues that cheap print, even the semi-pornographic books of eighteenth-century France, played a key role in carrying Enlightenment ideas (Darnton 1995). Moreover, Enlightenment print was also at the heart of a growing European and American sociability that had political and cultural repercussions: contemporaries shared their reading in clubs, coffee houses and salons, spreading ideas that chipped away at the established order. Another consequence was that such 'print communities' facilitated the emergence of national identity, especially in states such as the Dutch Republic, Spain, France and Britain, by helping to foster similar imaginative boundaries and shared national cultures. In Britain, for example, the 'news revolution' promoted by the flourishing of periodicals after governmental control on them lapsed in 1695 may have helped to strengthen ties, or a sense of 'imagined community' (Anderson 1983).

Print, then, was arguably part of a revolution in science, religion and ideas; it helped create revolution in seventeenth-century England and bring down the ANCIEN RÉGIME in France. And it led to cultural transformations across Europe.

The Case Against A 'Print Revolution'

Reluctant to place so much emphasis on one new technology, some scholars perceive a wider early modern communications revolution (Behringer 2006). An item of print only had impact once it was disseminated and that relied on improvements in marketing but even more fundamentally in the means of transport. Over the early modern period space and time shrank, as better roads, ships, canals and postal services improved communications. The Habsburgs developed a postal system in the early sixteenth century; and by the end of the eighteenth century there were about 2,500 postal stations in Germany and France. Travelling time between towns was cut dramatically. Thus, whereas in 1500 it took thirty days to go from Hamburg to Augsburg, by 1800 this had been cut to just five for postal couriers (Behringer 2006, 364). News—both manuscript newsletters and then printed newspapers—flowed along such routes; indeed, it depended on them. Without these developments in transport infrastructure the impact of the 'print revolution' might have been rather more restricted.

Historians have also argued that the revolution from a hand-written (scribal) and oral culture to a print culture has been exaggerated (Crick and Walsham 2004, 'Introduction'). Workshops of late medieval scribes had already created large numbers of books and manuscripts that proliferated across Europe. Indeed, whereas for Simplicissimus the character of print shaped the way he wrote, scribal practices and styles could in turn influence print which aped letter forms or imitated manuscript formats. Nor was scribal production suddenly replaced by printing. Hand-written copies of texts continued to flourish at least until the late seventeenth century, especially where censorship restricted the activities of authors and publishers. For much of the early modern period a literate, rather than a print, culture was what mattered, with a key divide between those who possessed or had access to texts and could read them, and those who did not.

Just as scribal practices remained vibrant, oral culture was not undermined or even replaced by 'print culture' ('Popular Culture(s)' in Part IV). Rather, print and oral culture existed in mutually reinforcing and stimulating ways: what was talked about found its way into print, and what was printed was talked about. Indeed, periodicals aimed at the middling sort—such as the *Tatler*—appeared with the specific intention of providing men and women in taverns, markets, clubs, salons and coffee houses with topics of conversation, and learned journals like the Royal Society's *Philosophical Transactions* stimulated debates all over Europe.

The case for a print revolution argues that it was instrumental in spreading knowledge and information. Yet it can be argued that print spread disinformation. Contemporaries used print but they also distrusted it. This was less the case in the scientific and cultural worlds but more so in the religious, political, social and economic arenas. Far from verifying and establishing 'truth' and 'reason', print could be used to distort and invert them. Paradoxically, then, although print 'fixed' texts, it could unfix truth. Indeed, partisans of all stripes believed their rivals engaged in deliberate attempts to mislead readers. In those circumstances, traditional forms of gauging credit—for example, through social or religious status—remained highly important. Distrust was further boosted by the ubiquitous anonymity of the medium—almost half the number of titles had no attributed author—which apparently allowed writers to lie without fear of reprisal (Figure 6.2). The developing nature of the book trade also encouraged the more disreputable end of the trade, especially in France and England, where by the eighteenth century a 'grub street' of impoverished authors, printers and publishers readily invented stories or took both sides of an argument in order to stoke the public appetite. As Filippo di Strata put it: 'The pen is a virgin, the printing press a whore' (Brooks 2005, 4). Print was a business, like any other, that pandered to markets. The profits were as much financial as cultural or intellectual.

Nor, it could be argued, was the print revolution necessarily one that undermined the Ancien Régime; indeed, it could even support and strengthen the role of authoritarian governments. The type of print products available remained surprisingly traditional. Theological debate kept a high profile in the output of the eighteenth century, for all the so-called secularizing tendency of the Enlightenment. Printed satire may have helped to delegitimize notions of a sacred monarchy or an unquestioned Church, but religious texts, sermons, schoolbooks, proclamations and government apologists served to defend it. And print could enhance and enforce authority within the state. Bureaucratization, centralization, more effective fiscal powers, militarization and the defence of ideologies of order were all facilitated by better communications. Moreover, the financial revolutions of the eighteenth century, which saw large amounts of private money invested in governmental debts and loans, relied to an important extent on information being available to investors via the newspapers and other forms of print. Indeed, the activities of

Figure 6.2 This anti-cavalier broadside ballad was published, probably with parliamentary approval, in 1642 at the outsetof the English Civil War and as part of the enormous printed propaganda campaigns that broke out from 1640. An attack on the pillaging behaviour of cavalier soldiers, copies could be sent all over the country by post and they could be pasted onto whipping posts in market-places, on church doors and on the walls in alehouses—in any place where both cavaliers and roundheads could see them. Anon., *The English Irish Soldier* (1642): British Library, London.

the state stimulated printed news: the 'coranto', an early form of newspaper, which developed at the beginning of the seventeenth century in the Netherlands, from an earlier French example, concentrated entirely on foreign affairs and European conflicts.

Finally, even if there was a print revolution in the sense of the greater production and availability of the press, it is hard to establish a clear correlation between text and action. Because propaganda was available, does that guarantee that its message would be followed?

Was the French Revolution the result of the Enlightenment and the Enlightenment the result of the press?

Assessment

It is certain that distribution and accessibility of texts increased Europe-wide from the fifteenth century onwards. Historians and literary scholars have pointed to revolutions not just in reading habits and print formats but also in religion, science, politics and wider cultural belief-systems that seem attributable to the press. Yet how far they actually were remains hotly contested. On the one hand, there are many who see the press as really instrumental in fostering a religion of the word, such as Protestantism; as disseminating ideas that both spread a rebirth of classicism and undermined the established order; and as contributing to the state and national identity as well as to a culture of entertainment and new forms of writing. On the other hand, there are scholars who stress that print did not provoke a radical break with the past and that its impact was often dependent on other technologies, especially transport. Far from undercutting an oral and literate culture, print merely reinvigorated it in different ways; print was not always available, especially among the poor and less well-off; print did not fix truth and reason but promulgated lies, propaganda and polemical irrationalities as one author railed against another. Moreover, the correlation between text and behaviour is uncertain.

Yet these are not mutually exclusive interpretations. We might simply want to build important caveats into our analysis of the transformative power of print. Indeed, in this respect it is helpful to think of the ways in which modern digital technologies coexist with older ones, are taken up at different rates with varying degrees of enthusiasm and foster new ways of thinking and behaving. When we evaluate such questions we are thrown back to problems faced by those who lived in the early modern period. Do changes in communicative practices change the way we think and what we say? Should we embrace transforming technologies or be sceptical about them or both? Are there justifiable limits on the freedom of expression or publishing copyright? How do we discern lies and misinformation, and what can we do about them? These are early modern questions that have a twenty-first-century urgency.

Discussion Themes

1. Is the term 'print revolution' misleading?
2. Did changes in communicative practices change belief and behaviour in early modern Europe?
3. Was print necessarily subversive of authority?

Bibliography

(A) Sources

Bacon, Francis (1620), *The New Organon: Or True Directions Concerning the Interpretation of Nature*, London

Grimmelshausen, Johan Jacob (1989), *Simplicissimus* [1668/9], trans. S. Goodrich, Sawtry

(B) Literature

Anderson, Benedict (1983), *Imagined Communities: Reflections on the Origin and Spread of Nationalism*, London

Behringer, Wolfgang ed. (2006), 'Communication in Historiography', special issue of *German History*, 24:3

Blanning, T. C. W. (2002), *The Culture of Power and the Power of Culture: Old Regime Europe 1660–1789*, Oxford

Brooks, Douglas A. ed. (2005), *Printing and Parenting in Early Modern England*, Aldershot

Cressy, David (1980), *Literacy and the Social Order: Reading and Writing in Tudor and Stuart England*, Cambridge

Crick, Julia and Walsham, Alexandra eds (2004), *The Uses of Script and Print, 1300–1700*, Cambridge

Darnton, Robert (1995), *The Forbidden Best-Sellers of Pre-Revolutionary France*, London

* Eisenstein, Elizabeth L. (1979), *The Printing Press as an Agent of Change: Communications and Cultural Transformations in Early Modern Europe*, 2 vols, Cambridge

Ginzburg, Carlo (1980), *The Cheese and the Worms: The Cosmos of a Sixteenth-Century Miller*, Baltimore, Md.

* Grafton, Anthony, Eisenstein, Elizabeth L. and Johns, Adrian (2002), 'AHR Forum: How Revolutionary was the Print Revolution', *American Historical Review* 107, 84–128

Houston, R. A. (2002), *Literacy in Early Modern Europe*, 2nd edn, London

Pettegree, Andrew (2002), 'Printing and the Reformation', in: *The Beginnings of English Protestantism*, ed. P. Marshall and A. Ryrie, Cambridge

Raven, James, Small, Helen and Tadmor, Naomi eds (1996), *The Practice and Representation of Reading in England*, Cambridge

Scribner, Robert (1981), *For the Sake of Simple Folk: Popular Propaganda for the German Reformation*, London

Sharpe, Kevin (2000), *Reading Revolutions: The Politics of Reading in Early Modern England*, New Haven, Conn.

Zaret, David (2000), *Origins of Democratic Culture: Printing, Petitions and the Public Sphere in Early Modern England*, Princeton, NJ

(C) Web resources

'English Broadside Ballad Archive', University of California, Santa Barbara: <http://www.english.ucsb.edu/emc/ballad_project/>

'The Gutenberg Bible' (c. 1454), British Library: <http://prodigi.bl.uk/gutenbg/file1.htm#top>

'Index Librorum Prohibitorum' (1557–), IHSP: <http://www.fordham.edu/halsall/mod/indexlibrorum.html>

'John Foxe's *Book of Martyrs*', Humanities Research Institute, Sheffield: <http://www.hrionline.ac.uk/johnfoxe/>

'Stephen Fry and the Gutenberg Press', BBC 4 programme in 'The Medieval Season': <http://www.bbc.co.uk/bbcfour/medieval/gutenberg.shtml>

Peter the Great and Westernization, 1689–1725

John M. Thompson

The thud of axes slicing into wood resounded through the walls of the small log house on the riverbank. Peter, tsar of Russia, stirred in his sleep, then sat up quickly. Seeing daylight under the door, he cursed himself and jumped out of bed, throwing on his clothes as he hastened outside. He liked to be first on the job, but already carpenters perched on top of and around the frames of several large ships nearby. After momentarily warming his hands over a fire alongside several just-arisen workmen, Peter picked up his own hammer and axe. Energetically, he clambered up the scaffolding surrounding a galley under construction and threw himself into the work. Peter looked supremely happy. As he wrote in a letter at that time, "We are eating our bread in the sweat of our face."

No one seemed surprised to see his tsarist majesty, the autocrat of all the Russians, the "most pious father of his people," laboring as hard as any peasant in the shipyard. Most of his coworkers were already accustomed to the unorthodox ways of the young tsar, and they respected him for his skill as a shipwright and his willingness to tackle the toughest jobs. On this occasion, in March 1696, both Peter's talents and his leadership were being tested to the fullest. Reigning tsar for only two years, he had suffered a serious defeat at the hands of the Turks the previous summer, and there was already considerable grumbling against him in Moscow. In 1695, Peter had tried to capture the fortified town of Azov, which commanded the entrance to the Sea of Azov at the mouth of the Don River (see Map 5). Peter's army besieged Azov, but because Peter had no support ships on the river, the Turks were able to relieve the garrison with reinforcements and supplies brought in by sea. Peter finally had to retreat.

John M. Thompson, "Peter the Great and Westernization, 1689-1725," *Russia and the Soviet Union: A Historical Introduction from the Kievan State to the Present*, pp. 99-115, 378. Copyright © 2012 by Taylor & Francis Group. Reprinted with permission.

Undaunted, Peter, as soon as he returned to Moscow in December, decided to resume the attack the following summer, but with a Russian fleet to control the river. That meant he had only five months to build from scratch the armada he needed, twenty-five seagoing galleys and over a thousand barges for troops and supplies, an almost impossible task even under the best of conditions! Yet Peter had little to work with. It was winter, with numbing cold, ice, and shortened days; there was no shipyard anywhere in southern Russia; no one in that region knew how to build large ships; and there was no prepared timber or other supplies for ship construction. As a recent biographer of Peter observed,

> Peter's plan, then, was to build the shipyards, assemble the workmen, teach them to mark, cut and hew the timber, lay the keels, build the hulls, step the masts, shape the oars, weave the ropes, sew the sails, train the crews, and sail the whole massive fleet down the Don River to Azov. All within five winter months![1]

Despite bad weather, delays in the arrival of skilled craftsmen, and the desertion of many conscripted laborers, Peter, to everyone's astonishment, drove the project through to completion. In early May, he sailed down the Don at the head of his mininavy, which compared favorably with Turkish and Western ships of the time, and by the end of July, he had captured Azov. In the triumphal procession several miles long that entered Moscow the following October to celebrate this important Russian victory, Tsar Peter walked on foot, among other captains of the Russian galleys, wearing a plain black uniform with only a white feather in his hat indicating he had any special status.

As this episode illustrates, Peter the Great was determined to use modern techniques and weapons to strengthen his country and unstintingly applied his considerable energy to this task. Russia had already begun to change under the impact of new ideas and increasing contact with Europe, [...] and doubtless, even without Peter, Russia would have eventually been transformed into a more modern society. What Peter did was to accelerate this transition greatly. At the same time, because he forced the pace of change, he widened the gulf between Westernized and old Russia. In their hearts, many Russians refused to accept the reforms Peter insisted on.

Moreover, in some respects, Peter the Great failed. On the surface, to be sure, Russian society, or at least the upper classes, appeared to adopt European ideas, technology, and attitudes; in retrospect, however, the result can be seen as a rough and uneven patchwork of the new and the traditional, with many anomalies and incongruities. Even today, three hundred years later, it is apparent that Russian society still suffers from a split personality, with part of the national outlook secular, rational, and tolerant and part zealous, emotional, and xenophobic.

Russia, like all traditional societies that have come in contact with Western science, technology, and power, really had no choice but to modernize. To ignore or reject Europe's influence meant isolation, backwardness, and eventual subjugation. Peter saw this clearly and did everything possible to propel Russia into the modern era. He competed successfully with his powerful, nearest, western neighbors, Sweden and Poland, and he greatly increased Russian security and prestige. He also set in motion far-reaching changes in almost every sector of Russian life. Yet he did not tamper with the institution of serfdom, which meant that society-wide modernization could not develop in Russia until after the liberation of the serfs in 1861.

Peter's impact was muted for two related reasons. First, unlike the western European nations, Russia lacked the resources to move quickly to a basic overhaul of its institutions and way of life. It had a relatively small population of about fifteen million, and as we have seen, at the end of the 1600s, it was still a poor country with low agricultural productivity, few cities, limited trade, and no substantial surplus. For Peter, even to make headway in establishing Russia's place in the European state system and in raising the level of culture in the country required a ruthless mobilization of Russia's available means and heavy exactions on the population.

Second, again unlike the West, Russia lacked many of the institutions and attitudes that could help carry out modernization. In the West, a reforming church, an entrepreneurial class, a developed higher-educational system, and well-established guilds and other associations all stood ready to assist any king or group of leaders who proposed modernizing techniques and changes. But in Russia, Peter and his advisors had to act almost alone: the established church was apathetic and the Old Believers hostile; the merchants weak and the nobles as a group were divided, indifferent, and recalcitrant; education was almost nonexistent; corporate bodies were absent; and the bulk of the population formed a conservative opposition. It is no wonder that many believed Peter to be the Antichrist and that he could make progress only by compulsion and through his astounding energy and will.

Peter's Coming of Age

Peter, like Ivan the Terrible, did not have a happy childhood, punctuated as it was by fights among noble families vying for power and by periods when the boy tsar was isolated and ignored. Peter was born in 1672, the first son of the second wife of Tsar Alexis. His mother, Natalia Naryshkin, a member of a prominent family, was politically ambitious but traditional and conservative. As a young man, Peter quickly rejected her position and point of view.

On his death, Tsar Alexis was succeeded by Feodor, his eldest surviving son by his first wife, Maria Miloslavsky. After a reign of six years, Feodor died in 1682 without an heir. A hundred years earlier, a similar succession crisis had opened the door to the Time of Troubles, but this time the Narysh kins quickly had Peter, a boy of ten, proclaimed tsar. Their claim was almost immediately contested, however, by the Miloslavsky faction, backed by special army regiments known as *streltsy*, or musketeers. During the subsequent fighting, Peter saw some of his mother's supporters murdered. It was finally agreed that Ivan, Peter's elder half-brother, would be senior tsar and Peter junior tsar. An older daughter of Alexis, Peter's half-sister Sophia, ruled as regent, with some effectiveness, until 1689, when a disastrous military campaign in the south against the Crimean Tatars led to her political downfall. Sophia was packed off to a convent, and Peter, who seemed uninterested in exercising power, permitted his mother and her family and supporters to manage affairs of state. After five years, his mother died, and in 1694, at the age of twenty-two, Peter began to direct policy. In 1696, the sickly co-tsar, Ivan died, and Peter assumed full authority.

In the 1680s, while Sophia was in charge, Peter had been shunted off to a village outside Moscow, where he was largely left to his own devices. As a result, he had little formal schooling but did a great deal to educate himself, particularly in practical matters about which he was intensely curious. Moreover, he was able to choose his own companions and develop his own interests. He surrounded himself with a motley crew of Russians and a few foreigners, selected not because of birth or position but because Peter liked them or because they had talents he wanted to tap. As recreation, Peter was allowed to form his own "play" army, with which he first displayed his love of organization and his genius at military tactics. These young playmate-soldiers later formed the core of the first guards regiment in Russia, military units that lasted until 1917.

Peter's Personality and Character

Gargantuan is an adjective frequently used to describe Peter the Great, and it is indeed apt. Physically, he was huge and very strong. Doubting that Peter was "nearly seven feet tall," on my first visit to a Moscow museum that displayed a dummy of Peter in battle dress, I put my six-foot, five-inch frame alongside it. To my surprise, Peter towered comfortably above me, certainly not seven feet in height but probably a commanding six feet, eight inches tall. Living in an era when most people were only a little over five feet tall, how Peter must have dominated any meeting or gathering!

His energy; his appetite for food, drink, and work; and his enthusiasm and intellectual curiosity were all virtually boundless. He wanted to do everything, know everything, see everything. He drove his officials, soldiers, and people hard, but he drove himself harder. Determined to make Russia stronger and better, he worked as single-mindedly for education and science as he strove fiercely for victory in battle. He cajoled and goaded his countrymen, and when all else failed, he coerced them down the path of modernization.

Darker sides to his personality and character should not be overlooked. He was often rude and inconsiderate. He was frequently ruthless and cruel. He personally participated in the torture and execution of some members of the streltsy who had rebelled against his rule.

Like so many extremely talented and determined people, Peter tried to do too much. He took on more than he could manage; as a result, some of his actions were haphazard and some of his reforms uncoordinated and incomplete. Nonetheless, he accomplished more than a dozen others could have.

Characteristic of his outlook and behavior was the extended trip to western Europe Peter undertook early in his reign. As a youth, he had absorbed from specialists residing in the foreigners' quarter of Moscow information and techniques in a wide range of civil and military trades. Peter was particularly fascinated with shipbuilding and navigation. Although he had helped establish shipyards and construct vessels from 1694 to 1696, Peter wanted to learn still more and looked naturally to the West. In addition, he hoped that in the course of visiting European nations, he might enlist their support in his continuing struggle against the Ottoman Empire.

Consequently, he set out in the spring of 1697 as part of a delegation of over two hundred Russians. Peter attempted to travel incognito as simply a member of the group, but his size made him easily identifiable. Moreover, as the first tsar to travel in Europe, he was the center of attention not only among European governments but among the general public as well. He spent almost a year and a half abroad, visiting Holland, England, and the Hapsburg empire; he was about to continue to Italy when political turmoil in Russia compelled him to return home.

His "grand embassy" was largely successful. Peter spent the most time in Holland, acquiring a great deal of information about seafaring and boatbuilding, and hiring a number of Dutch specialists to work for him back home. He learned a great deal there and in other countries about European attitudes, customs, and education, although his own rowdy behavior at times shocked the Europeans. He did not succeed in forging an alliance against the Turks, but he established personal ties with European officials that were useful in his later diplomatic pursuits. Most of all, he returned to Moscow with his head crammed with ideas about ways to modernize his tradition-bound homeland.

Peter in War and Diplomacy

Peter greatly changed Russian society but not Russian foreign policy. He consistently pursued objectives abroad that were very like those of his predecessors as far back as the fifteenth century. Of highest priority was securing Russia's vulnerable borders, particularly in the south and the west. Next came the task of expanding Russia's contacts and territory, especially in ways that would liberate Russia from its long isolation as a landlocked country. Finally, Peter, like Ivan the Terrible and the first Romanov tsars, encouraged exploration and expansion in Asia in search of new opportunities and trading partners.

The main threat to Russia in the south came from the Crimean Tatars, descendants of the Mongols who periodically attacked the tsarist state from their well-defended khanate based on the Crimean Peninsula in the Black Sea. Since the late 1400s, the Tatars had been under the protection of the Turks, and the Ottoman Empire was therefore the target of Peter's first campaign. In 1695, shortly after assuming full authority as tsar, he attacked Azov, finally subduing it in 1696 with the help of his newly constructed southern fleet, as we saw at the start of the chapter.

Later on, after a second war against the Turks in which Peter narrowly escaped a major defeat, he had to give back Azov and dismantle his Black Sea fleet. Nevertheless, he had set a precedent for Russian expansion to the Black Sea, and by the end of the eighteenth century, Russia had established a firm foothold along the northern shore of that important inland waterway.

[...] Ivan the Terrible made a major effort to reach the Baltic Sea but was ultimately defeated. In the Great Northern War, which lasted the greater part of Peter's reign, from 1700 to 1721, the modernizing tsar renewed this struggle. His two main objectives were to break the power of Sweden, at that time the dominant country in northern central Europe, and to open trade and contact directly with Europe via the Baltic Sea, his "window to the West." Although partners in the anti-Swedish coalition shifted with the fortunes of war, Poland and Russia were Sweden's main opponents during most of the Great Northern War.

When the war began, Sweden seemed at a disadvantage: not only had most of the states of the region allied against her, but Sweden's new king was a youth not yet twenty, Charles XII. Charles, however, proved to be a formidable adversary, an energetic and talented leader, and a military genius. Before his death on the battlefield at the age of thirty-seven, he had conducted some brilliant campaigns and won a number of major victories.

One of his first triumphs was the defeat of Peter and a much larger Russian army at Narva in the Baltic region in late 1700. Dismayed but not discouraged, Peter began at once to rebuild and reorganize his whole military establishment, including training methods, artillery, and supply. As we shall shortly see, civil government was also mobilized completely behind the war effort.

Luckily for Peter, Charles XII, although he probably could have forced Russia's withdrawal from the war had he pursued an offensive toward Moscow, turned his attention southward against Poland, which he considered the main enemy. Peter the Great took maximum advantage of this respite, expanding and reshaping his army and developing a fleet for use in the Baltic Sea. Beginning in 1701, the Russians captured most of the territories of Estonia and Livonia (present-day Latvia) along the Baltic shore, and in 1703, Peter founded a city strategically located in the northeastern corner of the Baltic Sea at the mouth of the Neva River (see Map 5). Soon named St. Petersburg (after the saint, not the tsar), it served as one of the two capitals of Russia from 1713 until 1918.

Charles XII finally defeated the Poles and thus could focus fully on the Russians. In 1708, he and his army crossed into Russia from Poland, but instead of heading directly for Moscow, the Swedes turned south into Ukraine, hoping to win over the Cossacks and to establish a firm base there. Several thousand Cossacks did join forces with Charles XII, but the majority of Ukrainians remained loyal to Peter. After a preliminary battle in which Peter captured some reinforcements and relief supplies intended for Charles XII, the main struggle between the Russians and the Swedish forces was joined in July 1709 at Poltava. Outnumbered almost two to one, the Swedes fought heroically but finally suffered a crushing defeat:

> At 9 o'clock ... the Swedish army turned and moved south to get into a position parallel to that of the Russians. ... Opposite ... [were] two packed lines of Russian infantry ... supported by seventy field guns. ... The Russian first line of twenty-four battalions was 10,000 strong, the second [of eighteen battalions] 8,000. ... The enemy superiority in numbers was terrifying. So was their superiority in firepower.

The Swedes attacked first to gain a moral advantage. [Swedish General] Lewenhaupt led a charge with armes blanches [bared swords] by the Swedish right wing which made the Russians fall back and gave the Swedes some field guns to turn against their enemy. But a gap appeared between the elite regiments of the right and those of the left, which could not keep up the same pace. Russian troops poured into the gap and widened it. Panic gripped men whose colonel was wounded and the Swedish line began to give way. Even Lewenhaupt when he came on the scene could not make the men stand. ...

Within half an hour the battle was over. The Swedes were either casualties of the battle or ... fled to the safety of the baggage and reserve regiments at Pushkarivka.

Charles XII on his stretcher [from an earlier wound] had been at the head of the right infantry wing. When the panic spread to that sector of the thin line, his cry of "Swedes, Swedes" went unheeded. His stretcher was hit by musket bullets and destroyed. It looked as if the king would become a prisoner of the Russians. ... Lewenhaupt's call that the king was in danger brought, however, a front of soldiers willing to delay the enemy by laying down their lives for his. Charles forced himself on to a horse, the bandages on his foot came undone, and blood dripped from [his] wound that opened with the unwonted activity. The horse was shot under him and was replaced. ...

The Russians did not pursue the Swedes. The fight had been one between infantry in the main, and the foot soldiers of Tsar Peter were nearly as shaken as those of Charles. ... The Swedes had left some 10,000 on the battlefield, 6,901 dead and 2,760 prisoners of the Tsar. Russian losses were relatively light: 1,345 killed and 3,290 wounded.[2]

Charles managed to escape southwest into Turkish territory. But Russia's reconstructed army had acquitted itself well under Peter's personal leadership, and Peter had every reason to be proud of the progress his Europeanizing program had achieved. He quickly followed up the victory at Poltava, capturing the Baltic coast from Riga to southern Finland in 1710, which secured his new city, St. Petersburg.

Shortly thereafter, however, he became embroiled with the Ottoman Empire again, and the war with Sweden, though essentially settled at Poltava, dragged on for over another decade. Peter made further gains along the Baltic shore, and finally, the Peace of Nystadt in 1721 brought the Great Northern War to an end, confirming Russia's possession of territory between St. Petersburg and Finland as well as of what are today the countries of Estonia and Latvia. Russia at last had secure access to the Baltic Sea and, through it, to western Europe. Even more importantly, Russia replaced Sweden as the dominant power in northern central Europe and was able to concentrate its energies during the rest of the century on a contest with Poland for supremacy in eastern Europe. As British historian B. H. Sumner succinctly summed up the outcome, "Peter made Russia a power in Europe and all three knew it." From the Great Northern War to the present, Russia has been a major player in the game of European power politics, and its influence in Europe seems likely to continue into the foreseeable future.

In recognition of his success, Peter was given the title of emperor and the word "great" was appended to his name; from that time on, the tsarist state was known as the Russian empire. Moreover, by adding Balts and Finns, Peter extended the multinational character of the empire, a feature that persisted to 1991. Finally, it can be argued, Russia had reached the geographic limits, at least in the west, of any expansion dictated by security considerations. In fact, however, the empire's expansion continued steadily into the 1860s.

Although Peter's main concerns in foreign affairs were his wars with Turkey and Sweden, he had a continuing interest in Asia. He maintained relations with China, encouraged explorations and contacts in the Pacific and with Mongolia and central Asia, and occupied Persian territory along the Caspian Sea (though it was returned shortly after his death). He even planned an expedition to establish ties with India. Peter, a leader of vision, clearly understood that because of Russia's location in Eurasia, it was bound to have increasing intercourse with the Asian peoples and cultures lying to the southeast. Besides, he was curious; he wanted to know more about these other societies, and he encouraged Russians to study them.

Peter's Reforms

In undertaking major changes in Russian society and government, did Peter have a grand design, or was he driven helter-skelter from one reform to another by the need to keep his war machine going? Proponents of the latter view point out that Russia was at peace for only a little over two years during the whole period of Peter's reign and that in a society as little developed economically as Russia, the major wars Peter waged demanded an all-out effort and overshadowed any other purpose or activity. On the other hand, those who believe Peter had a plan can point to his own justifications for the changes he made and to reforms he undertook that were quite unrelated to the military mobilization of Russia.

As in so many historiographic controversies, the answer seems to lie somewhere between the two positions. Peter certainly had a definite purpose: he intended to introduce into Russia the modern ideas, technologies, methods, and institutions he had learned about or observed on his mission to Europe. These, he was convinced, would both make Russia stronger and improve the welfare of his people. On the other hand, Peter certainly did not have a carefully worked out and consciously timed scheme for Europeanizing the country. He often did things impulsively and in an uncoordinated fashion. And certain measures were clearly related directly to the war effort and to the support of his new army and navy.

Though not a philosopher or theoretician, Peter the Great had a practical sense of the sort of state and society he was trying to shape. His models were the European nations of his time, monarchies with effective bureaucracies and commercial economies. Peter accepted completely the concept of autocracy, the idea of centralized absolutism. The governmental reforms he carried through were designed not to limit the tsar's rule but to make it more effective. He did try to change the ideology of autocracy by secularizing and depersonalizing the tsar's role. The tsar was to remain an absolute ruler, but not for his own sake or even for God's. Instead, the tsar-emperor was to serve the state, as everyone else did. Peter wanted the people to obey not the tsar as a person or a patriarch but as a symbol of sovereignty, as the first servant of the state. The bulk of the population, however, continued to see the tsar as both a "father" and a ruler anointed by God.

Consonant with his view of the tsardom was Peter's belief that all should serve the state. Neither religion nor wealth nor birth should exempt one from fulfilling a primary obligation to that entity. Civil and military service were the highest callings, and everything should be done to ensure that the army and the bureaucracy were efficient, honest, and just.

So also should economic life benefit the state. Peter accepted the tenets of mercantilism, then the dominant economic theory in Europe, holding that production should be stimulated and trade managed in such a way as to accrue maximum advantage to the state. At the same time, the state should encourage and support science, technology, and education, which were needed for effective governance and for expanding the economy.

As already noted, Peter carried out a complete overhaul of the Russian army and founded the Russian navy in order to better wage war against the Ottoman Empire and Sweden. In his military reforms, Peter changed almost everything, from A to Z, from the design, production, and procurement of weapons and ships; through the recruitment, training, and supply of enlisted men and officers; to transport, deployment, and battlefield tactics. From Peter's time on, Russia had a professional army and navy that rivaled those of any European power.

To ensure the manning and command of his armed forces (and his civil service as well), Peter required that everyone serve. To be sure, the Muscovite tsars had established this principle earlier, but Peter made the obligation universal and lifelong and saw that it was enforced. Nobles served with their units as long as they were fit, and peasant recruits were drafted for life (the term was reduced to twenty-five years later in the 1700s). Peter also decreed that appointment and advancement in civil and military service would be awarded according to ability and merit, not privilege, birth, or "pull." To this end, he set up the Table of Ranks, fourteen parallel grades in the civil and military service. Peter provided his own best example, working his way up in both the army and navy until he became a general and later an admiral. Peter encouraged upward social mobility. A person who attained the eighth rank of the civil service, for example, automatically became a noble.

Moreover, Peter chose his own closest advisors not primarily from the old boyar and gentry families but from all classes in society, selecting individuals he thought had special skills or unusual ability. Alexander Menshikov, Peter's most trusted confidant, whom he later made a prince, was of humble origins and reputedly worked as a street vendor in Moscow before becoming the tsar's orderly and rising to prominence. Other high officials in Peter's reign included several Swiss, Scots, and Germans, a former serf, a shepherd, and a clerk. At the same time, one of his ablest generals was a member of an old noble family.

Peter did not, however, alter serfdom. He seemed unaware that it was probably an inefficient system of agricultural production, apart from the moral issues it raised. Yet in other areas of economic life, Peter did his best to stimulate activity and output. He established hundreds of small manufacturing enterprises, most, to be sure, primarily to supply the armed forces, and he introduced a number of new products and trades into Russia. He provided subsidies to promote exports and assisted native Russian artisans. Because of the heavy costs of his wars, however, the Russian economy hardly flourished in the Petrine era, and some estimates suggest that Russia was worse off at the end of his reign than at the beginning.

There is certainly no doubt that the average citizen carried a heavy fiscal burden under Peter's rule, as the state budget more than doubled between 1700 and 1725. Peter and his advisors were ingenious at devising new taxes, including some intended to discourage traditional practices, such as those on beards and Old Believers. A reform of lasting significance was Peter's decree changing the basis of taxation on the peasantry from the household to the individual. It was suspected, probably correctly, that peasants were crowding together in ever larger households in order to spread the burden of the steadily increasing exactions levied by the central government. In order to prevent this and to make sure everyone paid, Peter's government carried out a crude census and then decreed a "soul tax" that assessed each adult male. There is some speculation that this led to the setting up of new households and eventually to a marked rise in fertility and population later in the century. In any case, since both serfs and household slaves were counted and taxed without distinction, Peter's fiscal policies further erased any lingering distinction between them: all became the movable property of their owners.

In a related fashion, a reform Peter designed with another purpose in mind helped eliminate the difference between estates held for service and those that were hereditary without any legal service obligation. In a decree of 1714 (abrogated after his death), Peter attempted to end the traditional practice of dividing an estate among all the male heirs since it resulted in ever smaller and less efficient landholdings. The new single-inheritance (or primogeniture) law required designation of one son as sole heir, with the eldest male child receiving title if no one else was named. At the same time, the decree made no distinction among estates, assuming that all were hereditary and that all estate owners owed service.

Peter's desire to make the tsarist system work better led to much tinkering with government institutions and procedures. The result was a patchwork of the old, the adapted, and the European. Because he was frequently away campaigning, Peter originally established the Senate, a senior council of about a dozen officials, to rule in his absence. After a while, the Senate came to have considerable administrative and judicial power and turned into a permanent institution of the empire. Peter ceased appointing boyars, and the boyar *duma* and *zemskii sobor* both disappeared. Peter thoroughly reorganized the central bureaucracy, setting up a series of "colleges" to handle such matters as foreign affairs, the army, the navy, justice, finance, mining, and commerce. Modeled on Swedish institutions, the colleges were to be run by a council or collegial group. In theory, this system would prevent abuse of power by one individual and provide a wider range of experience and judgment in making important decisions. In practice, the colleges were quite unwieldy but nevertheless lasted for almost a century.

In provincial and municipal government, Peter took some bold initiatives, but his reforms were largely unsuccessful. As the Russian empire grew, it became harder and harder to manage and govern, a problem that not only Peter but his successors failed to overcome.

Though Orthodox, Peter engaged at times in drunken and blasphemous parodies of church rituals and celebrations while relaxing with his friends. As in other fields, he called freely on the talents of several educated and able clerics, but he saw little role for the traditional church in the modernized Russia he was trying to mold. Since the general thrust of his policies was to secularize society, he tried to minimize the church's role in Russia. To make sure the church would be subservient to the state, Peter left the patriarchate vacant when Patriarch Hadrian died in 1700. Later, he abolished the post, replacing it with the Holy Synod, a body of high clerics supervised by a lay official, the ober-procurator of the Holy Synod. This arrangement lasted until 1917 and permitted the government to keep a tight rein on church activities and policies. Not yet recovered from the turmoil of the Schism, the church could do little to resist its subjugation by Peter.

Peter was an enthusiastic supporter of education. Training schools for the armed services naturally received high priority, but Peter also encouraged lay schools. He was particularly eager to advance the sciences and technology and laid plans for a national academy of sciences, which came into being shortly after his death. He established the first general hospital and surgical school at Moscow in 1706. Later, he reorganized medical affairs under the Medical Chancery headed by a foreign-educated imperial physician.

To make education more accessible to the average citizen, he oversaw a simplification of the Old Church Slavonic alphabet. To disseminate culture, he sponsored the first newspaper and greatly expanded book printing in Russia. The number of titles issued during his reign rose annually from six or seven to forty-five, and the content of these books broadened to include scientific and secular as well as religious topics. Peter's efforts in education, though extensive, were in fact only a tiny beginning. As one of the young Russians he sent abroad to study observed, "How can I learn geography without knowing the alphabet?" Russia needed to establish a much broader base of elementary and secondary schools and a better organized system, tasks that Catherine the Great undertook later in the 1700s.

To a considerable extent, Peter's most lasting reforms were cultural and psychological. His symbolic gestures, such as cutting off boyars' beards or forcing them to wear European dress, seem almost silly, but behind them was his relentless determination that the Russian elite change their outlook and attitudes, giving up the parochial, religious, old-fashioned ways and ideas of Muscovy for the worldly, secular, progressive lifestyle and thought of Europe. Many resisted or ignored him, but in the long run, Peter did succeed in orienting Russian society in a different direction, in forcing it to look to the future instead of the past. This wrenching change of direction had two fateful consequences, however. It alienated the educated elite from the mass of the people, and before long, it led to a fundamental questioning of Russian society as a whole and to ideas of revolution.

Resistance to Peter

In attempting to transform Russia, Peter was determined and ruthless. As early as 1696, he established permanent political police to persecute his opponents. Nevertheless, many Russians openly criticized his reforms, and millions more passively resisted, clinging stubbornly to the old ways. For the majority of peasants, Peter's reign meant not only new burdens but the introduction of strange and unorthodox customs, both of which they deeply resented. Many believed Peter was the Antichrist and feared the end of the world was near.

The most important rebellion against Peter broke out in southeastern Russia, centered in the city of Astrakhan, in 1705. Peter was then heavily engaged in the Great Northern War and could ill spare troops to send against the rebels. Moreover, since the leaders of the uprising espoused a broad range of popular grievances against both central and local government, the insurrection could easily have spread to other parts of southern Russia, the traditional seedbed of rebellion. Peter's opponents in Astrakhan included runaway serfs, Old Believers, and Cossacks but also many conservative Russian citizens outraged by the combination of new taxes and iconoclastic policies that Peter had imposed on them. In appealing to the Don Cossacks for help, the rebels declared,

> We wish to inform you of what has happened in Astrakhan on account of our Christian faith, because of beard-shaving. ... How we, our wives, and our children were not admitted into churches in our old Russian dress. ... Moreover, in the last year, 1704, they imposed on us, and collected a [new] tax. ... They also took away all our firearms ... and our bread allowance [for those serving as frontier guards].[3]

The rebels' anger soon turned to violence, with the killing of the military governor and several hundred officials and nobles. A regular army under one of Peter's leading generals was required to suppress the uprising. Some of its leaders were publicly executed in Red Square as an example to the population.

Nevertheless, in 1707 and 1708, a new insurrection erupted, this time in the south, led by a disgruntled Don Cossack named Kondratii Bulavin, who exhorted his followers to reject serfdom and the government. With a motley army of over fifty thousand, Bulavin occupied several key towns and tried to persuade the Dnieper Cossacks to join him, but he was finally defeated by government troops.

At the same time that he was suppressing these revolts, Peter had to contend with sporadic uprisings among the Bashkirs, a Turkic people on the eastern Russian frontier who resented Russian domination and the taxes of Peter's government.

Those in government circles and among the old boyars and conservative churchmen who opposed Peter's policies hoped to use the heir to the throne, Peter's son Alexis, as the spearhead of their discontent. Intelligent but weak willed and dissolute, Alexis, under pressure from Peter, renounced his right to the throne. Soon afterward, he went into self-imposed exile abroad. He was finally persuaded to return to Russia, but before long, his name was linked to plotting against Peter. Relations between father and son had never been good, and now Peter acted willfully against Alexis. In 1718, a broadly composed, extraordinary tribunal sentenced Alexis to death, but shortly thereafter, he died or was murdered in prison. Five years later, Peter promulgated a new succession law, declaring that the tsar had the right to name the heir to the throne, but he died in 1725 without doing so.

Significance of Peter the Great

Within fifty years of Peter's death, some writers were arguing that his reign had greatly benefited Russia, while others claimed that it had ruined the country. This controversy became a major issue in the intellectual history of modern Russia, reaching a high point during the 1840s in the polemics between the Westernizers, who approved Peter's policies, and the Slavophiles, who denounced them [...]. In the 1860s, conservative Russian publicist Michael Katkov concluded that Peter's rule was "a catastrophe that ... disrupted the organism of national life and ... deprived [us] of the instinct and feeling of personal life ... remaking us into senseless imitators doing everything on order of the government." Soviet historians generally approved of Peter's reforms (lavishly so in the period of Stalin's dictatorship), although concluding that they reinforced an absolutist system controlled by the aristocracy and a few rich merchants.

Perhaps Peter's reign can best be summed up as a series of paradoxes (which, incidentally, help explain why it is so controversial):

- Peter coerced Russia into modernization, but it was coming anyway.
- Peter had a vision of a more efficient, modernized Russia, but his reforms were often haphazard, forced upon him by military necessity and the pressure of events.
- Peter wanted to drive barbarism out of Russia but relied on barbaric methods to achieve that goal.
- Peter wanted to change and improve Russian society but left it with serfdom, an entrenched, privileged nobility, and a cumbersome and often corrupt bureaucracy.
- Peter cared about the welfare of his people, but his wars and fiscal demands left them burdened, exhausted, and resentful.

- Peter sought good government and encouraged individual merit, but his reign heightened the arbitrary power of the state.
- Peter saw Russia's distant future but failed to convince most Russians of that destiny.
- Peter set a fast pace and employed coercion to make progress, but this practice alienated most Russians and undercut the changes he was trying to make.
- Peter made Russia a great power in Europe, but he achieved this through aggression against Russia's neighbors and at great cost to Russia.

However one assesses these contradictions in Peter's record, three major conclusions concerning his reign emerge. First, he was clearly one of the most influential personalities in modern history, like Napoleon, Lenin, and Gandhi. Russia undoubtedly would have meandered into modern times at some point, but Peter greatly accelerated the process and, in so doing, changed Russian society fundamentally.

Second, Peter propelled Russia onto the European stage and made her a great power. Since 1700, Russia has been a major actor in European and world affairs.

Finally, Peter put on the agenda for all Russians fundamental questions with which they are still struggling. How can Russian society react to new ideas and technology and still be true to its own traditions and unique culture? Must the West be imitated, or can Western attitudes and methods be modified and adapted to serve Russian needs and interests? Is it possible to fuse Russian beliefs and Western thought? What is the true essence of Russian civilization?

Further Reading

Anisimov, Evgennii V. *The Reforms of Peter the Great: Progress through Coercion in Russia*. Armonk, NY: 1993.

Bushkovitch, Paul. *Peter the Great*. New Haven, CT: 2001

Cracraft, James. *The Petrine Revolution in Russian Culture*. Cambridge, MA: 2004.

_____. *The Revolution of Peter the Great*. Cambridge, MA: 2003.

Engel, Barbara Alpern. *Women in Russia, 1700–2000*. Cambridge, UK: 2004.

Hughes, Lindsey. *Peter the Great: A Biography*. New Haven, CT: 2002.

_____. *Sophia: Regent of Russia, 1657–1704*. New Haven, CT: 1990.

LeDonne, John P. *Absolutism and Ruling Class: The Formation of the Russian Political Order, 1700–1825*. New York: 1991.

_____. *The Russian Empire and the World, 1700–1917: The Geopolitics of Expansion and Containment*. New York: 1997.

Marsden, C. *Palmyra of the North*. London: 1942 (a description of St. Petersburg).

Meehan-Waters, B. *Autocracy and Aristocracy*. New Brunswick, NJ: 1982.

Sunderland, Willard. *Taming the Wild Field: Colonization and Empire on the Russian Steppe*. Ithaca, NY: 2004.

Notes

1. Robert K. Massie, *Peter the Great* (New York: 1980), 142.

2. R. M. Hatton, *Charles XII of Sweden* (New York: 1968), 299–300.

3. George Vernadsky, ed., *A Source Book for Russian History from Early Times to 1917*, vol. 2 (New Haven, CT: 1972), 349.

New Causes

Why Did the Industrial Revolution Happen, and Why Did It Happen in Eighteenth-Century Britain?

Peter N. Stearns

Explaining the industrial revolution is a challenge to analysts of history. New kinds of debates have surfaced recently, particularly through attempts to take a more global approach. Identifying the factors that caused the industrial revolution is vital not simply as a historical exercise but as the basis for understanding the complexity of the challenges awaiting societies that tried to establish an industrial revolution even after Britain showed the way. The variety of developments that combined to create the first industrial revolution had somehow to be replicated, though not necessarily in identical fashion. This same daunting variety helps explain why a number of regions have not managed to launch full-scale industrialization to this day. Complex causes persist as a factor in world affairs.

Not surprisingly, historians have offered different emphases. Occasionally, industrialization is presented as flowing from a few dramatic inventions and from some new thinking about the economy, notably Adam Smith's market-oriented theories issued in 1776 that stressed the importance of vigorous economic competition free from government controls as a means of generating innovation and growing prosperity. Inventions were involved, of course—but why did they occur? And why did Britain produce more inventions than other countries (followed, in the formative decades of industrialization, by France and the United States)? New economic theories helped produce some policies favorable to industrialization, but these did not cause the process; they came too late, and they affected too few people. Any explanation of the industrial revolution must account for new behaviors on the part of literally thousands of people: the entrepreneurs who gradually moved toward a factory system, the workers who staffed the factories, the investors who provided the capital, the

Peter N. Stearns, "New Causes: Why Did the Industrial Revolution Happen, and Why Did It Happen in Eighteenth-Century Britain?," *The Industrial Revolution in World History*, pp. 41-52. Copyright © 2012 by Taylor & Francis Group. Reprinted with permission.

consumers who eagerly accepted the machine-made products. A number of powerful factors had to combine to generate a change as substantial as even the early phases of industrialization.

For the industrial revolution to occur, considerable investment funds were required—the new machines were expensive, far costlier than any manufacturing equipment previously devised, even in the very small factories that characterized much early industry. Also needed was access to raw materials, including textile fibers, but particularly coal and iron, the sinews of the industrial revolution. Government interest in supporting economic innovation was a factor, and various kinds of specific government policies helped. Of major importance was an available labor force that did not have more agreeable employment options, for although some workers might be attracted to the industrial life because of high pay for their particular skills, the excitement of innovation, and greater independence from traditional family and community controls, most workers entered factories because they had little choice. Finally, industrialization, particularly in its first manifestation in Britain, required an aggressive, risk-taking entrepreneurial spirit that would drive businesses to venture into innovation. All these ingredients must be considered in connection with the causes of the industrial revolution. A list of this type helps guide the assessment of causation, and it may sort out why some societies could respond to industrialization more quickly than others—but it does not explain why it happened. Take raw materials, for example. A large seam of coal ran from Britain through Belgium and northern France to the Ruhr Valley in Germany, and the most intense early industrialization developed along this coal seam. Iron ore deposits also existed in western Europe, in some cases close to the coal sources. Without these raw materials—and especially coal as the energy source for smelting metal and powering the steam engine—early industrialization would have been impossible. Western Europe also had abundant wool and, through already established colonial trade, initial access to cotton (grown in the southern colonies of British North America and in parts of Asia).

On the whole, however, raw materials form preconditions for industrialization, not active causes; several other societies were in as good a position as Europe when it came to resources, and we will see a few cases where industrialization occurred without a particularly good resources base.

Other factors, more plausible as active causes, turn out to have their own complexities. The scientific revolution occurred in western Europe just a century or so before industrialization began in Britain. A few discoveries, like some that came out of studying the behavior of gases, proved directly relevant, as in Watt's work on the steam engine. But historians have shown pretty clearly that the new scientific activity did not on the whole link to early industrial technology; the marriage would occur only toward the mid-nineteenth century, when industrialization was already well underway. More general effects of modern science may still apply, as we will see, but specific links fall short.

Similar difficulties affect linkage between Europe's growing commercialization and early industrialization. It is certainly true that many Europeans had become familiar with production for the market, and that consumer interest in buying goods was unquestionably rising by the early eighteenth century. Like science, all this formed part of a favorable context. But direct connections are hard to prove. It turns out that China, an older commercial society, was as well positioned as Europe in this area, in terms of living standards and experience with a market economy. Furthermore, the European banks that had grown with greater trade rarely lent money to industrial activities, seeing them as too risky, and few established merchants participated. Early industrialists were more likely to emerge from craft backgrounds, though there were some exceptional landowners and traders involved.

Europe's growing role in world trade forms a more direct backdrop than commercialization in general. From the late fifteenth century onward, western European countries, ultimately headed by France, the Netherlands, and Britain, had won increasing control over international commerce. European ships and merchant companies dominated international trade, even in some cases in which exchanges did not directly involve Europe at all. Increasingly, a hierarchy emerged in the international economy, in which Europeans acquired minerals and agricultural goods from other areas (including their colonies in the Americas, India, and elsewhere) and in return sold manufactured products, including fine furniture, cloth, and metal goods such as guns. Because Europeans could price their goods to include the cost of processing, they were in general able to profit from the exchange. Not all parts of the world actively engaged in trade with western Europe at this point, but parts of eastern Europe (which sent grain, furs, and timber supplies), the Americas (precious metals, sugar, and tobacco), and India and Southeast Asia (spices, tea, and gold) added steadily to western Europe's wealth. The active slave trade that Europeans ran between Africa and the Americas was another source of profit.

Europe's role in preindustrial world trade set up the industrial revolution in several ways. Growing amounts of commercial experience developed through the trading companies, and new technologies relating to shipbuilding and warfare received impetus. Governments were encouraged to pay attention to the importance of fostering trade, though this attention at times led to heavy-handed efforts at control. Trade leadership helped stimulate a taste for new products. Growing interest in cotton cloth originated first from trade with India, particularly in Britain. The British government then sought (from the 1730s onward) to encourage cotton manufacturing at home and to prevent undesirable dependence on foreign manufacturing by banning cotton imports; this ban had the additional effect of reducing India's economic vitality and opening India to British goods. At the same time, Britain used its holdings in India and particularly the southern colonies in North America to provide raw cotton for its new textile branch. Trade also provided capital through the growing wealth of many business and landowning groups.

Most directly, experience in global competition pushed manufacturing innovation directly. European trading companies, for example, began handling printed cotton cloth from India as early as the sixteenth century. They could make money selling these colorful goods not only in Europe but in other markets. However, some European businessmen began wondering if the goods could not be made in their own countries, with even more profit possible. The deterrent was the experience and low cost of Indian artisans. But if machines could be devised to do the printing more efficiently, this competitive barrier could be overcome. From Switzerland to

Britain, from the late seventeenth century onward, Europeans began experimenting with new technologies, and by the mid-eighteenth century were ready to supply the market with factory-made goods. Here was a concrete case in which Europe's industrial revolution, which was to have such dramatic effects on the wider world, stemmed in great part from Europe's changing position in the wider world.

Three Approaches: Minimal, Western, and Global

Three approaches currently vie for attention in explaining the industrial revolution, though they overlap to some extent.

The first approach, and the most recent, urges that Europe, even including Britain, was not very different from other leading manufacturing centers like China and India; therefore, a causation scheme that relies heavily on European distinctiveness is off the mark. This view again follows from historians' growing realization that China and India benefited hugely from the world economy of the sixteenth and seventeenth centuries, earning huge profits in U.S. silver for their exports. Just like Europe, in broad outline, China had a strong merchant sector, widely sought manufactured exports, and much available labor. So why did Europe industrialize first? Colonies provide part of the answer by supplying cheap raw materials, new capital, and some additional spur to export manufacturing for colonial markets. There was also the sheer accident that British coal mines, unlike the Chinese mines, flooded easily and so encouraged the invention and use of the steam engine to pump out water. It turned out that the engine had wider applicability as well. Beyond this specific comparative calculation, recent work has reemphasized the importance of changes in European culture. If the scientific revolution is not applicable directly, it did encourage a new faith in the progress of knowledge and technology that provided prestige for inventors and businesspeople and thus a unique context in which industrialization could take root. China, it turns out, despite a host of favorable ingredients, did not offer this precise mixture, and then a set of additional impediments hampered its ability even to respond to Europe's industrial example.

The second explanation is more familiar, with less reference to precise comparison, in looking at particular features of the European situation by the eighteenth century. One recent study by Robert Allen, for example, simply asserts that Britain industrialized because its wage costs were rising but it had unusually cheap coal: technological innovation resulted directly from this very simple economic calculus. Then, once Britain's industrial success became clear, by the early nineteenth century, other Western countries had to follow suit because of competitive example. Most scholars would still add to this intriguingly barebones approach, pointing out for example that it is still vital to explain why Western countries were so quick to follow Britain's lead but other regions were not. They would add in, of course, the changing culture, throughout the West, that followed from the scientific revolution. They point to European governments eager to encourage economic growth as part of military competition, and thus willing to improve infrastructure (initially, roads and canals) and banking facilities, while backing merchant activities as well. The surge of new consumerism that flowed through western Europe in the seventeenth and eighteenth centuries created new eagerness for goods like cheap but fashionable clothing and tableware. Stylish clothing, indeed, became so important that theft rates soared in the eighteenth century, a sure sign of a growing market for less expensive, but eye-catching, machine-made goods like colorful cotton cloth. A combination of developments in European society, then, from politics to popular culture, set a stage in which Britain had specific reasons for its pioneering innovations but in which Western nations more generally were poised to install an even more dramatic set of changes.

The third pattern of explanation plays down a specifically European focus—which can so easily exaggerate distinctive Western qualities—in favor of focusing on shifting global relationships and outright European exploitation of its commercial and military position. From world trade, including the slave trade, Europe gained new levels of capital essential for taking risks on new inventions. From world trade, supplemented by an increasingly commercial domestic economy, Europeans developed a growing middle class (from which most of the new industrialists would emerge) and a taste for pleasurable goods that would feed the expanding consumer markets. From world trade, Europeans learned about the appeal of cotton cloth (from India) and porcelains (from China), which spurred the efforts to generate factory substitutes back home. From world trade, Europeans learned the profits to be made in selling processed goods globally, while seeking cheap raw materials in return. And if this imbalance could be enhanced by special measures, like British efforts to discourage Indian cotton production in favor of Britain's nascent industry, so much the better. The industrial revolution, in this model, emerged from the disproportionate advantages Europe was already gaining in the world's markets, and of course it would extend the international imbalances even further in the nineteenth century. The emphasis is on the global context of the industrial revolution and also on the special position Europe had already achieved in this context, which explains both industrialization and the West's long (though not permanent) leadership in the whole process.

All three approaches have analytical merit. They can, of course, be combined to some degree. But a certain amount of choice, particularly between seeing the industrial revolution as a global economic result from the outset and viewing it as the product of some special Western combination, is essential. The debate, in other words, stimulates a more precise assessment of historical factors, but it ultimately requires some reasoned prioritization.

Trigger: Why the Eighteenth Century?

All the factors pushing for the industrial revolution accelerated by the eighteenth century. The results of new science began to impact a wider culture; the Enlightenment, as an intellectual movement, brought new interest to technical progress and more discussion of the most effective economic policies; the growth of consumer expectations encouraged new markets; and Europe's world trade position improved steadily, particularly with new moves into India. The rapid expansion of domestic manufacturing gave some workers new spending money and growing urban contacts, which promoted new kinds of purchases and prepared an industrial labor force. Growing global trade helped build up domestic capital and provided further evidence of wider markets for manufactured goods.

Capping these developments, and arguably providing a final push, were the effects of a true population explosion, coming after several decades, in the seventeenth century, of demographic stagnation. Food was crucial. The lack of major agricultural changes in Europe between the late Middle Ages and the 1690s was ironic, given Europe's commercial advance. By the 1690s, this anomaly had begun to yield, the result being an agricultural basis for further economic change, via population growth. After long hesitations because the goods were not mentioned in the Bible, western Europeans began to grow calorie-rich New World crops, headed of course by the potato. Again, larger world history fed industrialization. Further, with the Dutch leading, new methods of draining and fertilizing expanded the available land and fertility. With more food came more people.

Rapid population growth resulted from new food supplies and other developments such as a temporary lull in major plagues. There was also a pause in the most devastating kinds of warfare between 1715 and 1792. Increased population pushed workers to seek new (even unpleasant) kinds of jobs, provided growing markets for inexpensive manufactured goods, and prodded even some prosperous families to seek economic innovation. An eastern French family, the Schlumbergers, was a case in point. In the 1760s the head of the family ran an artisan shop, producing cloth but displaying no particular business dynamism. He had twelve children; that all of them lived to adulthood was somewhat unusual but illustrative of the impact of population growth in a single-family context. Simply in order to provide for his brood in the accustomed respectable middle-class fashion, Schlumberger had to expand his textile operations, hiring domestic manufacturing workers and then tentatively introducing some powered equipment. His children, building on their father's example, became dynamic industrialists in the early nineteenth century, creating large textile and machine-building factories and sponsoring the first local rail line. Population upheaval promoted economic dynamism in a number of ways and at various levels of the initial industrialization process in western Europe.

Britain as a Special Case

Finally, why was Britain—which was among the several areas of western Europe in which relevant changes had been taking shape—in the vanguard? Within the larger west European context, there were several special features in Britain. Population growth was extremely rapid in the eighteenth century, and this helped free available labor from agriculture. British landlords successfully pried land away from smallholding farmers through the government's Enclosure

Acts. These required farmers to enclose their fields, usually by planting hedges, but the expense was beyond many small farmers, who had to sell out to the landlords. British agriculture became dominated by large estates, and although these employed many workers, they did not absorb a growing population as readily as peasant-dominated agriculture proved able to do elsewhere, and this created a labor force eager for new options. The enclosed estates, in turn, increased agricultural market production, providing food for growing cities.

British artisans were also unusual. Most urban artisans in western Europe belonged to guilds, which tried to protect members' working conditions by limiting new technology and preventing any employer from creating undue inequality or threatening wage rates by hiring too many workers. Guilds were ideal for a relatively stable economy, but they definitely inhibited both rapid labor mobility and changing techniques. Britain had once boasted a guild system, but it had virtually disappeared by the eighteenth century. The result was twofold: employers had unusual freedom to bring new workers into established branches of production, and they were at liberty to tinker with new methods—perhaps the most important single source of Britain's lead in inventions.

Britain's extensive international trade provided capital and markets and also supplies of vital materials such as cotton. The British aristocracy was more favorable to commerce than its counterparts on the European continent; some British landlords directly participated in setting up new mines and manufacturing, and tolerance for commercial development was high. The British government favored economic change. Tariff regulations in the eighteenth century, such as the barriers to the importation of cotton cloth from India, spurred new industries. Other laws that discouraged the export of new machinery or designs impeded rapid imitation elsewhere of British gains. Laws made the formation of new companies relatively easy and officially banned combinations of workers—what we would call unions—and this ban, in turn, constrained protest. During the eighteenth century a number of local governments began to build better roads, and then a wave of canal building developed at the end of the century. The new infrastructure facilitated the movement of both raw materials and finished goods. At the same time, the British government did not attempt to regulate manufacturing extensively. Other European governments, though often eager to promote economic growth, tended to control manufacturing with regulations about product quality, techniques, and some working conditions. The British state was less interventionist. This was not always an advantage, as we shall see in other industrialization cases, but it may have served well in setting a favorable framework for the first industrial revolution.

Simple luck in terms of natural resources also aided Britain, which is where the point about low energy costs comes in. There were excellent holdings in coal and iron, which were often located quite close together. The island nation had not only coastal waterways but good navigable rivers, which further facilitated the transport of the two materials that were so vital to early industrialization but were extremely heavy and costly to move over land. Britain was also running low on timber supplies by the early eighteenth century and had to search for alternative fuels, notably coal. This necessity, in turn, spurred industrial development, from the adaptation of the initial steam engine for mine pumping to the use of coal for smelting iron.

Finally, Britain apparently provided an optimal setting for producing individuals inclined to taking risks in business. Good market opportunities and an extensive preindustrial manufacturing system formed part of this framework. New ideas about science and material progress spread more rapidly in Britain than in most other European countries. A relatively small government meant limited chances for success by seeking bureaucratic jobs. Furthermore, Britain tolerated a number of Protestant religious minorities such as the Quakers, though this indulgence was incomplete: Protestants who were not members of the established Anglican Church could not attend universities or gain government employment. This ambivalence encouraged members of these minorities, eager to demonstrate God's favor, to seek opportunities in business. Certainly the Protestant minorities produced a disproportionate number of early manufacturers, who were stimulated by a belief that disciplined work, frugality, and economic drive were pleasing in the sight of God, and who were eager to get ahead where the chances lay—through entrepreneurial initiative.

In sum, Britain concentrated many of the changes developing generally in western Europe and added an array of special factors ranging from flukes of nature to new forms of callous manipulation of agricultural labor. Quite possibly the more general shifts taking place throughout Europe would have generated an industrial revolution elsewhere by the early nineteenth century; the uniqueness of the British combination should not be exaggerated. Nevertheless, the fact was that Britain came first and that its leadership can be explained.

For at least a half century the nation's effective monopoly on the industrial revolution was scarcely challenged. British industry enabled the country to hold up against the much larger population of France during the wars of the French Revolution and the Napoleonic era. By the 1830s Britain's industrial lead was so obvious, and its related need and ability to export cheap machine-made manufactured goods were so great, that the government changed its basic tariff policy. Britain became a pioneer in free trade, allowing imports of food and raw materials that helped keep prices (and wages) down while relying on manufacturing exports to balance the trade exchange and even to show a tidy national profit.

Britain was indeed pouring manufactured goods into the markets of the world. Machine-made textiles cut into customary production not only in Latin America but also in Germany. British iron products undersold traditional charcoal-smelted metal in France. Here, obviously, was a rude challenge. But here also was an opportunity. Britain's success in industrialization added another ingredient to the changes taking place in western Europe. Continental businesses and governments began to wake up to the possibility of copying British machine design and factory organization, realizing they must stir themselves lest they be engulfed in a British industrial tide. The industrial revolution began to spread.

Figure 8.1 In the 1800s, England's industries expanded and improved, causing towns such as Sheffield, located in northern England, to grow in population and importance. Sheffield factories produced high-quality steel, silver-plated items, and other metal goods. (Courtesy of the Mansell Collection Limited.)

For after Britain took the industrial lead, the whole question of causation takes on a different cast. The British model, and British success (including military success against Napoleon's forces), became causes in their own right for societies ready and able to recognize the message. Still, however, the analytical challenge is not over, for some societies imitated quickly, a fact suggesting that they had conditions very similar to those spurring industrialization in Britain or that they could supply alternative spurs. Other societies did not or could not follow up so readily, because they were defined by different economic, political, and cultural factors. In fact, the next industrial revolutions extended the phenomenon in the West alone; only later would some other societies follow suit (though often with impressive results), in a process that remains globally uneven to the present day.

It may seem surprising that historians are still debating the causes of industrialization. After all, the subject has been under discussion for decades. It is true that historians often like controversy, staking out new positions against old assumptions. It's also true that historical explanations are always hard to pin down, and a huge change like the industrial revolution is particularly challenging. Debate continues because of improvements in historical methods—for example, in quantitative assessments of components like British fuel and labor costs. It continues as well because certain factors, like cultural change, are inherently hard to pin down. It continues because the very evolution of industrialization itself prompts new considerations of global factors or comparative analyses. The results of debate, even if never quite definitive, have allowed certain old assumptions to be overturned. They contribute to an understanding of what this major and still quite recent development is all about. And they help us understand what other societies have had to do—what causes they have had to generate—to join the industrial parade.

READING 9

European Interests and Imperialism

Arthur Goldschmidt Jr. and Lawrence Davidson

In the eighteenth century, the West achieved and then maintained military, political, and economic superiority over the Middle East. This had not been the usual power relationship before. It may not be so in the future. Neither the rulers nor the subjects of the Ottoman Empire—or any other Muslim country—wanted this subordination to the European Christians, whom they had formerly looked down upon. But what could they do? Whereas once the Muslims had controlled the commercial routes between Europe and Asia and had dictated the terms of trade to both, now Europeans were selling their manufactures to the Middle East in exchange for raw materials and agricultural products. Europeans living or trading in Muslim lands dwelled in special quarters of the big cities and did not have to pay local taxes or obey local laws and regulations. Whereas once the Mediterranean Sea and the Indian Ocean had been dominated by Muslim navies (or pirates), now European sailing ships—military and merchant—controlled the high seas. Earlier, the Ottoman sultan could choose the time and place to attack Christian Europe and then dictate peace terms; now his armies were at the mercy of Austria's Habsburgs and Russia's czars. To the Muslims, accustomed to victory on the battlefield, these changes seemed a cosmic error. Was God punishing Muslims who had lost their purity of intention and strayed from his plan for their community?

Ottoman Weakness

We can trace the changing relationship between the Middle East and the West by a series of dated events. In 1683 the Ottomans failed to take Vienna, the capital of the

Habsburg Empire; in 1699 they signed a treaty at Karlowitz, ceding Hungary to the Habsburgs and the Aegean coast to the Venetians; in 1718 they gave up more of their European lands; in 1774 they lost the Crimea and allowed Russia to protect *their* Orthodox Christian subjects; and in 1798 Napoleon Bonaparte occupied Egypt and invaded Palestine. Meanwhile, other Muslim dynasties, such as the Mughals of India, the Safavids and their Persian successors, the Central Asian Uzbeks, and the Sharifian rulers of Morocco, were also fading before the mounting might of eighteenth-century Europe. But the Ottomans were closest to the new powers, viewed themselves as *ghazi*s fighting for Islam, and stood to lose the most if the Europeans partitioned their lands.

Some Symptoms and Causes

Some popular histories may tell you that the Ottoman rulers cared nothing for their empire's fate. Enchanted by the charms of the harem, dulled by wine or hashish, hamstrung by janissary revolts or quarreling court factions, the sultans lost interest in maintaining their regime or defending their lands. By the same token, the venal viziers tried to keep the sultans out of their way in order to profit from the corruption of the system. Bureaucrats bought their offices and sold subordinate posts to others, while everyone in power gouged the poor peasants and workers on taxes and fees (which were really assessed bribes). The janissaries, who should have been the backbone of the Ottoman army, became a hereditary caste of merchants and artisans who failed to keep in training or to learn how to use such modern weapons as muskets and bayonets. Worse, they overturned their soup pots and went on a rampage if anyone dared to call for reforms. As long as the state fed and paid them, they saw no need to reform or to let other troops take their place. The *ulama* became *juhala* (ignoramuses) steeped in superstition and untouched by the growth of knowledge taking place in Europe. Landowners and merchants were robbed by brigands, against whom they had no protection. Peasants suffered from greedy landlords and tax farmers; many ran away to become brigands themselves. So turned the sad cycle. The easy answer is to blame incompetent or impotent sultans. As the Turks used to say, "The fish stinks from the head."

The Reforming Sultans and Viziers

There is, as usual in such popular accounts, a germ of truth in all this. The sultans were getting worse. No one denies the insanity of Sultan Ibrahim (r. 1640–1648), who allegedly had his 280 concubines tied up in sacks and drowned in the Bosporus. Mustafa II (r. 1695–1703) insisted on leading his troops into battle and was decisively beaten by Prince Eugen of Savoy, the military genius of the age, costing the Ottomans the province of Hungary and their military prestige. Alcohol abuse and harem intrigues afflicted the later sultans far more than they had the first ten. Some members of the ruling class milked the Ottoman system to enrich themselves while failing to perform their duties. But one of the secrets of Ottoman longevity was that the system went on producing capable sultans and viziers who saw the corruption and introduced reforms. Among the reforming sultans were Osman II (r. 1618–1622), whose attempt to form a new militia led to his being killed by revolting janissaries; Murad IV (r. 1623–1640), who executed 25,000 rebellious subjects in a single year; Mahmud I (r. 1730–1754), the first to bring in Europeans to teach new fighting techniques; and Selim III (r. 1789–1807), who introduced a comprehensive reform scheme, the *nizam-i-jedid*, which we will soon describe.

What about the reforming viziers? The Koprulu family produced six grand viziers who enhanced Ottoman security abroad and imposed political, social, and aesthetic changes at home. The first, Mehmet (d. 1661), was taken from his Albanian Christian parents by the *devshirme* and started his career working in the imperial kitchen. As grand vizier to Sultan Mehmet IV (r. 1648–1687), he defeated the Venetians and quashed revolts in Transylvania and Anatolia, executing thousands in the process. His son, Ahmet, strengthened the vizierate, checked the Habsburgs, and took Crete as well as parts of Poland. Mehmet's brother led the Ottoman troops to the gates of Vienna in 1683 but failed to capture the city. A nephew of Mehmet Koprulu, serving Mustafa II, reduced taxes on consumer goods, set up factories, and hoped to restore farm production to its earlier level.

Another vizier was Damad Ibrahim, best known for diverting Sultan Ahmed III (r. 1703–1730) into building pleasure palaces and tulip gardens. But he also brought in European artists, commissioned Turkish translations of Western scientific works, and introduced the first Ottoman printing press. Even in this dark age of Ottoman history, some sultans and viziers tried to bring in some light. More westernizing reformers would arise in the nineteenth century; you will read about them later. However, reforms alone could not save the Ottoman Empire.

The European Powers and the Eastern Question

We think the key to the Ottomans' predicament—but also, paradoxically, their salvation—lay in Europe. Without the Renaissance, the Reformation, the age of exploration and discovery, the expansion of trade, the Enlightenment, and the Industrial Revolution, the West would not have surpassed the Muslim world in the eighteenth century. The Ottoman Empire had not experienced all the changes these movements brought to Western culture. But neither had such traditional Ottoman foes as Venice, Poland, and Spain; by 1750 they no longer menaced Ottoman security. Habsburg Austria still played its customary role as Christendom's chief defender against Islam. But Austria's leadership was paling before a new star rising in the north, czarist Russia. Many Westerners believed that Russia would have taken over all Ottoman lands but for the firm opposition of the other European states. To test this belief, let us look at the Middle East policies of the most important European countries of the nineteenth century—the Great Powers: Russia, Austria, Britain, and France.

The Koprulu Family of Viziers

For most of its existence, Ottoman rule mixed a hereditary succession with the promotion of administrators and military officers on the basis of merit. The empire did have a long run of luck with its hereditary sultanate, but that could not last forever. After the reign of Suleyman I, the luck of the Ottomans turned bad. Weak and incompetent rulers inherited power. This was not the only problem facing the empire, but without strong and capable leaders, other problems — military, economic, and governmental — could not have been solved. As noted in the text, there is an old Turkish saying that the fish begins to rot at the head, and so it did. Problems in the sultanate affected the rest of society.

The Ottoman decline lasted more than three hundred years, allowing time for people within the ruling class to try repeatedly to solve problems. These efforts were usually undertaken by strong viziers who would appear now and then to reverse the empire's fortunes. The most famous of these men came from one family of Albanian heritage, the Koprulus.

There is a pattern in the behavior of the Koprulu viziers. Each was given dictatorial or near dictatorial powers by sultans or their regents (often their mothers) who could not or would not rule directly. Each vizier could rule brutally when needed to root out corruption, rebellion, or incompetence. Most of them used the stick far more often than the carrot to achieve their ends. And, finally, the Koprulus, each one learning from his precursor in an informal apprenticeship, were very successful. A key fact, though, is that none of their reforms endured. This ultimate failure had many reasons, but one of them lies in the very definition of Ottoman success.

Among other things, the people expected the Ottoman government to expand its borders. They wanted a strong government not only to maintain stability and tradition, or to defend the faith, but also to enlarge Dar al-Islam (land of Islam). Thus, ending corruption, suppressing rebellion, dismissing the incompetent, and instituting discipline — all of which the Koprulus did well — were not just ends in themselves. They were needed to wage war. Almost all of the Koprulus, having stabilized the empire, quickly directed its renewed energies toward waging war. And most of the time, the newly reformed institutions proved too fragile to withstand eventual defeat by a powerful Western foe. Finally, the fifth Koprulu vizier, Huseyin (r. 1697–1702), recognized the futility of these efforts and negotiated the Treaty of Karlowitz (1699), in which the sultan ceded Hungary to the Austrians, marking the beginning of the end, militarily and diplomatically, for the Ottoman Empire.

Custom and tradition are hard to alter. They usually change only over long periods of time or under extreme circumstances. The first four Koprulus used the fruits of their labors to promote the age-old custom of expansive war. Only when the empire's state of exhaustion became obvious did the fifth Koprulu change this pattern of behavior. By then he had very little choice.

Czarist Russia

Unlike the other Great Powers involved in the Ottoman Empire, Russia had experienced Muslim rule under the Mongol Golden Horde. Russia had emerged in the fifteenth century as a small but independent state, centered on Moscow and close to the sources of central Eurasia's main rivers and portage routes. Some historians argue that the expansionist policy of Muscovite rulers was made possible by their control of these rivers and dictated by their ceaseless quest for outlets to the high seas. Rivers flowing into the Baltic Sea or the Arctic Ocean are apt to be icebound for half the year; therefore, Russia needed the Black Sea as a warm-water outlet for trade. In the seventeenth century this body of water was almost completely surrounded by Ottoman lands. As a result, Peter the Great and his successors fought several wars against the empire in the eighteenth century to ensure Russian access to the Black Sea. By the middle of the nineteenth century, the Russians could regard the Black Sea as mainly theirs, but their ships still had to pass through the Ottoman-ruled Bosporus and Dardanelles (the Straits) to reach the Aegean and hence the Mediterranean. So Russia sought control of the Straits, or at least assurances that the Ottomans would not bar passage to its warships and merchant vessels. Russia also wanted to rule the Straits to better defend its Black Sea ports against naval attacks from invaders.

Some Russians had an additional motive to seize the Straits: they wanted to rule that great city on the Bosporus—Istanbul. You know that up to the Ottoman conquest, it had been Constantinople, capital of the Byzantine Empire, hence the "Second Rome," and chief jewel of the Greek Orthodox church. When Constantinople fell, Russia became the leading Greek Orthodox country and declared Moscow the "Third Rome." A Muscovite prince married the niece of the last Byzantine emperor. Their descendants, Russia's czars, sometimes sought to gain control of Constantinople (which they called Czargrad) and restore the power and prestige of Greek Orthodoxy to the level of Roman Catholicism. Besides, many Orthodox Christians lived under Ottoman rule, mainly in the Balkans. Austria captured some of them in the early eighteenth century, but the Habsburgs, being Catholic, were unsympathetic. Mother Russia would be a better protector for the Serbs, Bulgars, Albanians, Romanians, and Greeks seeking freedom from Muslim rule, for they were nearly all Orthodox. So when Catherine the Great defeated the Ottomans in 1769–1774 and thus could set the terms of the peace treaty, she secured Ottoman recognition of Russia's right to intervene diplomatically on behalf of Orthodox Christians living within the Ottoman Empire. The wording of this Treaty of Kuchuk-Kainarji is ambiguous, but Russians claimed later that it set a precedent for relations between Russia and Turkey (as the Ottoman Empire came to be called by the Europeans).

Later on, the Russians maintained that they had something else in common with many of the sultan's Balkan subjects—namely, that they were Slavs. The term *Slav* denotes membership in a language group. Russian and Ukrainian are Slavic languages; so, too, are Bulgarian, Polish, Serbian, and Croatian. During the nineteenth century, some Balkan peoples espoused a kind of nationalism called pan-Slavism that aimed to unite within a single state all peoples speaking Slavic languages. Russia, the largest Slavic country, claimed to be its leader. Ottoman Turkey feared the divisive effect of pan-Slavism as much as it had Russia's earlier sponsorship of the Orthodox Christians. But pan-Slavism threatened such European neighbors as Prussia and Austria with their many Polish subjects; thus Russia had to mute its pan-Slavism when it wanted to placate those powers. Indeed, many Russian officials preferred upholding Ottoman integrity and friendly ties with the other European powers over unity with Orthodox Christians or their Slavic cousins.

In the nineteenth century, Russia's drive toward the sea, leadership of the Orthodox Christians, and encouragement of pan-Slavism combined at times to produce an aggressive Middle East policy. Russian troops entered the Balkans during the 1806–1812 conflict, the Greek war for independence in the 1820s, the 1848 Romanian uprising, the 1853–1856 Crimean War, and the 1877–1878 Russo-Turkish War. In the last of these struggles, Russian troops came within 10 miles (15 kilometers) of Istanbul and dictated the peace terms at San Stefano in February 1878. Because all the other Great Powers opposed Russia's military and political gains from that war, the sultan regained some of the Balkan lands in the comprehensive Treaty of Berlin, signed later that same year. Russian encouragement of pan-Slavism even helped cause the Balkan Wars of 1912–1913 and the outbreak of World War I in 1914. Although you (like us) may feel overwhelmed by all the twists and turns of the "Eastern Question" from 1774 to 1917, you may assume that the Ottomans viewed Russia as their main enemy for most (but not all) of that time.

The Eastern Question centered on whether Russia would gobble up Turkey's European possessions, especially the Straits, or be stopped from doing so by the other Great Powers. Although other countries at times accepted or even welcomed Russia's growing might (for example, when Russian forces helped defeat Napoleon in 1812–1814, or Hitler in 1942–1945, to jump ahead a bit), they usually tried to prevent a Russian capture of the Balkans and the Straits, lest it endanger the European balance of power.

Now, here is a concept you may want us to explain. No one could decree that each state would have as much power as all the others. After all, Britain had industrialized first, built up the strongest navy, and acquired a large overseas empire. France derived more of its wealth from farming than manufacturing, but it, too, had a big empire and a very strategic location. Austria and Russia each controlled vast areas with large and diverse populations, necessitating big standing armies. Prussia (which became Germany only in 1871) had a well-armed and disciplined army. The balance of power did not, therefore, ensure that each state had equal power; it did mean that no state or coalition could become strong enough to dominate all the other European countries. Failure to maintain that equilibrium had enabled Louis XIV and later Napoleon to impose French power over the rest of the continent, hardly an experience that the British or the Germans (or any other country) cared to relive. On the same logic, many people in the nineteenth century feared that if Russia ruled the Balkans and controlled the Straits, all Europe would be at the mercy of the czars. The West felt a similar dread of Soviet influence over Turkey (and over Central Asia and Afghanistan) during the cold war of 1945–1991. Even now, the realist theory of international relations stresses the need to keep a power balance among the world's countries.

Remember also that Russia was, like the United States, a continental power and an expanding one, except that the direction of its growth was eastward and southward. The Ottomans saw how the Islamized descendants of the Mongols, Tatars, and Turks who had occupied Central Asia fell under Russian control in the nineteenth century. While the West feared that Russian rule in the Balkans would upset the European balance of power, the czars were also building an Asian empire that menaced Persia, Afghanistan, and British India.

Habsburg Austria

Russia's rivals had positive reasons to get involved in Ottoman Turkey. The Habsburg Empire, for instance, bordered directly on Ottoman lands in southeastern Europe from the fifteenth to the nineteenth centuries. Having whetted its appetite by taking Hungary in 1699, Austria hoped to move down the Danube River toward the Black Sea. It also wanted to control lands south of the Danube, especially Croatia, Bosnia, and Serbia. The Habsburg emperors may have pursued commercial interests, but they also saw themselves as carrying on the old Crusading traditions against the Muslim Turks. During the nineteenth century, as each of the Balkan states wrested its independence from the Ottoman Empire, Austria would step forward as its patron, protector, and trading partner. Some seemingly traded one master for another. Bosnia and Herzegovina, two regions culturally and geographically close to Serbia (but with large Muslim populations), were placed under Habsburg military occupation as part of the 1878 Berlin Treaty. Thirty years later, with no prior consent from Ottoman Turkey (and to Russia's dismay), Austria annexed Bosnia and Herzegovina. But their acceptance of Habsburg rule was undermined by propaganda from nearby Serbia, leading to the 1914 assassination at Sarajevo of the heir to Austria's throne. You may know that this event ignited World War I. Some historians see Austria's Balkan policy as a cause of that great conflict once facetiously named "the War of the Turkish Succession."

Britain and the Middle East

Britain was a naval, imperial, and Indian power. Safe sea transport to India became a primary British concern once it had consolidated its Asian empire by defeating France in the Seven Years' War (French and Indian War) of 1756–1763. As long as most maritime transport between Europe and Asia went around South Africa, Britain hardly worried about the Ottoman Empire and at times even backed Russian expansionism in the Balkans. It did not, however, favor French control of Egypt and Syria, as we shall soon see. From about 1820, the growth of steamship transport and the improvement of overland communications made it faster and safer to transship people and goods across Egypt or the Fertile Crescent, both nominally Ottoman lands, instead of taking the long route around Africa. Britain decided in the 1830s that the Ottoman Empire would be the best guardian of its routes to India and soon committed itself firmly to the empire's defense. It also had a commercial motive, for, as you will learn in the next chapter, Britain and the Ottoman Empire signed a treaty lowering their import duties on each other's goods. By 1850 the empire had become a leading buyer of British manufactures and a major supplier of foodstuffs and raw materials to Britain. The British also came to share Austria's suspicions of Russia's Balkan aims.

The largest European conflict between Napoleon's defeat and the outbreak of World War I was the Crimean War. Although many people think the war was sparked by a fight between Catholic and Orthodox priests in Jerusalem, the real cause was the fear of most European countries that Russia's growing strength in the Balkans in 1853 would threaten the balance of power in Europe. By leading the anti-Russian coalition, Britain proved that it would go to great trouble and expense to defend Turkey against Russian expansionism and thus to preserve the balance of power. On the same logic, Britain sent part of its fleet into the Dardanelles in 1878 as a warning, after Russia had occupied most of the Balkan lands. In Chapter 10 you will see how Britain's commitment extended to pressing westernizing reforms on the Ottoman rulers at these critical times. In a further attempt to secure its routes to India, Britain also took Aden in 1839, Cyprus in 1878, and Egypt in 1882, and made treaties with Arab rulers along the Gulf from Oman to Kuwait. Several times Britain sent troops to Afghanistan or Persia to deter the advancing Russians, whose hope of reaching the Gulf nearly equaled their drive to the Straits. Britain feared that the czars' land hunger might extend to the Himalayas, India, and even China. These nineteenth-century events foreshadowed Britain's attempt to dominate the Middle East after World War I.

France: Protector and Civilizer

The best friend of the Ottoman Turks was usually France. Its strategic location, with ports on both the Atlantic and the Mediterranean, made France a contender for mastery in Europe. Until the nineteenth century, its greatest Mediterranean rival was the Habsburg Empire, making France the ally of the Ottomans. France claimed to have the first Capitulations, and French merchants and investors usually led the Europeans doing business in the Ottoman Empire. When it needed military or naval experts, engineers, or teachers, the Ottoman government usually sought French ones. Young Ottomans were more apt to choose France than any other foreign country for higher education or advanced vocational training.

Religion, too, strengthened the French connection. When Russia tried to protect Orthodox Christians under Ottoman rule, France advanced similar claims on behalf of the Catholics. Because they were less numerous, the Turks minded them less. One fateful result was the special bond between France and Syria. And one key to this tie was a Christian sect, the Maronites, who predominated in what is now northern Lebanon. In the seventh century, the Maronites had stood for a position between Orthodox and Monophysite Christianity, giving them a unique identity. They later entered into communion with Rome during the Crusades but retained their traditional practices (e.g., having prayers in Syriac and married priests). From the seventeenth century, they had access to Western learning through a papal seminary for Maronites in Rome. When France emerged as the leading Catholic power, the Maronites welcomed French missionaries and merchants to Syria, where they built up a network of schools, churches, factories, and trading posts. France's primacy in Syria also rested on ties with other Christians. Some Christians were leaving their native churches, usually Orthodox but some Jacobite (Monophysite) and Nestorian, and entering into communion with Rome as Uniates. These Catholic converts, like the Maronites, studied in the French schools and traded with French merchants. Some adopted other aspects of French culture and viewed France as their patron and protector. When fighting erupted in 1860 between Syria's Muslims and Christians, Paris intervened to rescue the latter.

Strategically speaking, Egypt mattered more to France than Syria did. This concern was not widely felt in the eighteenth century, when Egypt's economy and society reached a low point owing to Ottoman neglect and Mamluk misrule, for the Mamluks, as will be explained later, retained their power in Egypt. But Napoleon Bonaparte, who called Egypt the world's most important country, occupied it in 1798. For three years Britain and Turkey engaged in military and diplomatic maneuvers to get the French troops out of Egypt. Following France's departure, a military adventurer named Mehmet Ali (the Arabs call him Muhammad Ali) seized power in Cairo. Using French advisers, he started an ambitious reform program, built up a strong army and navy, and took Syria from the Ottomans in 1831. France abetted and applauded Mehmet Ali's gains. Not so the other Great Powers, which saw these gains as a threat to the European balance of power and viewed Mehmet Ali as a French agent. It took British naval intervention to get his troops out of Syria in 1840, but Mehmet Ali stayed in power and founded a dynasty that would rule Egypt until 1952.

France played the lead role in yet another Egyptian drama. Mehmet Ali's son, Sa'id, granted a concession in 1854 to a French entrepreneur to build a ship canal across the Isthmus of Suez. The British tried to block the project, fearing that it would put the French in control of a major route to India. But once the Suez Canal was opened in 1869, Britain became its main user. Soon it bought the Egyptian government's shares in the controlling company; then it sent troops into Egypt (France was supposed to send troops, too, but failed to act at the critical moment) to quell a nationalist uprising in 1882. France's economic and cultural ties with Egypt remained strong, but by the end of the nineteenth century, despite French opposition, Britain dominated the Nile Valley. France did, however, take control of most of the rest of North Africa. After World War I, it would seek further compensation in Syria and Lebanon.

Conclusion

This brings to a close our rapid survey of Middle Eastern interests and policies of the major European powers. We went beyond the eighteenth century, hoping to give you a context for events occurring later on. You may ask why we focused on Russia, Austria, England, and France to the exclusion of all other countries. Admittedly, we have oversimplified the scenario somewhat. The complete cast of characters in the Eastern Question would include Swiss archaeologists, Belgian bankers, German military advisers, American Protestant and Italian Catholic missionaries, Greek grocers, and Armenian photographers. By 1900 the German, Italian, and US governments had also acquired bit parts in the political drama. Persia was becoming more important as well, especially as an object of Anglo-Russian commercial and military rivalry.

This chapter also treats the Middle East not as an area acting but as one acted upon. This, too, is a distortion. Even if it did lose lands in the Balkans and North Africa, the Ottoman Empire (increasingly called Turkey by the Europeans) remained independent throughout this time. Even though Western ambassadors and advisers tended to overdirect sultans and viziers, the scope of their actions was limited by Muslim conservatism and their need to block other countries from intervening. Likewise, Persia staved off the Russians and the British until both agreed to split the country into zones of influence in 1907. Most Middle Eastern peoples went on living their lives as if Europe were on another planet. The changes affecting them were the westernizing reform policies of their own rulers. It is to these reforms that we will now turn.

The Rise of Nationalism

Arthur Goldschmidt Jr. and Lawrence Davidson

Among the ideas the Middle East has imported from the West, none has been more popular and durable than nationalism. Often called the religion of the modern world, this ideology or belief system is hard to pin down. Drawing on the Western historical experience, we define nationalism as the desire of a large group of people to create or maintain a common statehood, to have their own rulers, laws, and other governmental institutions. This desired political community, or nation, is the object of that group's supreme loyalty. Shared characteristics among the peoples of Egypt and also among those of Persia stimulated the growth of nationalism in those two countries in the late nineteenth century. Other nationalist movements have grown up in the Middle East around shared resistance to governments, institutions, and even individuals regarded as foreign.

Nationalism was itself foreign to the world of Islam. In traditional Islamic thought, the *umma*, or community of believers, was for Muslims the sole object of political loyalty. Loyalty meant defending the land of Islam against rulers or peoples of other faiths. All true Muslims were meant to be brothers and sisters, regardless of race, language, and culture. Although distinctions existed between Arabs and Persians, or between them and the Turks, common adherence to Islam was supposed to transcend all differences. Nationalism should not exist in Islam.

Yet it does, though religion has deeply influenced nationalism in the Middle East. Arab nationalism at its start included Christians and even Jews, but its clearest expressions since World War II have been opposition to Christian control in Lebanon and to Jewish colonization in Palestine (Israel since 1948). The rhetoric of nationalism often confuses the Arab nation with the Islamic *umma*, as when an Arab nationalist

Arthur Goldschmidt, Jr. and Lawrence Davidson, "The Rise of Nationalism," *A Concise History of the Middle East*, pp. 163-180. Copyright © 2012 by Taylor & Francis Group. Reprinted with permission.

cause is termed a *jihad*. Other Middle Eastern nationalist movements were based even more firmly on religion and called on their people to resist oppression by others having a different faith. These include Greeks and Armenians among the Christians of the Middle East, as well as Turks and Persians among its Muslims. Political Zionism, which called for Israel's creation as the Jewish state, drew its inspiration from Judaism, even if many of its advocates were not themselves observant. In all three monotheistic faiths, the rise of nationalism has meant substituting collective self-love for the love of God, enhancing life on this earth instead of preparing for what is to come after death, and promoting the community's welfare instead of obeying God's revealed laws.

During the forty years before World War I, the peoples of the Arab world, Turkey, and Persia began to develop nationalist feelings. As this was the high-water mark of European imperialism, we can see rising nationalism as a natural reaction to Western power. But it was also the end result of a century of westernizing reform, with its enlarged armies and bureaucracies, modern schools, printing presses, roads and rail lines, and centralized state power. One could not learn Europe's techniques, most often taught in French, without absorbing some of its ideas. Middle Eastern students at French or German universities had ample exposure to Western ideas, even if they never heard lectures in political theory. There were newspapers and magazines being hawked in the streets, lively discussions in cafes, demonstrations, and encounters with Western orientalists (the nineteenth-century counterpart of our Middle East historians) who could explain what was happening in Europe to a Turkish, Egyptian, or Persian sojourner. Even the students who learned their technical skills in Istanbul, Cairo, or Tehran were apt to be exposed to Western ideas through their European instructors. Besides, their schools usually had reading rooms. A Middle Easterner studying engineering could read works by Rousseau or other Western writers.

In short, as Middle Easterners learned how to work like Europeans, some also started to think like them. They learned that bad governments did not have to be endured (indeed, many earlier Muslims had defied tyrannical rulers), that individuals had rights and freedoms that should be protected against official coercion, and that people could belong to political communities based on race, language, culture, and shared historical experience—in short, they could form nations. In the 1870s these liberal and nationalist ideas became current among many educated young Muslims of the Middle East, especially in the capital cities. While they faced the frustrations of these years and those that followed, their ideas crystallized into nationalist movements.

Many religious and ethnic groups formed nationalist movements in the Middle East before World War I. We will limit this chapter, however, to three that arose within existing states that had governments and some experience with westernizing reform: those of the Egyptians, the Turks in the Ottoman Empire, and the Persians under the Qajar shahs. Arab nationalism and Zionism will be covered later. Nationalism among such Christian peoples of the Ottoman Empire as the Greeks and Armenians will be treated only as they spurred the rise of Turkish nationalism.

Egyptian Nationalism

Western writers used to call Egypt "the land of paradox." Almost all its inhabitants were crowded into the valley and delta of the great River Nile, without which Egypt would have been only a desert supporting a few bedouin nomads. To European tourists a century ago, Egypt was filled with ancient relics—temples, obelisks, pyramids, sphinxes, and buried treasures—and haunted by pharaohs whose tombs had been violated by bedouin robbers or Western archaeologists. To most Muslims, however, Egypt was the very heart and soul of Islam, with its mosque-university of al-Azhar, its festive observance of Muslim holy days and saints' birthdays, and its annual procession bearing a new cloth that would be sent to cover the Ka'ba in Mecca. Egypt meant Cairo, with its hundreds of mosques and *madrasa*s, ornate villas and bazaars—survivals of a time when the Mamluks really ruled and the city stood out as an economic and intellectual center. To a student who has just been exposed to Mehmet Ali's reforms and the building of the Suez Canal, Egypt was the most westernized country in the nineteenth-century Middle East.

Imagine one of the newer quarters of Cairo or Alexandria in 1875, or the new towns of Port Said and Ismailia, their wide, straight avenues lined with European-style houses, hotels, banks, shops, schools, and churches. Horse-drawn carriages whiz past the donkeys and camels of a more leisurely age. Restaurants serve coq au vin or veal scallopini instead of *kufta* (ground meat) or kebab; their customers smoke cigars instead of water pipes. The signs are in French, not Arabic. The passersby converse in Italian, Greek, Armenian, Turkish, Yiddish, Ladino (a language derived from Spanish and spoken by Mizrachi Jews), or several dialects of Arabic. Top hats have replaced turbans, and frock coats have supplanted the caftans of yore. Each of these images fits a part of Egypt almost 140 years ago—but not all of it.

Khedive Isma'il

The ruler of this land of paradox was Mehmet Ali's grandson, Isma'il (r. 1863–1879), a complex and controversial figure. Was he a man of vision, as his admirers claimed, or a spendthrift who would ultimately bring Egypt into British bondage? His admirers cited the railroads, bridges, docks, canals, factories, and sugar refineries built during his reign. It was also the time when the Egyptian government paid explorers and military expeditions to penetrate the Sudan and East Africa and tried to abolish slavery and slave trading within its empire. The Egyptian Mixed Courts were set up to hear civil cases involving Europeans protected by the Capitulations. Public and missionary schools—for girls as well as boys—proliferated in the cities. The Egyptian Museum, National Library, Geographical Society, and many professional schools began under Isma'il.

But Isma'il's detractors point out that he squandered money to impress Europe with his munificence and power. Building the Suez Canal cost the Egyptian government much, for the state treasury had to reimburse the Suez Canal Company when it was forced to pay wages to the construction workers (the company had expected to get the peasants' labor for free). This was the fault of Isma'il's predecessor, Sa'id. But it was Isma'il who turned the canal's inauguration into an extravaganza, inviting the crowned heads and leaders of Europe to come—at Egypt's expense. Costing at least 2 million Egyptian pounds (worth $200 million in today's prices), it must have been the bash of the century, with enormous receptions, all-night parties, balls, parades, fireworks displays, horse races, excursions to ancient monuments, and cities festooned with flags and illuminated by lanterns. New villas and palaces sprouted up, streets were widened and straightened, old neighborhoods were demolished, and even an opera house was erected in Cairo. Giuseppe Verdi, the Italian composer, was commissioned to write *Aida* for the inauguration of that opera house. Isma'il also paid huge bribes in Istanbul to lessen his ties to the Ottoman government, changing his title from pasha (governor) to khedive (viceroy) of Egypt and obtaining the right to pass down his position to his son in Cairo rather than to a brother living in Istanbul. He also won a fateful privilege: to take out foreign loans without Ottoman permission.

Financial Problems

But where could the money have come from? Egyptian taxpayers could not have covered Isma'il's extravagance. His reign had begun during the American Civil War, which caused a cotton boom in Egypt. The British, cut off by the Northern blockade from their usual cotton supply, would pay any price for other countries' crops to supply the textile mills of Lancashire. The high demand for Egypt's cotton stimulated output and enriched both the Egyptian growers and the government. During this cotton boom, European investment bankers offered Isma'il loans on attractive terms. When the boom ended after the Civil War, Egypt's need for money was greater than ever, but now he could get credit only at high interest rates. In 1866 Isma'il convoked an assembly representing the landowners to seek their consent to raise taxes. Soon they were taxing date palms, flour mills, oil presses, boats, shops, houses, and even burials.

Isma'il adopted still other stratagems to postpone the day of reckoning. He offered tax abatements to landowners who could pay three years' taxes in advance. He sold Egypt's shares in the Suez Canal Company—44 percent of the stock—to the British government in 1875. When a British delegation came to investigate rumors of Egypt's impending bankruptcy, the khedive agreed to set up a Dual Financial Control to manage the public debt. But a low Nile in 1877, high military expenses incurred in the Russo-Turkish War, and an invasion of Ethiopia by Egypt put the Egyptian government deeper in debt. In August 1878 Isma'il, pressed by his European creditors, agreed to admit an Englishman and a Frenchman to his cabinet; he also promised to turn his powers over to his ministers. At the same time, he secretly stirred up antiforeign elements in his army. This was easy, for the Dual Control had cut the Egyptian officers' pay in half. A military riot in February 1879 enabled Isma'il to dismiss the foreign ministers and later to appoint a cabinet of liberals who began drafting a constitution, much as the Ottoman Empire had done in 1876. Britain and France, guarding their investors' interests, asked the Ottoman sultan to dismiss Isma'il. He did. When Isma'il turned over the khedivate to his son, Tawfiq, and left Egypt in July 1879, the state debt stood at 93 million Egyptian pounds. It had been 3 million when he came to power in 1863.

The Beginnings of Nationalism

Isma'il's successes and failures made him the father of Egypt's first nationalist movement. His new schools, law courts, railroads, and telegraph lines drew Egyptians closer together and helped to foster nationalist feeling. So did the newspapers he patronized in hope of creating a positive public image. The Suez Canal and related projects drew thousands of Europeans into Egypt; they became models for modernization and at the same time targets of native resentment.

Muslim feeling, always strong but usually quiescent, was aroused at this time under the influence of a fiery pan-Islamic agitator, Jamal al-Din, called al-Afghani (despite his claim of being an Afghan, he really was from Persia), who came to teach at al-Azhar. Afghani would pop up in almost every political movement that stirred in the late nineteenth-century Middle East. He soon clashed with the *ulama* and quit al-Azhar to form a sort of independent academy that attracted many young Egyptians who would later become political leaders or Islamic reformers. Two of them were Muhammad Abduh, the greatest Muslim thinker of the late nineteenth century, and Sa'd Zaghlul, leader of Egypt's independence struggle after World War I. Afghani, like Isma'il, encouraged journalists; but his protégés were bolder ones, often Jews or Christians who turned more readily to secular nationalism than did the Muslims whom Afghani wanted to stir up.

Isma'il's financial crisis, which tied Egypt to Western creditors and to their governments, shamed Egyptians, especially members of his representative assembly. Once a subservient group of frightened rural landlords, it had now turned into a vociferous body of antigovernment critics. But the key breeding ground for nationalism was the army. Sa'id had started admitting Egyptian farmers' sons into the officer corps and had promoted some of them rapidly, whereas Isma'il withheld their promotions and pay raises in favor of the traditional elite, the Turks and Circassians. Frustrated, the Egyptian officers formed a secret society to plot against their oppressors. It later would become the nucleus of the first National Party.

Isma'il's deposition set back the nascent nationalists. During his last months in power, the Egyptian officers had joined with government workers, assembly representatives, journalists, and *ulama* to back the drafters of a constitution that would give to Egyptians some of the rights and freedoms Europeans enjoyed in their own countries. But Tawfiq, the new khedive, thought it safer to back the European creditors than the Egyptian nationalists. He dismissed the liberal cabinet, restored the Dual Control, banned the newspapers, and exiled Afghani and other agitators.

Ahmad Urabi

The nationalists seemed to be in eclipse, but we suspect that Khedive Tawfiq secretly encouraged them. Sa'd Zaghlul and Muhammad Abduh could still demand constitutional rule in the official journal they edited. The disgruntled Egyptian officers continued to meet. In February 1881 these men, led by Colonel Ahmad Urabi, mutinied and "forced" Tawfiq to replace his Circassian war minister with a nationalist, Mahmud Sami al-Barudi. Seven months later, 2,500 Egyptian officers and soldiers surrounded the khedive's palace and "made" him appoint a liberal cabinet. Moreover, they demanded a constitution, parliamentary government, and an enlarged army. The same demands were sought by the civilian nationalists; they were also feared by the European creditors, who wondered how Tawfiq or Urabi would ever find money to pay for these reforms.

Ahmad Urabi

Urabi (1841–1911) was an Egyptian military officer and national hero. Urabi was born to a relatively well-to-do peasant family in the village of Qaryat Rizqa, the son of a village shaykh who made sure Ahmad received a strong traditional Islamic education. He entered the Egyptian army as a teenager and moved up through the ranks quickly. He held the rank of lieutenant colonel by age twenty. He had a charismatic personality and was an excellent public speaker. His gifts would be borne out by his eventual achievements.

Several problems afflicted Egypt during Urabi's time. The Egyptian army was more a patronage bureaucracy than a true fighting force, and its officer corps was divided into competing ethnic groups. Native Egyptians faced discriminatory treatment in the army by officers of Circassian and Turkish origin. In addition, the indebtedness of the khedives and the strategic location of Egypt and the Suez Canal combined to make that country matter greatly to Europe's imperial powers, particularly Great Britain. Finances and strategy would encourage European intervention in Egypt.

Urabi acted out of both personal interests and patriotism. For instance, when Khedive Tawfiq, acting under the influence of Turkish officers in the army, passed a law barring peasants from becoming officers, Urabi, reacting out of self-interest, organized resistance among the Egyptian soldiers and forced the law's repeal. He also forged an alliance between the army officers and Egyptian nationalists seeking to limit the growing influence of Europeans in Egyptian affairs. Additional pressure on the khedive (who may have encouraged the nationalists) brought Urabi into the government as war minister. It is from this position that he and other nationalists contested the Egyptian budget, with its Anglo-French Dual Financial Control.

In the end Europe's power overwhelmed Urabi and those who sought real independence for Egypt. The British were not willing to risk their investments or control of the Suez Canal by supporting Egyptian nationalism. When they invaded Egypt in 1882, Urabi's charismatic leadership was no match for Britain's Gatling guns. Urabi's forces were defeated in the Battle of Tel al-Kebir. Urabi fled to Cairo, where he finally surrendered. By this time the khedive had switched sides, thrown in his lot with the British, declared Urabi a rebel, and wanted to have him sentenced to death. The British high commissioner in Cairo, Lord Dufferin, recognizing that Urabi's death would make him a martyr, had the sentence commuted to permanent exile in Ceylon.

Long disdained by civilian nationalists, Colonel Urabi has now become a national hero in Egypt. His resistance against foreign invasion was an important milestone in Egyptian national history.

During the next year Egypt came as close as it ever would to democratic government (if you take the Egyptian nationalist view of history) or anarchy (if you buy the British interpretation of what happened). A liberal cabinet drafted a constitution and held elections as Egypt's debts rose further. In January 1882 Britain and France sent a joint note, threatening to intervene to support Tawfiq (they really meant to restore the Dual Control). The nationalists called their bluff, declaring that Egypt's new parliament, not the British and French debt commissioners, would control the state budget. Barudi took over the premiership and Urabi became war minister, threatening the Turkish and Circassian officers in Egypt's army. The nationalists even thought of ousting Tawfiq and declaring Egypt a republic. More likely, though, they would have replaced him with one of his exiled relatives, a strange treatment for their secret patron.

As nationalism was new in Egypt, could an outsider have inspired these moves? A few English liberals helped the movement, and France's consul in Cairo may have encouraged Urabi; however, the outside supporters were probably the Ottoman sultan and a dispossessed uncle of Tawfiq living in Istanbul. This fact may make the movement seem less than wholly nationalist. One scholar argues that what we call the National Party was really a constellation of several groups with various political, economic, and religious interests. Still, the movement had become popular by June 1882. What destroyed it was Britain's determination to dispatch troops to protect European lives and investments in Egypt and to defend the Suez Canal, which had become vital to British shipping.

Riots in Alexandria caused a general exodus of Europeans, and both British and French gunboats dropped anchor near the harbor. Then the British fired on Alexandria's fortifications, somehow much of the city caught fire, and British marines landed to restore order (as the French ships sailed away). Urabi declared war on Britain, but Tawfiq declared him a traitor and threw in his lot with the British in Alexandria. Other British Empire troops entered the canal and landed at Ismailia. Defeating Urabi's army was easy, and the British occupied Cairo in September 1882. Barudi's cabinet was dismissed, the nationalists were tried for rebellion, Urabi was exiled, the constitution was suspended, the nationalist newspapers were banned, and the army was broken up by Tawfiq and his British advisers. The early nationalists had proved a weak force. Their party had been divided among Egyptian officers resenting privileged Turks and Circassians in the army, civilians seeking parliamentary rule, and reformers like Afghani and Abduh who wanted an Islamic revival.

Lord Cromer and the British Occupation

The British government that sent troops to Egypt in 1882 expected a brief military occupation. As soon as order was restored, Britain's troops were supposed to leave, and Egypt was to resume being an autonomous Ottoman province. But the longer the British stayed, the more disorder they found to clean up and the less they wanted to leave Egypt. The financial situation in particular needed drastic economic and administrative reforms. The British agent and consul general in Cairo from 1883 to 1907, Lord Cromer, was a talented financial administrator. With a small (but growing) staff of British advisers to Egypt's various ministries, Cromer managed to expand the Nile irrigation system to raise agricultural output, increase state revenues, lower taxes, and reduce the public debt burden. His officials were competent, devoted to the Egyptians' welfare, and honest. Cromer's epitaph in Westminster Abbey would call him the "regenerator of Egypt."

He may have been so, but Cromer is not well remembered in Egypt today. Egyptians living in his era felt their own advancement in government jobs or the professions was blocked by the numerous foreigners holding high posts in Cairo. Besides, they objected to Cromer's policy of limiting the growth of education. Some were angry that the Egyptian army, despite its British officers, lost the Sudan in 1885 to a rebellion led by the self-styled *Mahdi* (Rightly Guided One). After British and Egyptian troops regained the Sudan in 1898, it was placed under a condominium, with Britain effectively in control. Opposition to the continuing British occupation of Egypt came from a few British anti-imperialists; the French, who (despite their large economic stake in Egypt) had failed to intervene in 1882; and the Ottoman Turks, who resented losing another province of their empire. As long as there was no internal opposition, though, these groups could do little to thwart British rule.

The Revival of Egyptian Nationalism

Major resistance began when Abbas, Khedive Tawfiq's seventeen-year-old son, succeeded him in 1892. High-spirited and proudly guarding what he felt were his khedivial prerogatives, Abbas fought with Cromer over the right to appoint and dismiss his ministers and over control of the Egyptian army. Although the British consul won the battles by bullying the ministers and asking his own government to send more troops to Egypt, he lost the trust of the youthful khedive. Seeking to undermine Cromer, Abbas created a clique of European and native supporters. Among the latter was an articulate law student named Mustafa Kamil, who emerged as a potent palace propagandist in Europe and Egypt. In the ensuing years, he converted what had been Abbas's secret society into a large-scale movement, the (revived) National Party. He founded a boys' school and a daily newspaper to spread nationalist ideas. As his popularity grew, Mustafa came to care more about obtaining a democratic constitution and less about upholding the khedive's prerogatives. He and his followers always demanded the evacuation of British troops from Egypt.

In 1906 an incident occurred that spread Mustafa Kamil's fame. A group of British officers entered a village called Dinshaway to shoot pigeons. Due to some misunderstandings between the villagers and the officers, a fracas broke out. A gun went off, setting a threshing floor on fire. Another bullet wounded a peasant woman. The villagers began to beat the officers with clubs. One of the latter escaped, fainted after running several miles, and died of sunstroke. The British authorities, suspecting a premeditated assault, tried fifty-seven farmers before a special military court, which found many of them guilty of murder. Four were hanged, and several others were flogged in the presence of their families as an object lesson to the Dinshaway villagers. These barbarous sentences appalled Mustafa Kamil, most Egyptians, and even many Europeans, for at that time people were shocked by atrocities that now seem tame. Mustafa exploited this reaction to win new followers and hasten Cromer's retirement. He publicly established the National Party in December 1907 but tragically died two months later.

Mustafa's successors disagreed about their tactics and aims. Was the National Party for Muslims against Christian rulers or for all Egyptian people opposed to the British occupation? If the latter, could Egypt expect support from its nominal overlord, the Ottoman Empire? Should the party seek national independence by peaceful or by revolutionary means? If the latter, would it oppose Khedive Abbas and other large landowners? Should it seek economic and social reform or stress evicting the British from Egypt? How could a party mainly of lawyers and students, with few backers in the Egyptian army, persuade Britain to leave?

More moderate leaders argued that constitutional government should precede independence. Muhammad Abduh, who had backed Urabi in 1882, later worked for the regeneration of Islam and the reform of al-Azhar University, encouraged by Lord Cromer. Abduh's followers, together with some secular intellectuals and large landowners, formed the Umma Party in 1907 to counter the Nationalists. The British consul who replaced Cromer in 1907 neutralized the Nationalist threat by wooing Khedive Abbas and the more conservative landowners to Britain's side. The next consul won peasant support through his agrarian policies. By 1914 the Nationalist leaders were in exile. Only after World War I would the Egyptians build up enough resentment against British rule to form a truly national and revolutionary movement.

Ottomanism, Pan-Islam, and Turkism

The rise of Turkish nationalism was hampered by the fact that until the twentieth century no educated Ottoman, even if Turkish was his native tongue, cared to be called a Turk. The Ottoman Empire, though Westerners called it Turkey, was definitely not a Turkish nation-state. It contained many ethnic and religious groups: Turks, Greeks, Serbs, Croats, Albanians, Bulgarians, Arabs, Syrians, Armenians, and Kurds, to name but a few. Its rulers were Sunni Muslims, but it included Greek Orthodox, Armenian, and Jewish subjects organized into *millet*s (which functioned like nations within the state), as well as many smaller religious groups. Its inhabitants were either *Osmanlilar*, who belonged to the ruling class, or *re'aya*, who did not, with nothing in between.

Early Nationalism in the Ottoman Empire
Nationalism in the modern sense first arose among the Greeks and the Serbs (peoples exposed to Western or Russian influences), then spread to other subject Christians. As independence movements proliferated in the Balkans, the Ottoman rulers worried more and more over how to hold their empire together and counter the Russians, who openly encouraged Balkan revolts. Westernizing reforms were their first solution, but these raised more hopes than could be met and did not create a new basis of loyalty. The reformers espoused the idea of Ottomanism (loyalty to the Ottoman state) as a framework within which racial, linguistic, and religious groups could develop autonomously but harmoniously. To this the New Ottomans of the 1870s had added the idea of a constitution that would

set up an assembly representing all the empire's peoples. The constitution was drafted in 1876—the worst possible time, with several nationalist rebellions going on in the Balkans, war raging against Serbia and Montenegro (two Balkan states that had already won their independence), the Ottoman treasury nearly bankrupt, Russia threatening to send in troops, and Britain preparing to fight against the Turks to protect the Balkan Christians and against the Russians to defend the Ottoman Empire (a policy as weird to people then as it sounds now). Moreover, the New Ottomans had seized power in a coup, put on the throne a sultan who turned out to be crazy, and then replaced him with his brother, Abdulhamid II (r. 1876–1909), whose promises to uphold the new constitution were suspect.

Well, they should have been. The ensuing Russo-Turkish War put the empire in such peril that no one could have governed under the Ottoman constitution. Sultan Abdulhamid soon suspended it and dissolved parliament. For thirty years he ruled as a dictator, appointing and dismissing his own ministers, holding his creditors at bay, fomenting quarrels among the Great Powers to keep them from partitioning the empire, and suppressing all dissident movements within his realm. Europeans and Ottoman Christians viewed him as a cruel sultan, reactionary in his attitudes toward westernizing reforms and devoted to the doctrine of pan-Islam. This movement alarmed Russia, Britain, and France, with their millions of Muslim subjects in Asia and Africa. It is interesting that Istanbul, seat of the sultan-caliph, became the final home of that wandering pan-Islamic agitator, Jamal al-Din al-Afghani.

Abdulhamid is remembered for his censors and spies, his morbid fear of assassination, and his massacres of Armenians (some of whom were plotting against his regime). Scholars trying to rehabilitate his image have claimed he furthered the centralizing policies of the earlier Tanzimat reformers, noting that the Ottoman Empire lost no European lands between 1878 and 1908. Even though Muslims at home and abroad hailed him as their caliph, Sultan Abdulhamid was incompetent, paranoid, and cruel. The empire's finances were controlled by a European debt commission, freedoms of speech and assembly vanished, the army came to a standstill, and the navy deteriorated. The ablest reformers went into exile. Midhat, leader of the New Ottomans, was lured back with false promises, tried for attempted murder, locked up in the Arabian town of Taif, and secretly strangled there.

Many Ottomans, especially if they had attended Western schools, felt that the only way to save the Ottoman Empire was to restore the 1876 constitution, even if they had to overthrow Abdulhamid first. A number of opposition groups were formed. All of them tend to get lumped together as the "Young Turks," a term possibly borrowed from the "New Ottomans." Many were not Turks, and some were not even young, but the term has stuck. The key society was a secret one formed by four cadets—all Muslims but of several nationalities. It became known as the Committee of Union and Progress (CUP). Its history was long and tortuous, with moments of hope interspersed with years of gloom, centering at times on exiled Turkish writers living in Paris or Geneva, at others on cells of Ottoman army officers in Salonika and Damascus. Gradually, many Ottomans adopted the CUP's goals: that the empire must be militarily and morally strengthened, that all religious and ethnic groups must have equal rights, that the constitution must be restored, and that Sultan Abdulhamid must be shorn of power. Otherwise, Russia would take what was left of the empire in Europe, including Istanbul and the Straits. The Western powers would carve up Asiatic Turkey, as they had partitioned Africa and divided China into spheres of influence.

The Young Turks in Power

The CUP was Ottomanist, not Turkish nationalist, as long as it was out of power. Fearful of the reconciliation between Britain and Russia in 1907, the CUP inspired an army coup that forced Abdulhamid to restore the Ottoman constitution in 1908. Every religious and ethnic group in the empire rejoiced; the committee, even if its leaders were Turks, was backed by many loyal Balkan Christians, Armenians, Arabs, and Jews. Most wanted to be Ottoman citizens under the 1876 constitution. Western well-wishers expected Turkey to revive. Elections were held for the new parliament, the tide of democracy seemed to be sweeping into Istanbul, and the CUP started so many changes that we still call vigorous reformers "Young Turks." Indeed, their rise to power portended the many revolutions that have changed the face of Middle Eastern politics since 1908.

But if we examine what really happened to the Ottoman Empire under the Young Turks, we must give them lower marks for their achievements than for their stated intentions. They did not halt disintegration, as Austria annexed Bosnia, Bulgaria declared its independence, and Crete rebelled, all in late 1908. Their hopes for rapid economic development were dashed when France withdrew a loan offer in 1910. The next year Italy invaded the Ottoman province of Tripolitania. Russia incited Bulgaria and Serbia to join forces in 1912 and attack the empire in Macedonia. In four months the Turks lost almost all their European lands. Even Albania, a mainly Muslim part of the Balkans, rebelled in 1910 and declared its independence in 1913. And the Arabs [...] were getting restless.

How could Istanbul's government, as set up under the restored 1876 constitution, weather these problems? After the CUP won the 1912 election by large-scale bribery and intimidation, the army forced its ministers to resign in favor of its rival, the Liberal Entente. It took another military coup and a timely assassination in 1913 to restore the CUP to power. By the outbreak of World War I, the Ottoman government was a virtual triumvirate: Enver as war minister, Talat as minister of the interior, and Jemal in charge of the navy. Though these men had led the 1908 revolution to restore the 1876 constitution, democracy was dead in the Ottoman Empire.

Turkish Nationalism

Amid these crises, the CUP leaders became more and more Turkish in their political orientation. Their early hope that the Great Powers and the empire's minorities would back their Ottomanist reforms had been dashed. The powers grabbed land and withheld aid. The minorities grumbled, plotted, or rebelled. What could the Young Turks do? Some stuck to their Ottomanist guns. Others argued for pan-Islam, which would have held the loyalty of most Arabs and won needed support from Egypt, India, and other Muslim lands. But the new wave was pan-Turanism. This was the attempt to bring together all speakers of Turkic languages under Ottoman leadership, just as pan-Slavism meant uniting all speakers of Slavic languages behind Russia. Indeed, as most speakers of Turkic languages were then under czarist rule or military occupation, pan-Turanism seemed a good way to pay back the Russians for the trouble they had caused the Ottoman Empire. Some of the leading pan-Turanian advocates were refugees from Russian Central Asia or Azerbaijan, but it was hard for the Ottoman Turks to forget their traditional ties to Islam or their own empire. Few believed in a distinct Turanian culture. The CUP's efforts to impose Turkish in the schools and offices of their Arabic-speaking provinces stirred up Arab nationalism, further weakening the empire. The committee could not influence Central Asian Turks. The Turks' ethnic and linguistic nationalism caused more problems than it solved, until they limited their national idea to fellow Turks within the Ottoman Empire. The idea was not unknown. A Turkish sociologist named Ziya Gokalp was writing newspaper articles to promote what he called Turkism, but this idea would become popular only after World War I. By then it was too late to save the Ottoman Empire.

Nationalism in Persia

Persia did not westernize as early as Egypt and the Ottoman Empire, but it had a compensating advantage when it came to developing Persian nationalism. Let us look at what historians and political scientists usually cite as nationalism's components: (1) previously existing state, (2) religion, (3) language, (4) race, (5) lifestyle, (6) shared economic interests, (7) common enemies, and (8) shared historical consciousness. If you test Egyptian or Turkish nationalism against these criteria, you will find that they fall short on several counts. Not so Persian nationalism. The Qajar dynasty may have governed ineptly, but it was heir to a Persian political tradition traceable to the ancient Achaemenids, interrupted by Greek, Arab, Turkish, and Mongol invasions. Persia was predominantly Muslim, but its uniqueness was ensured by its general adherence to Twelve-Imam Shiism, whereas its Muslim neighbors were mainly Sunni. Its chief written and spoken language was Persian, although many of the country's inhabitants spoke Turkish, while numerous Muslims in India and the Ottoman Empire read and wrote Persian well. "Race" is a treacherous term to use in a land so often invaded and settled by outsiders, but certainly the Persians viewed their personal appearance as distinctive. Their culture had withstood the tests of time, invasions, and political change. Both visitors and natives hailed the Persian way of life: its poetry, architecture, costumes, cuisine, social relationships—and even its jokes. The economic interests of nineteenth-century Persia seem to have been, if not homogeneous, at least complementary among city dwellers, farmers, and nomads. No other Middle Easterners could match the Persians' strong historical consciousness, expressed in their monumental architecture, painting, epic poetry, written history, and music, glorifying twenty-five centuries as a distinctive people.

Early Resistance to Foreign Power

It should not surprise you, therefore, to learn that a Persian nationalist movement arose between 1870 and 1914. Basically, it was a reaction against the threat of a Russian military takeover, against growing dependence on the West, and against the divisive effects of tribalism in the rural areas. It was facilitated by the spread of roads, telegraphs, and both public and private schools. Nasiruddin Shah's policy of selling to foreign investors the rights to develop Persia's resources alienated his own subjects. In 1873 he offered a concession to one Baron de Reuter, a British subject, to form a monopoly that would build railways, operate mines, and establish Persia's national bank. Russian objections and domestic opposition forced the shah to cancel the concession, although the baron was later authorized to start the Imperial Bank of Persia. In 1890 Nasiruddin sold a concession to an English company to control the production, sale, and export of all tobacco in Persia. [...] a nationwide tobacco boycott, inspired by the same Afghani you saw earlier in Egypt, forced the cancellation of this concession. The boycott gave westernized Persians, Shiite *ulama,* and bazaar merchants enough confidence in their political power to spur the growth of a constitutionalist movement in the ensuing years.

Many observers noted the mounting problems of the Qajar shahs, their economic concessions to foreigners, the widening disparities between rich landowners and poor peasants (owing to the shift from subsistence to cash-crop agriculture), and Persia's growing dependence on Russian military advisers. Well might they have wondered how long it would take for Russia to occupy Persia. Persians knew about the British occupation of Egypt, Sultan Abdulhamid's weakness, and the foreign penetration of China. If the Russian troops did not come, some asked, would British investors take over Persia more subtly? Russia was Persia's main enemy, but Britain was a close second. The shah, surrounded by corrupt courtiers, had sold most of his inherited treasures and spent the proceeds of his foreign loans on palaces, trips abroad, and gifts to his family and friends.

The Constitutionalist Movement

Patriotic Persians felt that the remedy to these ills was a constitution that would limit their rulers' arbitrary acts. The idea spread among bazaar merchants, landlords, *ulama,* army officers, and even some government officials and tribal leaders. Secret societies sprang up in various cities, notably Tabriz (Azerbaijan's main city) and Tehran (Persia's capital). The spark that set off the revolution was an arbitrary act by the shah's prime minister, Ayn al-Dowleh, who had several merchants flogged for allegedly plotting to drive up the price of sugar in the Tehran bazaar. The merchants took refuge in the royal mosque (which, by a time-honored Persian custom called *bast,* gave them sanctuary from arrest), but Ayn al-Dowleh had them expelled. This move enraged Tehran's *ulama* and swelled the number of protestors, who moved to another mosque. Desiring peace, the shah offered to dismiss his minister and to convene a "house of justice" to redress their grievances. But he failed to act on his promises. When the shah was incapacitated by a stroke, Ayn al-Dowleh attacked the protestors, who organized a larger *bast* in Tehran. Meanwhile, the *mujtahid*s, or Shiite legal experts, sought *bast* in nearby Qom and threatened to leave Persia en masse—an act that would have paralyzed the country's courts—unless their demands were met. Tehran's shops closed. When Ayn al-Dowleh tried to force them to open, 15,000 Persians took refuge in the British legation, camping on its lawn for several weeks during July 1906. Finally the shah bowed to popular pressure. He fired Ayn al-Dowleh and accepted a Western-style constitution in which the government would be controlled by a Majlis, or representative assembly. So great was his aversion to the Persian nationalists, however, that only pressure from Britain and Russia (plus the fact that he was dying) kept him from blocking the constitution before it could take effect.

The Persian nationalists achieved too much too soon. In 1907 Britain and Russia reached an agreement recognizing each other's spheres of influence in Persia. Britain was to have primary influence over the southeast, close to its Indian empire. Russia acquired the right to send troops and advisers to the heavily populated north, including the key provinces of Azerbaijan and Khurasan, plus Tehran itself. Russia backed the new shah enough to enable him to close the Majlis in 1908. Though one of the main tribes helped the constitutionalists to regain control of Tehran and then to reopen the Majlis in 1909, Persian nationalism now lacked the fervent popular support it had enjoyed three years earlier. The Majlis got bogged down in debates and achieved nothing.

Oil Discoveries

Persians might have welcomed news from Khuzistan, located in the southwest, where a British company had begun oil exploration in 1901. In 1908 it made its first strike. By 1914 thousands of barrels were being piped to a refinery on the Gulf island port of Abadan. When Britain's navy switched from coal to petroleum just before World War I, the future of Persian oil looked even brighter. But to the nationalists this growing industry was cold comfort. It was far from Tehran, in lands controlled by tribal shaykhs. The revenues were going mainly to British stockholders—not to the Persian government, let alone its impoverished subjects. In the last years before World War I, Persia as a whole seemed to be drifting toward becoming a Russian protectorate.

Conclusion

Nationalism in the West earned a bad name in the twentieth century, partly due to the destruction caused by two world wars, partly because of the excesses of such dictators as Mussolini and Hitler, and maybe also because our intellectual leaders have become more cosmopolitan. Even in the Middle East, people now attack secular nationalism and exalt Islamic unity. Nearly everyone recognizes the artificial character of most of the so-called nations set up by foreign imperialism.

Generally speaking, Middle Eastern nationalist movements fared badly before World War I. They did not increase the power, the lands, or the freedom of the Muslim states in which they arose. Except for a few successful moments, which now seem like lightning flashes within a general gloom, these movements did not win any wide popular support. There is no nationalism in Islam, said the critics, so these movements could appeal only to youths who had lost their religion because of Western education. Even when the movements reached a wider public, their success was due to popular misunderstandings. The uneducated majority often mistook the nationalist triumphs for Muslim victories. And these were few indeed.

You may wonder why we told you so much about these unsuccessful nationalist movements. Why learn about them? History is not just the story of winners; sometimes we study losers whose grandchildren would be winners. History is more than a collection of mere facts, names, and dates; we must also learn how the peoples whom we care about view their own past. Ahmad Urabi and Mustafa Kamil are heroes to the Egyptian people today; Khedive Isma'il and Lord Cromer are not. In Istanbul, you can buy postcards that bear pictures of the leading New Ottomans. Every Turkish student sees the Young Turks as a link in the chain of national regenerators going from Selim III to Kemal Ataturk. The 1906 constitution remained the legal basis of Iran's government until 1979, and the Islamic Republic still honors the Shiite leaders and bazaar merchants who joined forces against the shah to make the older constitution a reality. For the peoples of the Middle East, these early nationalist movements were the prologue for the revolutionary changes yet to come.

The Industrial Revolution Outside the West

Peter N. Stearns

Before the 1870s no industrial revolution occurred outside Western society. The spread of industrialization within western Europe, although by no means automatic, followed from a host of shared economic, cultural, and political features as well as frequent and familiar contacts. The quick ascension of the United States was somewhat more surprising: the area was not European and had been far less developed economically during the eighteenth century. Nevertheless, extensive commercial experience in the northern states and the close mercantile and cultural ties with Britain gave the new nation advantages in its rapid imitation of Britain. Abundant natural resources and extensive investments from Europe kept the process going, joining the United States to the wider dynamic of industrialization in the nineteenth-century West.

Elsewhere, conditions did not permit an industrial revolution, an issue that must be explored in studying the international context for this first phase of the world's industrial experience. For almost a century, the West held a virtual monopoly in the industrial domain. Yet the West's industrial revolution did have substantial impact. It led to a number of pilot projects whereby initial machinery and factories were established under Western guidance. More important, it led to new Western demands on the world's economies that instigated significant change without industrialization; indeed, these demands in several cases made industrialization more difficult.

Pilot Projects: Russia

Russia's contact with the West's industrial revolution before the 1870s offers an important case study that explains why many societies could not quickly follow the lead of nations like France or the United States in imitating Britain. Yet Russia did

Peter N. Stearns, "The Industrial Revolution Outside the West," *The Industrial Revolution in World History*, pp. 89-106. Copyright © 2012 by Taylor & Francis Group. Reprinted with permission.

introduce some new equipment for economic and military-political reasons, and these initiatives did generate change—they were not mere window dressing.

More than most societies not directly part of Western civilization, Russia had special advantages for reacting to the West's industrial lead and special motivations for paying attention to this lead. Russia had been part of Europe's diplomatic network since about 1700. It saw itself as one of Europe's great powers, a participant in international conferences and military alliances. The country also had close cultural ties with western Europe, sharing in artistic styles and scientific developments—though Russian leadership had stepped back from cultural alignment because of the shock of the French Revolution in 1789 and subsequent political disorders in the West. Russian aristocrats and intellectuals routinely visited western Europe. Finally, Russia had prior experience in imitating Western technology and manufacturing: importation of Western metallurgy and shipbuilding had formed a major part of Peter the Great's reform program in the early eighteenth century.

Contacts of this sort explain why Russia began to receive an industrial outreach from the West within a few decades of the advent of the industrial revolution. British textile machinery was imported beginning in 1843. Ernst Knoop, a German immigrant to Britain who had clerked in a Manchester cotton factory, set himself up as export agent to the Russians. He also sponsored the British workers who installed the machinery in Russia and told any Russian entrepreneur brash enough to ask not simply for British models but for alterations or adaptations, saying "That is not your affair; in England they know better than you." Despite the snobbery, a number of Russian entrepreneurs set up small factories to produce cotton, aware that even in Russia's small urban market they could make a substantial profit by underselling traditionally manufactured cloth. Other factories were established directly by Britons.

Europeans and Americans were particularly active in responding to calls by the czar's government for assistance in establishing railway and steamship lines. The first steamship appeared in Russia in 1815, and by 1820 a regular service ran along the Volga River. The first public railroad, joining St. Petersburg to the imperial residence in the suburbs, opened in 1837. In 1851 the first major line connected St. Petersburg and Moscow, along a remarkably straight route designed by Czar Nicholas I himself. U.S. engineers were brought in, again by the government, to set up a railroad industry so that Russians could build their own locomotives and cars. George Whistler, the father of the painter James McNeill Whistler (and thus the husband of "Whistler's mother"), played an important role in the effort. He and some U.S. workers helped train Russians in the needed crafts, frequently complaining about their slovenly habits but appreciating their willingness to learn.

Russian imports of machinery increased rapidly; they were over thirty times as great in 1860 as they had been in 1825. Whereas in 1851 the nation manufactured only about half as many machines as it imported, by 1860 the equation was reversed, and the number of machine-building factories had quintupled (from nineteen to ninety-nine). The new cotton industry surged forward, most production being organized in factories using wage labor.

These were important changes. They revealed that some Russians were alert to the business advantages of Western methods and that some Westerners saw the great profits to be made by setting up shop in a huge but largely agricultural country. The role of the government was vital: the czars used tax money to offer substantial premiums to Western entrepreneurs, who liked the adventure of dealing with the Russians but liked their superior profit margins even more.

But Russia did not really industrialize at this point. Modern industrial operations did not sufficiently dent established economic practices. The nation remained overwhelmingly agricultural. High-percentage increases in manufacturing proceeded from such a low base that they had little general impact. Several structural barriers impeded a genuine industrial revolution. Russia's cities had never boasted a manufacturing tradition; there were few artisans skilled even in preindustrial methods. Only by the 1860s and 1870s had cities grown enough for an artisan core to take shape—in printing, for example—and even then large numbers of foreigners (particularly Germans) had to be imported. Even more serious was the system of serfdom, which kept most Russians bound to agricultural estates. Although some free laborers could be found, most rural Russians could not legally leave their land, and their obligation to devote extensive work service to their lords' estates reduced their incentive even for agricultural production. Peter the Great had managed to adapt serfdom to a preindustrial metallurgical industry by allowing landlords to sell villages and the labor therein for the expansion of ironworks. But this mongrel system was not suitable for change on a grander scale, which is precisely what the industrial revolution entailed.

Furthermore, the West's industrial revolution, although it provided tangible examples for Russia to imitate, also produced pressures to develop more traditional sectors in lieu of structural change. The West's growing cities and rising prosperity claimed rising levels of Russian timber, hemp, tallow, and, increasingly, grain. These were export goods that could be produced without new technology and without alteration in the existing labor system. Indeed, many landlords boosted the work-service obligations of the serfs in order to generate more grain production for sale to the West. The obvious temptation was to lock in an older economy—to respond to new opportunity by incremental changes within the traditional system and to maintain serfdom and the rural preponderance rather than to risk fundamental internal transformation.

The proof of Russia's lag showed in foreign trade. It rose, but rather modestly, posting a threefold increase between 1800 and 1860. Exports of raw materials approximately paid for the import of some machinery, factorymade goods from abroad, and a substantial volume of luxury products for the aristocracy. And the regions that participated most in the growing trade were not the tiny industrial enclaves (in St. Petersburg, Moscow, and the iron-rich Urals) but the wheat-growing areas of southern Russia, where even industrial pilot projects had yet to surface. Russian manufacturing exported nothing at all to the West, though it did find a few customers in Turkey, central Asia, and China.

The proof of Russia's lag showed even more dramatically in Russia's new military disadvantage. Peter the Great's main goal had been to keep Russian military production near enough to Western levels to remain competitive, with the huge Russian population added into the equation. This strategy now failed, for the West's industrial revolution changed the rules of the game. A war in 1854 pitting Russia against Britain and France led to Russia's defeat in its own backyard. The British and French objected to new Russian territorial gains (won at the expense of Turkey's Ottoman Empire), which had brought Russia greater access to the Black Sea. The battleground was the Crimea. Yet British and French steamships connected their armies more reliably with supplies and reinforcements from home than did Russia's ground transportation system, with its few railroads and mere 3,000 miles of first-class roads. And British and French industry could pour out more and higher-quality uniforms, guns, and munitions than traditional Russian manufacturing could hope to match. The Russians lost the Crimean War, surrendering their gains and swallowing their pride in 1856. Patchwork change had clearly proved insufficient to match the military, much less the economic, power that the industrial revolution had generated in the West.

After a brief interlude, the Russians digested the implications of their defeat and launched a period of basic structural reforms. The linchpin was the abolition of serfdom in 1861. Peasants were not entirely freed, and rural discontent persisted, but many workers could now leave the land, and the basis for a wage labor force was established. Other reforms focused on improving basic education and health, and although change in these areas was slow, it, too, set the foundation for a genuine commitment to industrialization. A real industrial revolution lay in the future, however. By the 1870s Russia's contact with industrialization had deepened its economic gap vis-à-vis the West, but it had also yielded a few interesting experiments with new methods and a growing realization of the need for further change.

Pilot Projects: Asia, Latin America, and Africa

Societies elsewhere in the world—those more removed from traditional ties to the West or more severely disadvantaged in the ties that did exist—saw even more limited industrial pilot projects during the West's industrialization period. The Middle East and India tried some early industrial imitation but largely failed—though not without generating some important economic change. Latin America also launched some revealingly limited technological change. Only eastern Asia and sub-Saharan Africa were largely untouched by any explicit industrial imitations until the late 1860s or beyond; they were too distant from European culture to venture a response more quickly.

Prior links with the West formed the key variable, as Russia's experience abundantly demonstrated. Societies that had regular familiarity with Western merchants and some preindustrial awareness of the West's steady commercial gains mounted some early experiments in industrialization. Whether they benefited as a result compared with areas that did nothing before the late nineteenth century might be debated.

India and the Middle East
One industrial initiative in India developed around Calcutta, where British colonial rule had centered since the East India Company founded the city in 1690. A Hindu Brahman family, the

Tagores, established close ties with many British administrators. Without becoming British, they sponsored a number of efforts to revivify India, including new colleges and research centers. Dwarkanath Tagore controlled tax collection in part of Bengal, and early in the nineteenth century he used part of his profit to found a bank. He also bought up a variety of commercial landholdings and traditional manufacturing operations. In 1834 he joined with British capitalists to establish a diversified company that boasted holdings in mines (including the first Indian coal mine), sugar refineries, and some new textile factories; the equipment was imported from Britain. Tagore's dominant idea was a British-Indian economic and cultural collaboration that would revitalize his country. He enjoyed a high reputation in Europe and for a short time made a success of his economic initiatives. Tagore died on a trip abroad, and his financial empire declined soon after.

Other early industrial ventures included some factory cotton production, around Bombay, which among other things began to support training for some Indian textile engineers—ultimately reducing dependence on foreigners. By the 1870s cotton cloth made in Indian factories began to replace British goods in Chinese markets. And a British entrepreneur set up some metal production in southern India.

These first tastes of Indian industrialization were significant, but they brought few immediate results. The big news in India, even as Tagore launched his companies, was the rapid decline of traditional textiles under the bombardment of British factory competition; millions of Indian villagers were thrown out of work, even though some manual textile production would survive past 1900. Furthermore, relations between Britain and the Indian elite worsened after the mid-1830s as British officials sought a more active economic role and became more intolerant of Indian culture.

A further step in India's contact with the industrial revolution took shape in the 1850s, when the colonial government began to build a significant railroad network. The first passenger line opened in 1853. The principal result, however, was not industrial development but a further extension of commercial agriculture (production of cotton and other goods for export) and an intensification of British sales to India's interior. Coal mining did expand, but manufacturing continued to shrink. There was no hint of a full industrial revolution in India. Among other things, the British colonial government had no real interest in Indian industrial growth, even purchasing weapons from England rather than supporting the rich tradition of Indian arms manufacturing.

Imitation in the Middle East was somewhat more elaborate, in part because most of this region, including parts of North Africa, retained independence from European colonialism. Muslims had long disdained Western culture and Christianity, and Muslim leaders, including the rulers of the great Ottoman Empire, had been very slow to recognize the West's growing dynamism after the fifteenth century. Some Western medicine was imported, but technology was ignored. Only in the eighteenth century did this attitude begin, haltingly, to change. The Ottoman government imported a printing press from Europe and began discussing Western-style technical training, primarily in relationship to the military.

In 1798 a French force briefly seized Egypt, providing a vivid symbol of Europe's growing technical superiority. Later, an Ottoman governor, Muhammed Ali, seized Egypt from the imperial government and pursued an ambitious agenda of expansionism and modernization. Ali sponsored many changes in Egyptian society in imitation of Western patterns, including a new tax system and new kinds of schooling. He also destroyed the traditional Egyptian elite. The government encouraged agricultural production by sponsoring major irrigation projects and began to import elements of the industrial revolution from the West in the 1830s. English machinery and technicians were brought in to build textile factories, sugar refineries, paper mills, and weapons shops. Ali clearly contemplated a sweeping reform program in which industrialization would play a central role in making Egypt a powerhouse in the Middle East, equal to the European powers. Many of his plans worked well, but the industrialization effort failed. Egyptian factories could not, in the main, compete with European imports, and the initial experiments either failed or stagnated. More durable changes involved encouragement of the production of cash crops like sugar and cotton, which the government required in order to earn tax revenues to support its armies and its industrial imports. Growing concentration on cash crops also enriched a new group of Egyptian landlords and merchants. But the shift actually formalized Egypt's dependent position in the world economy, as European businesses and governments increasingly interfered with its internal economy. The Egyptian reaction to the West's industrial revolution, even more than the Russian response, was to generate massive economic redefinition without industrialization, a strategy that locked peasants into landlord control and made a manufacturing transformation at best a remote prospect.

Spurred by the West's example and by Ali, the Ottoman government itself set up some factories after 1839, importing equipment from Europe to manufacture textiles, paper, and guns. Coal and iron mining were encouraged. The government established a postal system in 1834, a telegraph system in 1855, and steamship building and the beginning of railway construction from 1866 onward. These changes increased the role of European traders and investors in the Ottoman economy. Again, the clearest result of improved transport and communication was a growing emphasis on the export of cash crops and minerals to pay for the necessary manufactured imports from Europe. An industrial example had been set, and as in Egypt, a growing though still tiny minority of Middle Easterners gained some factory experience, but no fundamental transformation occurred.

Latin America and Africa

Latin American nations, newly independent after 1820, had strong historical ties with western Europe. Although cultural links to Spain and Portugal did little for industrialization—these areas lagged within Europe—the broader European connection was solid, and Western merchants, led by the British, expanded commercial ties. Because of economic disorder following the independence wars, little imitation was possible until about 1850; more pressing problems of political consolidation commanded greatest attention. A steam-driven sugar mill was set up as early as 1815 in Brazil, however, and the number of engines, all imported, had risen to sixty-four by

1834. Coffee processors began acquiring steam equipment at this time also, and by 1852 the nation boasted 144 engines in all. Individual businessmen also established some cotton textile factories, meeting about 10 percent of national demand. These were interesting developments; they enhanced the operations Brazilians performed on some of their leading export crops, but they served largely to confirm Brazil's concentration on these sectors. The effort led neither to a more general industrial development focused on internal demand nor to a balanced set of innovations that would foster Brazilian industries in machine building and metallurgy. Nor did great interest arise on the part of the government at this point. As was true elsewhere, the difference between important technical imitation and a real industrial revolution, even if partly imitated, remained clear. Most Brazilian workers and most sectors of the Brazilian economy did not move toward industrialization. Change was real but came mainly in the form of a growing emphasis on export crops.

Patterns elsewhere were even more diffuse. Cuba had first built a rail line in 1838 (from Havana to Guines), and other Latin American nations began to sponsor railroad development in the 1850s, using capital borrowed from European banks and equipment purchased from Europe. Twenty years later Brazil had 800 miles of track. Paraguay inaugurated steamship and rail lines after 1858; the nation also built Latin America's first iron foundry. The country was unique in the region in hiring British technicians using tax revenues, thus avoiding dependence on foreign loans. This promising start was cut short by loss in a war with Argentina, Uruguay, and Brazil. Chile inaugurated its first rail line in 1852 after some previous development of steam-powered flour mills, distilleries, sawmills, and coal mines. Mexico lagged in rail construction, with only 400 miles in 1876. And many other Latin American nations envisaged only short lines connecting seaports to the interior, not nationwide networks. Overall, early rail development helped spur mineral and food exports—the cash-crop economy—while increasing reliance on foreign banks and technologies.

Developments of preliminary industrial trappings—a few factories, a few railroads—did provide some relevant experience on which more intensive efforts could build (mainly after 1870). A few workers became factory hands and experienced some of the same upheaval as their Western counterparts in new routines and pressures on work pace. Many sought to limit their factory experience, leaving for other work or for the countryside after a short time; transience was a problem for much the same reasons as in the West: the clash with traditional work and leisure values. Some technical and business expertise also developed. By the 1850s a number of governments were clearly beginning to realize that some policy response to the industrial revolution was absolutely essential, lest Western influence become still more overwhelming. On balance, however, the principal results of very limited imitation tended to heighten the economic imbalance with western Europe, a disparity that made it easier to focus on nonindustrial exports. This, too, was a heritage for the future.

Sub-Saharan Africa, in contrast, avoided any significant contact with the industrial revolution until the late nineteenth century, ignoring or shunning even modest imitation. The region faced great economic changes after 1820, mainly because of the effective ending of the Atlantic slave trade. This reduced tremendous pressures on Africa's labor force (though the East African slave trade with the Middle East actually accelerated for a time), but it also cut the revenues available to West African merchants and governments. Some attempts were made to expand traditional industries, but there was no basis for major technical change, and no capital was available for venturing in new directions. African societies had long-standing experience with ironworking and other relevant technologies, and they had a substantial commercial tradition. Weakened governments and major economic dislocation, however, made quick response to Europe's transformation virtually impossible. Economic innovation focused on agriculture, particularly the area of vegetable oil production, where there were export possibilities that brought in some earnings to compensate for the loss of the slave trade.

China

Chinese industrial history has generated a huge scholarly literature in recent years because it has become increasingly clear that, in principle, an industrial revolution could have occurred in China almost as readily as in the West. Chinese production levels and living standards in the eighteenth century were essentially on the same levels as in places like Britain. The giant nation continued to introduce important technological changes, for example in spinning. Also, until late in the nineteenth century, China was not significantly affected by competition from European-made factory goods. Rather, what seems to have happened was a focus in government policy on military defense, particularly against the threat of land-based invasions from potential enemies, such as Russia. Internal unrest and a major famine in the 1870s provided further distraction. Overall, the costs of maintaining an overextended empire forestalled additional economic innovation for a crucial century—the same century that saw western Europe now racing ahead. Furthermore, given a long tradition of hostility to most outside influence, the Chinese were slow to register opportunities that might result from imitation of Western technologies. All this added up to a situation in which Chinese leadership sought to deal with the growing evidence of Western industrialization mainly by avoiding it.

As a result, early steps toward industrial change depended on pressures from the outside. Britain, which acquired the port city of Hong Kong in the 1840s, set up some initial factories in its new territory. No railroad was constructed until 1876, when a Western company built a line without government authorization. (The government's response was to tear up the line and let the remnants rust away.) The first successful railroad was opened in 1882 to carry coal from the Kaiping mines to a port. No textiles were produced by machinery in China proper until 1890, though some sluggish planning efforts preceded this project. In effect, until almost the end of the nineteenth century, the industrial revolution passed China by, partly, of course, because traditional manufacturing remained strong. The same held true for much of Southeast Asia and, until the 1860s, for Japan.

Restructuring the International Economy

Direct contact with industrial organization and technology formed a significant facet of world history during the middle decades of the nineteenth century, but it was overshadowed by a more general reorientation in international economic relationships as the West began to display its industrial muscle. Already the world's premier commercial society, the West, now including the United States, greatly increased its world role as a direct consequence of industrialization. Economic inequalities among major world societies accelerated, and some economies were durably redirected in response to Western pressure. The significance of international trade expanded as well, and several new institutions were created to facilitate this exchange.

The West's industrial revolution meant a flood of cheap manufactured goods directed toward world markets. Some societies could absorb new imports of textiles and metal products without facing massive dislocation. Russia, as we have seen, increased its imports, but its internal manufacturing sector, which included production of a wide array of goods in individual villages for local consumption, was sufficiently large that its overall manufacturing performance improved. Its relative economic position in the world declined because the country failed to keep up with Western gains, but its absolute levels held strong, aided by a modest amount of new technology in a few sectors.

The impact of Western imports in other cases was more disruptive. Latin American nations had gained their independence from Spain by 1820, but the attendant wars and internal strife inevitably weakened the domestic economies for a time. Simultaneously, the withdrawal of Spanish regulations had opened Latin American markets to massive imports of machine-made textiles from Britain. What had been a growing industry in the manual production of textiles at home was virtually crushed. Tens of thousands of people, urban and rural, were thrown out of work. Urban women were particularly hard hit as a major source of supplementary income disappeared. Poverty and prostitution increased rapidly as a result. Similar disruption of the traditional manufacturing sector occurred in India, where Britain had, even before outright industrialization, manipulated tariff regulations to discourage the once-thriving Indian cotton industry. These were cases in which the crippling of manufacturing thrust important economies backward toward fuller concentration on agriculture and mining.

The combination of Western industrial growth and the resultant disruption of the internal economies of many other areas steadily increased the inequalities in international economic performance. In 1800, Mexico's per capita income was about a third of that of Great Britain and half of that of the United States. Because of growing Western competition and internal disarray following the wars of independence, Mexican per capita national income actually fell until 1860; at that point it stood at a mere 13 percent and 14 percent respectively. It was a graphic illustration of the new balance sheet between industrializers and most of the nonindustrial regions.

Disruption and decline were not the whole story. The West's industrial revolution provided new economic opportunities for some regions outside the industrial orbit. A herding economy in the Mosul region of northeastern Turkey expanded rapidly in the mid-nineteenth century. Demand in the West for raw wool for its growing factories spurred a host of trade representatives to seek new sources of supply. Both the British and the French governments, through their local consular officials in this part of the Ottoman Empire, kept tabs on wool production, and Turkish merchants and urban authorities did the direct bargaining with the tribespeople. The British directly encouraged expansion of cotton production in Egypt because they sought a more reliable and cheaper source of supply than the southern United States offered, particularly after the disruptions of the U.S. Civil War. And of course opportunities to sell food to urban western Europe increased. Russia increased its grain exports, and other areas in east-central Europe, like Hungary, did the same. Latin American nations found new opportunities for export earnings by expanding their production of cash crops such as coffee, which added to existing commercial agriculture in sugar and tobacco.

A commercialized export economy expanded steadily in a growing number of regions in Africa, Latin America, and Asia. Local merchants and landlords found substantial profits in their changing economies. They helped press a growing number of workers, in particular former peasants but also immigrants, to change their work habits in a fashion not entirely dissimilar to patterns developing in the West's factory centers. Latin American landlords, backed by liberal governments, pried land from traditional Indian or mestizo villagers in order to expand coffee and sugar production. They then attempted to alter the work habits of these new agricultural laborers, trying to reduce the time spent on festivals and drinking and urging more regular and efficient work routines and a new sense of time. Along with local labor, immigrant workers fueled this new commercial economy. Brazil and Argentina began to recruit growing numbers of Spaniards, Italians, and Portuguese. In Brazil the many immigrant workers directed to the coffee-growing regions helped to propel this sector to a commanding position in the world coffee trade by the 1880s—56 percent of the total market share. Workers from India and Southeast Asia were sent under long-term indenture contracts to work on commercial estates in the Caribbean region and elsewhere.

Changes of this sort were vitally important, and they brought important profit opportunities to several local groups, merchants and landowners in particular but also some other elements like the herders in Mosul. At the same time, however, these shifts increased vulnerabilities on the world market, and they most definitely failed to generate any sort of economic parity with the industrial West. The simple fact was that the goods exported to the West—agricultural and mineral products almost exclusively—were not as valuable as the manufactured products that the West exported. The terms of trade favored the West. Furthermore, Western capitalists controlled many operations directly. They ran the shipping and most of the international trading companies. With their greater capital resources, they bought many mines and estates outright. For example, Westerners, including entrepreneurs from the United States, owned most railroads, banks, and mines in Colombia and Chile by the late nineteenth century.

The fundamental imbalance showed in many ways. Cash-crop and mineral exports involved little new technology, except in the transport systems used to get them out of their originating countries. These sectors were much more dependent than Western factories on very cheap labor, often kept in semiservitude by indenture contracts or company stores. The new working class being created around the world had some features in common with the worker of the industrial West, but it was far more miserable.

Local governments and businesses, seeking to develop their export opportunities and in some cases sincerely hoping to generate more diversified economies, frequently went into debt. The construction of modern port and rail facilities in Latin America, though vital to expanding the export sector, cost more than the exports easily paid for. The solution was to borrow from eager, capital-rich banks in western Europe and the United States; the result was a growing indebtedness that made additional investment more difficult and that invited Western interference, including military threats on occasion, in basic economic policy.

Impoverished workers and growing foreign debt made it difficult to imagine a real industrial revolution, though by the late nineteenth century some Latin American leaders saw industrialization as a valid goal. Latin America became a classic area of economic dependence, importing manufactured products and luxury goods from the West while trying desperately to stay afloat with low-cost exports.

Industrialization did have some role in a potentially positive development in nineteenth-century labor history: the abolition of the leading forms of slavery and serfdom, particularly in the Americas but ultimately on a global scale. Western reformers had pushed for abolition out of genuine humanitarian sentiment, though also, perhaps, to distract factory workers in their own societies from their miseries by calling attention to more degraded labor elsewhere. It was also true that slavery was too inflexible for certain economic operations now that world population growth ensured an adequate labor supply in the Americas. Ex-slaves welcomed their freedom. But low wages and more subtle forms of servitude, through debts to company stores, for example, constrained the impact of change in all the regions selling raw materials to the West. Work in the economies producing cheap export goods was typically unprotected and miserable—even in the southern United States.

Economic change created new gaps between Asia and Europe. How could an industrial revolution even be contemplated in nineteenth-century India? Even though India, unlike the Latin American nations, was still ruled from Europe—by an English government that had no interest in creating a new industrial rival—the result of Western industrialization had impoverished large stretches of the nation. Cotton manufacturing had drastically declined by 1833, with millions of Indian women and men, domestic spinners and weavers, thrown out of work by machines half a world away. The peasant economy became increasingly dependent, and it harbored unprecedented numbers of unemployed people. In the 1850s the British turned from a concentration primarily on sales to India to a new, parallel interest in cheap supplies. The railroads were introduced in the 1850s not only to facilitate the sale of British goods but also to encourage the production of raw materials such as jute and cotton. As commercial estates expanded with the aid of huge reserves of cheap labor, India became increasingly locked into a dependent position in the Western-dominated world economy.

Western industrialization further exacerbated the military imbalance of world power. Even earlier, Western armaments had ensured predominance on the seas and had allowed Europeans to establish colonies in a number of ports and on islands such as Java, Borneo, and the Philippines. With industrialization, Western forces gained even greater maritime potency by virtue of larger ships and bigger cannons; new advantages in land wars accrued as well, with factory-produced weapons. In the 1830s this growing military superiority, plus the insatiable thirst for new markets and sources of supply, began to usher in a new age of European expansion. To be sure, the Americas were now largely independent, though economic penetration continued nevertheless. But Africa, Asia, and the Pacific Islands offered almost irresistible allure. It became obvious that Polynesian islands such as Hawaii, discovered by Europeans in the eighteenth century, could be made over into additional sources of sugar and other goods; it was logical to take over the government as well. China, long proudly resistant to Europe's economic overtures, was forced open during the Opium Wars that began in 1839. European gunboats, backed by small forces of well-armed soldiers, did the trick. The carving of North Africa began. France seized Algeria beginning in the late 1820s. Britain and France disputed control of Egypt. In 1869 a French industrial concern completed construction of the vital Suez Canal, a major improvement in access to India and the rest of Asia, but it was the British who gained effective control in the 1870s. By this time also, European expeditions in Southeast Asia and particularly in sub-Saharan Africa were adding huge swaths of territory to Western empires old and new.

The industrial revolution directly prompted this last and greatest imperialist outburst from the West. Steamships enabled Europeans to sail upriver, giving them new entry into China and particularly into the previously unnavigable rivers of central Africa. Mass-produced repeating rifles provided new advantages in gunnery, and by the 1860s early versions of the machine gun offered even more deadly fire. When this basic muscle was added to the quest for secure markets and cheap supplies, the age of industrial imperialism was at hand. Completion of imperialist conquest and full economic exploitation of new holdings, particularly in Africa, came only after 1880, but the stage was clearly set as a direct result of the first phase of the industrial revolution. And the consequence of the new imperialism, in turn, was an even greater economic and political imbalance in the world at large.

Structural imbalance intensified Western scorn for peoples who seemed incapable of mastering advanced technology and modern organization. A variety of factors fed growing racism, but a rooted belief that performance in economy and technology measured the worth of a society played a growing role.

Finally, the first decades of industrialization's entry onto the world stage brought the West's initial attempts to create an international infrastructure. Forming part of this structure were international trading companies and shipping lines, which were expanded by the technology of the steamship. After 1850, telegraph lines were laid across the Atlantic and then to other regions outside the West; this development was vital to the transmission of commercial as well as political information. Also in the 1850s and 1860s international conferences (effectively confined to the Western powers) began to discuss world postal arrangements and worked to standardize some agreements on patents and commercial law. The world postal union, established in 1878, greatly facilitated international mailings; international copyright rules on works of literature and art were set in 1886. The globe was shrinking because of industrial technology and new levels of world trade, and unprecedented arrangements to reduce disputes and ease communication both reflected and furthered this contraction. Western control of the initial agreements was inevitable and ensured their application in other parts of the world as well; some of the consequences in terms of spreading new ideas and technical knowledge ultimately led in less predictable directions.

The Two Faces of International Impact

The most important short-term global result of Europe's hold on industrialization was the growing economic imbalance between the small number of industrial powers and most of the rest of the world. Beyond that, more and more regions had to alter their economies to produce low-cost goods for export to the industrial centers, hoping to stay afloat in a global economy that was out of their control. Important residues of these changes persist today, in continued imbalances and economic dependence. Even countries now achieving industrial success remember their period of weakness, and often push even harder in consequence.

But there was another outcome as well. The small industrial steps taken in Brazil, Russia, and India were the seeds from which later industrialization would sprout. They did not generate a full process of change at the time; they could not prevent growing weakness, including reliance on cheap exports. But from the standpoint of the twenty-first century, when countries such as Brazil and India loom as the world's next economic giants, the quiet first steps may have been more important, historically, than the brief but vivid exacerbation of inequality. Both patterns—the short-lived global hierarchy with the industrial West on top, and the small first moves toward industrial change in key nations in Asia and Latin America—mark the first stage of the industrial revolution in the world arena.

The first stage was certainly unique in one respect, for the growing imbalance created by the West's exploitation of its industrial lead would not be permanent. More striking modifications of the West's industrial monopoly would help set up the second phase of the industrial revolution in world history.

Discussion Questions

The Scientific Revolution

1. Why is the period from roughly 1500 to roughly 1700 usually referred to as the *Scientific Revolution* in Europe?

2. What is the author's argument for why the 1500s should instead be seen as a "Scientific Renaissance"? Do you agree with that alteration in thinking about this period? Why or why not?

3. According to the author, what distinguishes the 1600s from the 1500s? How did these distinctions lead to considering the 1600s a time of "Scientific Revolution?" Do you agree with this assessment? Why or why not?

From pen to print—a revolution in communications?

1. What three inventions "revolutionize[d] society" in the early modern period, according to the authors?

2. How did the printing press change the production of books in Europe? Describe this change in detail.

3. How did the printing press change European society more broadly? Give some examples.

4. How did the printing press factor into the Protestant Reformation and the European Enlightenment?

5. What are some arguments *against* the printing press having such an outsized impact on European history? Do you agree with any of them? Why or why not?

Peter the Great and Westernization, 1689–1725

1. In what ways was Peter the Great successful in his reformist policies as Russia's czar?

2. In what ways was he unsuccessful?

3. What specific factors prevented Peter from being more successful in modernizing Russia?

4. What were some ways Peter was actually not much of a reformer at all?

5. What were some of Peter's greatest reforms?

6   Why does the author characterize Peter's most lasting reforms as mostly "cultural and psychological"? Do you agree? Why or why not?

7   What did the resistance to Peter and his reforms look like? Were they successful? Why or why not?

8   What do you make of the author's list of Peter's "paradoxes" at the end of the chapter?

9   Ultimately, what is Peter the Great's legacy? Overall, is it a mostly positive legacy or a mostly negative one?

New Causes: Why did the Industrial Revolution happen, and why did it happen in eighteenth-century Britain?

1   What are some of the main reasons historians have offered to explain the timing of the Industrial Revolution? Are any of these reasons particularly compelling to you? Why? Conversely, do any of the reasons seem particularly unconvincing to you? Why?

2   According to the author, what were some of the most important "preconditions," as he calls them, for the Industrial Revolution? What does the term *preconditions* mean in this scenario?

3   Briefly explain the three approaches that currently exist among scholars for why the Industrial Revolution occurred. Which approach seems most reasonable to you? Why?

4   What factors in the 1700s specifically "triggered" the Industrial Revolution?

5   Why did Britain lead the way and industrialize first? Briefly discuss the several reasons Britain was, according to the author, "in the vanguard" of the Industrial Revolution.

6   Why do historians still argue over things like the causes of the Industrial Revolution, why it happened in the 1700s, and why Britain was first? We know the Industrial Revolution happened, we know it happened first in the 1700s, and we know it happened first in Britain—are the reasons *why* important or not? Explain your answer.

European interests and imperialism

1   What was the status of the relationship between the West and the Middle East before the 1700s?

2   How did that relationship change during the 1700s?

3   Why did the relationship change so dramatically? Further, why did it change *then* (i.e., the 1700s)?

4. How did Russia, starting with Peter the Great, affect the Ottoman Empire's strength, in particular in the 1700s and 1800s?

5. For how long do the authors say the Ottoman Empire declined? How did the empire's rulers contribute to that decline?

6. How did the Great Powers of Europe, primarily Britain and France but also Austria, interact with Russia and the Ottoman Empire during the 1700s and 1800s?

7. Further, what role did the Crimean War play in the intersection of these powers?

The rise of nationalism

1. What role did nationalism play over the last century and a half in the Middle East?

2. How have nationalism and Islam existed concurrently in the modern Middle East?

3. What role did Europe play in Middle East politics and the formation of national identities during the 1800s and through the first half of the 1900s?

4. How did Egypt function as both what the author calls "the very heart and soul of Islam" for Muslims and simultaneously "the most westernized country in the nineteenth-century Middle East"? Were these two identities compatible? Why or why not?

5. How did the Suez Canal affect Egypt's budding nationalism in the late 1800s? What role did Europeans, especially the British, play in its creation?

6. What distinct challenge did the Ottoman Empire face with regards to nationalism? Describe this in detail.

7. Who were the Young Turks? What role did they play in Ottoman politics in the late 1800s and early 1900s?

8. Unlike the Ottomans, what advantages did Persia have in developing its modern nationalism?

9. What particular events initiated modern Persian nationalism?

10. Were these various nationalist movements in the Middle East during the late 1800s and early 1900s generally successful? Why or why not?

The Industrial Revolution outside the West

1. In general, what effects did the West's Industrial Revolution have on the rest of the world?

2. Despite some important movements towards industrialization, why did Russia remain a mostly agriculture-based economy through the mid-1800s?

3. What role did Russia's loss in the Crimean War play in its early, but uneven, movements toward industrialization?

4. During the early to mid-1800s, how was India connected to the Industrial Revolution? What effects did those connections have on India's own industrialization?

5. How and why did Egypt and the Ottoman Empire fail to industrialize in the 1800s?

6. How did its connection to the West actually hamper Latin American industrialization?

7. How did sub-Saharan Africa change dramatically during the 1800s? How did this relate to industrialization?

8. Even though it seems like China could have industrialized during the 1800s, why didn't they?

9. How would the world look different, if at all, if China had industrialized during the 1800s?

10. What are some negatives for the rest of the world due to Western industrialization?

11. What are some positives?

UNIT III

THE FIGHT FOR A MODERN GLOBAL WORLD, 1900–PRESENT

Introduction

While numerous events and trends of the twentieth century have contributed to the creation of our modern global world, much of it was accomplished through warfare, competition, and destruction. The result has been an uneasy globalization of the world—one at some times more tolerant and diverse than ever before, and at other times more divisive and unhinged than at any time in human history. This unit follows that process through multiples lenses. First, the economic recoveries of the soon-to-be Axis powers from the Global Great Depression are explained. Second, the Cold War is discussed through superpower nationalism and the Chinese Civil War. Third, the amazing diversity of the twentieth-century Caribbean and African decolonization and independence movements are charted. Finally, the Cold War's effects on modern globalization itself are explored.

Undeniably, the two world wars of the first half of the twentieth century, and the global economic downturn during the intervening years set the destructive and divisive tone for the growth of modern globalization. John E. Moser's chapter entitled "Recovery Through Nationalism: The 'Have-Nots,' 1933–1936" looks particularly at the responses to the Global Great Depression by the three nations that would ally together as the Axis Powers during World War II: Germany, Japan, and Italy. The goal of all three was not economic redevelopment for its own good, but in the pursuit of national self-sufficiency—also called autarky, or even anti-globalization, if you will—through expansionism and, in Germany's case, racial homogeneity. Germany's National Socialists, Japan's ultra-nationalists, and Italy's Fascists all withdrew to varying levels from international trade during the mid- to late-1930s and pursued new or expanded empires. This would lead, eventually and perhaps inevitably, to the Second World War shortly thereafter.

After the destruction wrought during World War II, the uneasy peace of the Cold War that followed often broke out into "hot" wars—the first and most consequential of which was the Chinese Civil War. While Mao Zedong's Communist Revolution had been underway since the early-1920s, full-scale civil war broke out in China in 1946, following Japan's surrender and withdrawal the previous year. As Mark Chi-Kwan describes in "The Chinese Civil War and European Cold War, 1945-9," however, the Chinese Civil War was wrapped up and shaped, at least partly, by Cold War superpower politics. Namely, Stalin's quick realization that Mao's PRC (People's Republic of China) was going to be victorious in 1949 led to the USSR recognizing the PRC, while the US continued to hold out hope for a Chinese Nationalist resurgence. That calculation was incorrect and Mao would not let the US forget it.

While the Cold War was expansive, as shown by its effects on the Chinese Civil War, it is also often described in ideological, economic, or imperialistic terms. Malcolm Anderson argues in "The Cold War and Nationalism" that superpower nationalism stemming from the grand rivalry between the United States and the Soviet Union should also be included in any explanation of the Cold War. Anderson points out that while both superpowers often expressed their ideologies in universalist principles, it was actually their nationalist ideals that were at the heart of those ideologies. Most crucially, both sides saw their proselytizing of those principles as patriotic, not nationalistic, which had significant consequences for the rest of the globe.

One place in particular that exemplified both the effects of the Cold War and the massive diversity that was a hallmark of globalization was the Caribbean. Aisha Khan discusses the development of that diversity in her chapter, "Africa, Europe, and Asia in the Making of the 20th-Century Caribbean." Khan explains that the end of slavery in the 19th-century Caribbean meant that many Caribbean islands then saw a massive immigration of indentured laborers from Africa, South Asia, and China to make up for the loss of Afro-Caribbean slave labor. As such, the modern Caribbean is now defined by extreme diversity of races, languages, classes, religions, and culture with all of the expected complexity that accompanies it. As such, very few places are such good case studies in modern globalization, as the Caribbean.

Meanwhile, a place that has been at the crossroads of globalization with all of its attendant challenges is the African Continent, especially following World War II. Antony Best, Jussi M. Hanhimaki, and Joseph A. Maiolo argue in "Africa: decolonization and independence, 1945–2007" that the often simplistic view of modern Africa as being corrupt, poor, and violent overshadows the fact that no other place on the globe has changed as much politically as Africa has over the last half-century or so. Decolonization did cause significant upheaval throughout the continent, however, which was only exacerbated by the failure of Pan-Africanism and local leadership, along with the incursion of Cold War politics into many internal political struggles.

It was a confluence of all of these factors—world wars; global economic instabilities; the Cold War and its related hot wars; superpower politics, rivalry, and nationalism; migration and increasing diversity; decolonization and independence movements—that led to our modern, globalized world. Bruce Mazlish in his chapter on "Cold War and globalization: Unintended consequences" argues that while globalization was a logical outcome of the last century or so, it was a subconscious outcome, which has brought with it its own challenges. After World War II, the world was only "semi-globalized," due to there being two superpowers and their allies, with diametrically opposed ideologies and economies fighting for supremacy. Mazlish points to many facets of superpower competition—nuclear technology, missiles for military use and space exploration, satellites, the computer revolution, anti-colonialism, the United Nations, the creation of the "Third World," the rise of globalizing Islam, and the many hot wars associated with the Cold War—to explain the advent of globalization. He also claims these forces and pressures were what led to the collapse of the Soviet Union. Put another way, the USSR was unable to adapt to globalization. Furthermore, it was the Cold War itself and, most importantly, its unintended consequences that led to today's globalization, which is why our modern global world has been at least partly unmanageable and shows little sign of simplifying any time soon.

Recovery Through Nationalism

The "Have-Nots," 1933–1936

John E. Moser

In both Germany and Japan, the Great Depression served to discredit liberal democracy and capitalism and bring to power political forces committed to militaristic nationalism and foreign conquest. It is important to note, though, that the worldviews of the German National Socialists and Japanese ultranationalists were not shaped in any meaningful way by the crisis. In fact, while each group had used the prevailing economic distress as a bludgeon against its political opponents, it is not much of a stretch to say that neither had given much thought to the concrete steps that would have to be taken to promote recovery. The National Socialists and ultranationalists intended to bring about fundamental changes, both to their respective societies and to the international landscape, but had comparatively little interest in what they regarded as technical matters such as reducing unemployment and increasing industrial production. Of course, once in power they could not ignore such questions, as they understood that they would likely have no opportunity to pursue their larger goals unless they first secured some measure of domestic recovery. Their approach, however, was marked by considerable improvisation, and the involvement of technocratic experts who were not always on the same ideological wavelength as their superiors. The remarkably quick recoveries experienced by Germany and Japan during this period would solidify their respective regimes' hold on power, but the means they employed would create additional difficulties—problems that ultimately could be solved only through war.

It can be difficult to identify consistent views on economics in the ideologies of German National Socialism or Japanese ultranationalism, mainly because the leading figures in both movements had little formal knowledge of the subject as an academic

John E. Moser, "Recovery through Nationalism: The 'Have-Nots,' 1933-1936," *The Global Great Depression and the Coming of World War II*, pp. 120-135, 199. Copyright © 2015 by Taylor & Francis Group. Reprinted with permission.

discipline. (The same might be said of Franklin Roosevelt and his Brains Trust.) The case of Hitler is especially complicated since he was notorious for avoiding any firm commitment to particular policies in his speeches, preferring to tailor his words to fit his audiences. Nevertheless, it is possible to identify certain strands of economic thought in their respective worldviews. In each case the "third way" ideology of the late nineteenth century provided the foundations for their thinking.

First of all, it is important to note that there was nothing socialist about National Socialism, at least in the Marxist sense. Hitler and his followers utterly rejected fundamental socialist ideas such as the inevitability of class struggle and the ultimate elimination of national boundaries. It is true that, particularly early on, National Socialists embraced radical ideas such as abolition of "unearned" income (i.e., dividends), redistribution of wealth, and even nationalization of certain industries. Hitler himself was highly critical of the German bourgeoisie, which he believed had focused selfishly on its own material well-being at the expense of the nation as a whole. Nevertheless, he consistently defended private property, and frequently praised the work of individual entrepreneurs.

For National Socialists the interests of the nation trumped all other concerns, whether individual or class-based. This meant not that business owners should be dispossessed or that large firms should be dissolved, but that they should be forced to serve the needs of the German people. The state would, therefore, be the dominant force in the economy—as it would be in society at large. Hitler sometimes offered the model of the army as an ideal social organization, with a top-down command structure whose merit was ultimately based on the extent to which it served the national interest. Capitalists who were willing to accept government regimentation would be permitted to profit handsomely, but those who refused would be destroyed. When questioned about his use of the term "socialist," he admitted that it was "unfortunate" and that it should not be interpreted to mean that all "business *must* be socialized; it means only that they *can* be socialized if they offend against the interests of the nation. As long as they do not do that, it would be simply a crime to destroy business life."[1]

Up to this point National Socialism sounds very much like any other "third way" ideology, practically indistinguishable from early twentieth-century American progressivism or the National Efficiency movement in Great Britain. However, two additional elements to Hitler's ideology distinguished it from its intellectual half-siblings and help to explain why Germany under National Socialism would eventually unleash the most destructive war in human history.

The first of these elements was Hitler's desire to make Germany into a *Volksgemeinschaft*, a racially homogeneous "people's community." This meant eliminating social distinctions among Germans themselves so that service to the nation became the ultimate determinant of status. It also meant reducing to subservience—or eliminating altogether from German society—those who were not deemed racially "pure." In some ways *Volksgemeinschaft* could be traced to the eugenics movement [...], which was popular in the United States and Great Britain in the 1910s and 1920s. National Socialism, however, grafted onto this a romantic dualism in which the honest, guileless peasant, connected organically to the blood and soil of Germany, was contrasted against the urban, cosmopolitan Jew. The Jew, in Hitler's mythology, had been working for centuries to destroy the German race, using both Marxism and international "finance capitalism" as tools in this effort. The goal of *Volksgemeinschaft* was, first and foremost, the elimination of Jews from German national life.

The second element stemmed from the first. If the Jews secretly controlled international capitalism, the country's relative lack of natural resources placed it in a dangerous position. Germany lacked sufficient natural resources to support its large and growing population, and was thus dependent on foreign imports not only for strategic materials such as oil and rubber, but even for its food supply. Since the nineteenth century, therefore, the country had focused on industry, producing manufactured goods that could be exchanged for these imports. However, World War I demonstrated the danger of this dependence, as the British naval blockade had succeeded in starving the country into submission. The only way of avoiding such a fate in the future was to achieve national self-sufficiency—everything that the German people needed would be produced at home, using substitutes if need be.

The problem with Hitler's desire for autarky was that it could never be attained given Germany's current borders, or even with the borders of 1914. In order to feed and supply the population, the country needed *Lebensraum*—living space. As early as 1928 Hitler specified that at the heart of the National Socialist approach to foreign affairs lay "a clear, farsighted policy of space," focusing "all of its strength on marking out a way of life for our people through the allocation of adequate *Lebensraum* for the next one hundred years."[2] The land that he desired lay to the east—Poland and the Soviet Union—and it would have to be conquered and "Germanized"; that is, denuded of its current population and resettled with German farmers. In other words, National Socialism believed the country's economic problems could not ultimately be solved without war.

Of course, nobody—including Hitler—believed that Germany in 1933 was anywhere close to being ready to wage war. In the short term the new regime had to focus on creating *Volksgemeinschaft* while building the armed forces that would be necessary for the conquest of *Lebensraum*. An added complication was the fact that the NSDAP was neither large enough nor popular enough to run the country on its own. This meant that, at least for the time being, it had to cooperate with traditional German elites, such as those in banking, industry, and the army. In fact, only three of the members of Hitler's initial cabinet were National Socialists (although, significantly, one of these was the minister of the interior, giving the party effective control over the police). In an effort to reassure business owners, for the post of Reichsbank president he tapped none other than Hjalmar Schacht, who two years earlier had resigned from the same post in protest against what he saw as the profligate spending of the Weimar government.

If Hitler's regime was going to achieve his long-term goals, it first had to demonstrate that it was capable of tackling the problem of mass unemployment—and for this National Socialist ideology offered no clear remedies. Recovery, therefore, would come in large part by continuing the policies that had been put in place by Brüning, von Papen, and von Schleicher. The exchange controls first enacted in 1931 continued under Hitler, and taxes remained high. Public spending nearly doubled, with some of the new spending going to finance the so-called "Reinhardt Program" of public works. A compulsory National Work Program was set up in which unemployed workers were sent to work camps around the country, where they engaged in land reclamation, road and railway construction, and other projects. But while such undertakings as the construction of a network of superhighways—the famous Autobahn system—were well publicized in National Socialist propaganda, they really represented the continuation of policies developed by von Papen and von Schleicher. It is worth noting that while overall public-works spending during this period was considerably higher than it had been during the final years of the Weimar Republic, it remained much lower than it had been in the 1920s.

The regime was far more willing to spend on rearmament than on jobs programs, although the restrictions imposed by the Versailles treaty dictated that this be done quietly. In June 1933 Hitler's cabinet began planning for a standing army of 300,000 men, to be augmented by a reserve force twice that size. To build this force Hitler approved the spending of 4.4 billion RM per year for the next eight years. This was a colossal sum, representing more than 10 percent of Germany's gross domestic product that year, as well as three times what the government had spent on public works in 1932 and 1933 combined. It was also more than four times what the Weimar Republic had ever spent on the armed forces in any given year.

Of course, the immediate question was how to pay for these projects—a question that was made more difficult by Hitler's refusal to devalue the currency. In 1932 he had accused his opponents of planning to devalue, and he reassured his conservative allies that the stability of the reichsmark remained at the heart of his economic program. Not only had he experienced firsthand the disruptive effects of the hyperinflation of the early 1920s—indeed, the chaos of that period had encouraged him to attempt his 1923 *Putsch*—but he recognized that there was a certain advantage in sticking with Brüning's "gold standard on crutches." The decision by Great Britain (in 1931) and the United States (in 1933) to leave gold reduced the real value of German debts to those countries by as much as two-thirds; had Germany decided likewise it would have lost this important advantage.

Since Hitler would not devalue, he was forced to find other means of paying for his expansion of the army, and for this he turned to Schacht. It was under von Papen's chancellorship that Germany first began paying contractors with certificates that could be used for remittance of future taxes. Schacht built on this by creating a dummy company called the *Metallurgische-Forschungsgesellschaft*, Mefo for short, which issued what amounted to IOUs backed by the full faith and credit of the National Socialist regime. This bit of monetary legerdemain effectively created an alternate currency that allowed Germany to depart from financial orthodoxy without technically leaving the gold standard; by 1938 Mefo bills totaling roughly 12 billion RM had gone into circulation.

Schacht could use Mefo bills as a substitute for reichsmarks, but not for the foreign currency that Germany needed to purchase foreign imports. Of course, service on the country's commercial debts had been a constant drain on German reserves, but this had been manageable as long as Berlin was able to export its manufactured goods. The protectionist policies of Germany's leading trading partners [...] dealt a crippling blow to those exports, and since the country still needed to import food and other vital resources the Reichsbank's supply of foreign exchange had dwindled rapidly in 1931 and 1932. Already, under Brüning the government had begun rationing foreign currency so as to allow only the most vital imports, and von Papen had initiated the use of "blocked marks" for the purchase of foreign goods. The National Socialist regime kept these policies in place but then went a step further in May 1933, announcing that until such time as the country enjoyed a healthy trade surplus it could no longer spare foreign currency for service on Germany's long-term debts. Instead payments would be made in blocked reichsmarks, deposited in special Reichsbank accounts that could be used only to buy German products.

The new policy elicited protests from the United States and Great Britain, which led to concern in Berlin that the two powers might use the World Economic Conference in London as an opportunity to organize some kind of international effort against Germany. They need not have worried, as arguments over tariffs, war debts, and especially currency stabilization caused the conference to adjourn without having accomplished anything [...]. Apart from a moment of awkwardness when a member of the German delegation, Economics Minister Alfred Hugenberg, imprudently circulated an inflammatory memorandum demanding the return of Germany's colonies and land for settlement in eastern Europe, the conference could not have gone better from the regime's perspective. The formation of an Anglo-American bloc would have posed a significant obstacle to Hitler's plans, so the failure of the two powers to agree on any issue of substance came as a tremendous relief.

The new debt policy did not solve Germany's foreign-currency problem, however, since the country's export trade continued to languish in 1933–1934. The brutal nature of the regime, particularly its mistreatment of Jews, led to boycotts of German goods during this period, but the basic problem was that Hitler's insistence on a gold-backed reichsmark meant prices for German exports were 30 to 40 percent higher than comparable products on the world market. The government established a program of subsidies to help reduce prices, but the paperwork involved ended up slowing down the process. Meanwhile, Hitler's rearmament campaign diverted German industry from producing goods for export and at the same time caused increased demand for foreign imports, so that the country ran a significant trade deficit. As a result, Germany in 1934 faced a full-blown currency crisis. When Hitler took power in January 1933 the Reichsbank's reserves of gold and foreign exchange stood at 964 million RM (in December 1930 they totaled nearly 3 billion RM), but by September 1934 they had plummeted to 79 million RM—barely enough to cover a week's worth of imports.

The regime took a variety of steps to cope with the crisis. For example, it organized German coal producers into a cartel charged with developing synthetic oil, in the hope of reducing the country's dependence on petroleum imports. The leadership also altered its policy toward Jewish emigration. Up to this point it had sought to rid Germany of its population of roughly half a million Jews by encouraging them to emigrate voluntarily; 37,000 did so in 1933. However, German Jews held at least eight billion RM in personal property, and understandably they sought to take that property with them. The government, in an effort to keep wealth at home, imposed a high surtax on all wealth to be taken out of the country, and while this slowed the hemorrhage of foreign exchange, it also brought the flow of Jewish émigrés to a virtual halt—only 23,000 left in 1934, and 21,000 the following year. The National Socialists would ultimately have to resort to increasingly brutal methods to eliminate the Jewish population.

More provocatively, Hitler hoped to replenish Germany's stocks of gold and foreign currency through the annexation of neighboring Austria, which possessed considerable reserves of both. On orders from Berlin, Austrian National Socialists attempted a coup in late July, assassinating the conservative chancellor, Engelbert Dollfuss. Before German forces could occupy the country, however, Mussolini dispatched Italian troops to the Austrian border. Completely unprepared for war, Hitler backed down; most of Austria's National Socialists fled to German soil, although a few remained to conduct a campaign of terrorism against the regime in Vienna.

The regime's most effective strategy for stopping the loss of foreign currency proved to be Schacht's "New Plan" for trade, which he announced in September. Under this arrangement, a Supervisory Agency was established for each of thirty-five commodities for which Germany relied on foreign imports. No importer could purchase products from abroad without receiving a foreign-exchange permit from the relevant agency. The willingness of the agencies to do so would depend not only on how critical the import was to the country's needs (with rearmament at the top of the list), but also on the willingness of the exporting country to increase its purchases of German exports. Schacht therefore accompanied his announcement with a new campaign to conclude bilateral barter agreements with Germany's major trading partners. [...] [T]he United States—at the insistence of Cordell Hull—refused to sign any such agreement, so although the demands of rearmament dictated that Germany remain a major importer of certain US primary products such as scrap iron and steel, oil, copper, and grain, imports of American manufactured goods, as well as US imports of all German products, dwindled to insignificance. Great Britain, on the other hand, chose to negotiate—and the result was the Anglo-German Trade and Payments Agreement of November 1934.

The New Plan brought about a reorientation of German trade over the next several years. By spring 1938 Berlin had concluded barter agreements with twenty-five countries, most of them relatively poor states that relied on the export of raw materials and commodities. Trade with the industrialized world—even Great Britain, despite the 1934 agreement—declined, while commerce with Latin America, and particularly with southeastern Europe, increased dramatically. In a global economy that seemed to be dividing into regional trading blocs—the British-dominated sterling bloc, the French-led gold bloc, the Japanese yen bloc—a new reichsmark bloc emerged that included Hungary, Romania, Bulgaria, Yugoslavia, Greece, and Turkey. In the late 1920s only around 15 percent of those countries' exports (mostly grain and other foodstuffs) went to Germany; by the late 1930s the figure was 40 percent. Growing German commercial ties to eastern Europe had the additional benefit, from Berlin's perspective, of helping to undermine France's alliances in that region.

Another source of German imports during this period was the Soviet Union. On an official level relations between the two countries were actively hostile—Hitler and Stalin routinely denounced one another in the bitterest terms in their speeches, with Hitler frequently predicting a climactic war in which his people would save civilization by destroying "Judeo-Bolshevism." Stalin, for his part, was pursuing a "popular front" strategy in an effort to unite with Britain, France, and the United States in an anti-German coalition [...]. Nevertheless, a steady flow of Soviet resources (particularly oil and grain) came into Germany between 1933 and 1936. The reason was that the Soviet Union was the only power that actually owed Germany money, to the tune of 1.11 billion RM when Hitler took office as chancellor. For the Soviets, exports to Germany were a way of paying down this debt (as already mentioned, the Soviets had practically stopped importing foreign goods in 1932–1933); for the Germans these resources represented imports that did not hurt the country's balance of trade. By 1935, in fact, the German economy had begun to grow dangerously dependent on these imports, and this became a serious problem when by the end of that year the Soviets' debt had been wiped out almost completely. Stalin offered to continue selling oil and grain to Germany into 1936 in exchange for exports of weapons—aircraft and submarines in particular. When Hitler refused, the flow of Soviet imports stopped, with serious consequences for Berlin.

Still, the regime's program of improvisations and stopgap measures was effective, and according to most measures, by 1936 Germany seemed to have recovered completely from the worst features of the Depression. In four years per capita gross domestic product had grown by more than 35 percent, exceeding its 1928 precrisis high by nearly 9 percent. By 1935 the German economy had surpassed the French in terms of per capita GDP. Unemployment, which in 1932 had stood at nearly 6 million, was down to 1.5 million in 1936. Starting in 1935 there was a virtual halt of spending on job-creation projects; it was assumed that those still out of work would soon find jobs in the armaments industry.

But while Germany appeared to be in overall good economic health—an image assiduously promoted in National Socialist propaganda—there remained some very serious problems. German GDP may have surpassed its 1928 levels, but this was almost entirely the result of government spending; private investment remained 22 percent lower than it had been in 1928. Moreover, while Schacht's New Plan may have slowed the drain of foreign currency from the Reichsbank, it did not solve the underlying problem of the German trade deficit. Indeed, thanks to the recovery of world commodity prices in 1934–1935 Germany was forced to pay more for its imports, while exports during that same period kept declining. Since rearmament continued to have first claim on resources, any savings of foreign exchange had to come by reducing food imports. The situation was made even worse by a bad harvest in 1935. By the end of the year meat and dairy products were starting to disappear from the shelves of German shops, and queues for food were increasingly common in the cities. As a result, even though unemployment was becoming a thing of the past, the availability of jobs did not translate into improved living standards for ordinary Germans. In fact, death rates in Germany climbed even as the unemployment rate fell;

by 1935 the mortality rate from childhood diseases and pneumonia was one of the highest in the industrialized world, most likely thanks to protein deficiency.

Nevertheless, the recovery of Germany's industrial sector was widely heralded as the first great success of National Socialist economics, giving a tremendous boost to the regime's credibility, both at home and abroad. When, step by step, Hitler moved to secure absolute power in Germany—by claiming the right to rule by decree, abolishing all political parties aside from the NSDAP, and, finally (upon the death of von Hindenburg in August 1934), combining the positions of chancellor and president under the single title of *Führer*—there were few willing to stand in his way. Those who did were quickly and quietly dispatched to one of a growing number of concentration camps that had begun to spring up around Germany as early as March 1933.

By early 1936 the economy had recovered sufficiently that Schacht and many other members of the German business and banking communities were beginning to call for a return to the international economy. The regime's monetary, trade, and financial policies, they argued, had effectively given industry breathing space to help it get back on its feet. Now it was time for German firms to cut back on production for military purposes and return to manufacturing for export. A strategic devaluation of the reichsmark would bring the prices of German goods in line with the products of the rest of the industrialized world. German industry would be freed from the byzantine web of regulations that the regime had imposed on foreign trade, which had stifled entrepreneurial initiative. If exports did not rise, they warned, Germany would continue to hemorrhage gold and foreign currency until the value of the reichsmark could not be maintained—with runaway inflation as the inevitable result.

The problem with this line of argument was that it assumed that Hitler was just like any other Depression-era politician—that he sought nothing more than economic recovery. In fact, recovery for him was only the first step, a necessary precondition for an eventual war for *Lebensraum*. Already in 1935 he had announced that Germany would no longer be bound by the arms-limitation clauses of the Treaty of Versailles, and unveiled plans for a modern air force. In that year military spending jumped from just over four billion RM to between six and seven billion, nearly a billion of which was earmarked for the *Luftwaffe*. In 1933 Hitler needed the support of the conservative elites of German industry, but three years later his power was sufficiently established that he was prepared to strike out on his own. Needless to say, he had no intention of returning Germany to the path of international trade.

Although its major theorists would have denied it, Japanese ultranationalist ideology was in many ways similar to German National Socialism. Ultranationalists, who tended to be concentrated in the Japanese Army, liked to claim that their beliefs were rooted in authentic Japanese tradition and that they represented a repudiation of the Western ideas that had taken hold in Japan in the late nineteenth century. However, there were many points of agreement between Japanese and German nationalism. Both regarded individualism and rationalism as abhorrent, arguing that they had been responsible for the rise of dangerous nineteenth-century ideologies such as liberalism and Marxism. Both sought a radical transformation of society in which all citizens subordinated their personal interests to the community, as represented by a single leader—in the case of Japan, the emperor, who was held to be a god. Like the National Socialists, the Japanese ultranationalists believed in a national mission, in this case to liberate East Asia from Western imperialists (both capitalist and communist) and to form a self-sufficient bloc that was capable of competing with world powers such as the United States, Great Britain, and the Soviet Union. The ultranationalists did not share National Socialist racial theories, nor did they have any particular animus against Jews, but they did believe in the superiority of the Japanese "way," which they intended to impose on the peoples of East Asia.

While Hitler liked to speak of an inevitable clash between Germany and the Soviet Union, ultranationalists predicted a massive conflict with Britain and the United States. As one leading theorist, General Ishiwara Kanji, put it in 1933, this would be "mankind's last war, to be fought for the unification of world civilization."[3] Control of East Asia, by freeing Japan from dependence on trade with the Anglo-Americans, would guarantee access to the resources that Tokyo would need to wage such a protracted war. But unlike Hitler, the Japanese did not have to wait to rearm before moving to make their dreams a reality, since they possessed a powerful army and one of the world's best navies. Indeed, they had already taken a long step toward creating an East Asian bloc in the 1931 conquest of Manchuria.

The Depression had discredited Japan's financial community, *zaibatsu*, and political parties, leaving the army as the strongest force in national politics. However, the military did not yet dominate the country's political life to the extent that it would later in the decade. In the meantime it had to work with certain civilian leaders whose reputations had not been tarnished by Japan's disastrous experience with the gold standard. Chief among these was Finance Minister Takahashi Korekiyo, who more than anyone else was responsible for taking the yen back off gold in December 1931. The improvement in the Japanese economy that followed was able to keep civilian government alive for the next several years. Takahashi believed that increased government spending was needed to bring about recovery, and while the military captured the lion's share of this new money (spending on the armed forces more than doubled between 1931 and 1935), the long association between the army and farming groups dictated that some of it would be directed toward relief for rural Japan. Army Minister Araki Sadao, a general with ties to several ultranationalist groups, was a strong advocate for aid to unemployed fishermen, as well as programs to diversify crops, promote small-scale industry in the countryside, and provide relief for indebted farmers.

Much of the impetus for Japan's recovery, however, came from its depreciated currency, since the yen had lost roughly half its value by the end of 1932. This afforded Japanese exports a significant price advantage over the country's leading competitors, particularly in textiles and other consumer goods. Soon Japanese products were invading markets around the world—so much so that in 1933 the city of Osaka replaced Lancashire, England, as the world's leading producer of cotton goods. The French, British, Dutch, and US colonies of Southeast Asia became major purchasers of Japanese manufactures, which were far less expensive than European-made products, not only because of the devalued yen but also due to lower shipping costs. By

1934 nearly a third of all imports coming into the Dutch East Indies were made in Japan—this was a greater portion than those of the Netherlands itself, Germany, and Great Britain combined. But Japanese market penetration went far beyond Asia—the country's goods sold very well in India, the Middle East, and Africa. They were even showing up in Europe, where despite high tariffs they continued to undersell similar items that were produced domestically.

For the industrial powers of the West this was a serious problem, and not merely because of the Depression-induced rush to protect domestic industries. The flood of Japanese imports into French, British, Dutch, and US colonies threatened the economic links that helped to bind the people of these areas to their colonial masters. The presence of manufactured goods from an Asian country in the markets of places such as the Philippines, Malaya, and Senegal demonstrated that there was an alternative to economic domination by the West.

From the perspective of the colonial powers, this was reason enough to accuse the Japanese of underhanded trading practices and to erect further barriers against their products. From the United States and Great Britain came accusations that their East Asian competitors were subsidizing their exports, gaining an unfair advantage on world markets. But subsidization of exports had become extremely common among industrial powers during this period, and Japan's subsidies were comparatively low. As one official of the British Embassy in Tokyo reported, "There is no question of selling at below production cost, nor is there any evidence to show that goods for export are usually sold cheaper than goods for the domestic market."[4] In fact, Japanese industry had achieved a high level of efficiency during the 1920s. That Japanese exports enjoyed the benefit of a depreciated yen is clear, but every country that devalued its currency during this period was guilty of seeking the same benefit.

This made little difference to the industrial powers of the West, which one by one took steps to keep Japanese goods out of their colonies. In India, where by 1933 Japanese manufactures had captured half the market for imported cotton textiles, the British colonial authorities increased tariffs on non-British imports to 75 percent. That same year the government of the Dutch East Indies passed a Crisis Import Ordinance that set special quotas on the amount of Japanese goods that would be allowed to enter the country. The United States placed a quota on Japanese imports to the Philippines; even such a committed free trader as Cordell Hull was prepared to sacrifice his principles where the Japanese were involved. At the World Economic Conference in London, Tokyo's delegation pushed for a treaty prohibiting economic boycotts and preferential tariffs, but it came away empty-handed.

The move to check Japan's export trade did not seriously hinder the country's economic recovery, but it had some profound political effects. First, it forced hard choices on the cabinet in 1934–1935. Recovery had brought with it an increase in foreign imports, especially from the United States. To a certain extent this had been counterbalanced in 1932–1933 by the rapid growth in exports, but by 1934 this growth had begun to slow and Japan's balance of trade turned sharply negative. At the same time, Takahashi was becoming increasingly concerned that the mounting national debt could trigger runaway inflation. On his recommendation the cabinet announced that total spending for 1934 would have to remain at 1933 levels. The army and navy found this completely unacceptable, but a crisis was averted when the cabinet agreed to increase the military budget by slashing programs for rural relief. The army, it seemed, was more than prepared to sacrifice the interests of the countryside when they threatened the course of rearmament.

Second, the West's discriminatory trade practices served to convince many Japanese industrialists that they could not entrust their fortunes to the vicissitudes of international trade. Gradually they came to abandon their economic liberalism and join the military in striving for a Japanese-dominated bloc in East Asia that would provide a secure overseas market for their products. By the middle of the decade nearly two-thirds of Japan's exports were going to Asia—and over half of those went to Taiwan, Korea, and Manchuria, the three territories that were under direct Japanese control.

The quest for a "yen bloc" spurred further aggression against China. Direct fighting between Chinese and Japanese forces ended in May 1933 with the signing of the Tanggu Truce, under which Jiang Jieshi agreed to withdraw his forces from a 100-kilometer zone south of the Great Wall. By this time the Kwantung Army occupied not only Manchuria, but virtually all of Chinese territory north of the wall. Two years later the commander of Japanese troops in Tientsin concluded an agreement with Jiang's minister of war—the Ho-Umezu Agreement—in which the Chinese agreed to withdraw not only troops but all organs of the Nanjing government from Hebei Province, just outside Beijing. While local Japanese army commanders continued to promote economic development in Manchukuo—gradually diminishing the authority of the South Manchuria Railway in the process—they also set about creating an "autonomous region" in North China that would be subject to the army's economic control.

Jiang Jieshi felt powerless to resist any of this. Exhausted from long years of campaigning as part of the Northern Expedition [...] and engaged in sporadic fighting against a growing communist movement under the leadership of Mao Zedong, his forces were in no condition to take on the Japanese. At the same time, China was in the grip of its own economic crisis produced in part by US silver purchases [...] and exacerbated by the Kwantung Army's policy of encouraging the smuggling of silver through the parts of the country that were under its control. The result was widespread deflation—farm prices fell by more than 40 percent from 1932 to 1934, bringing misery to much of the country's peasant population. However, China's economic crisis did not last long. With assistance from Great Britain [...] the Central Bank of China issued a new paper currency—the fapi—in November 1935, and within a year and a half the amount of money in circulation tripled. As the value of the fapi decreased, farm prices climbed and Chinese exports once again became competitive on the world market. Nationalists began to urge Jiang to stop giving in to Japanese demands and defend the nation's sovereignty.

Meanwhile Japan's leaders were growing increasingly concerned about Japan's reliance on US exports. In 1936 the cabinet moved to stop the importation of American automobiles by setting up two corporations—Toyota and Nissan—for which the state provided half the capital. However, Japanese manufacturing could not come up with a substitute for oil, for which the country was almost entirely dependent on the United States. The navy in particular grew worried about shortages of petroleum, without which the fleet would be paralyzed. In July 1935, therefore, the navy set up a committee to investigate the possibility of obtaining oil from Southeast Asia—by peaceful means if possible, but by force if necessary.

By the end of 1935 war was becoming increasingly likely, although it was not yet clear whether the major theater of operations would be China or Southeast Asia (or both). The army and navy both demanded substantial increases to their budgets, but Takahashi had other ideas. Japan was nearing full employment; the Depression, he declared, was over. Heavy government spending had been a useful instrument for promoting recovery, but now it was no longer necessary. Prices had begun to creep upward, leading to fears of further inflation if spending were not reduced. In late 1935, therefore, he announced that the following year's budget would contain a series of cuts—including a sharp reduction in military spending—and that the cabinet had rejected a proposal to increase taxes on business profits.

Takahashi's announcement was a bold attempt to reassert civilian influence over the government. However, the new budget never went into effect, for on February 26, 1936, a clique of young army officers attempted a coup d'état, their boldest effort yet. Small detachments of soldiers quickly moved to secure strategic buildings in Tokyo, including the Ministry of War. Others carried out assassination attempts against certain officials whom the officers had accused of attempting to weaken the army and navy. Although the prime minister managed to escape (the assassins mistook his brother-in-law for him), Takahashi was among those who did not. The eighty-two-year-old finance minister was shot and stabbed as he slept in his bed.

To this day the extent to which the army's top commanders were involved in the rebellion remains unclear. The generals were certainly reluctant to try to stop the uprising, and stonewalled even after the emperor issued a direct order to suppress it. However, they eventually mobilized forces, and with some assistance from the navy forced the rebels to surrender three days later. Nineteen of the plotters were eventually given the death sentence, and dozens of other young officers were sent to prison. Nevertheless, the army and navy proved to be the big winners of February 26. From then on, no cabinet would dare to oppose the wishes of the armed forces for fear of ultranationalist violence. Although certain civilians would continue to serve on cabinets, they all understood that the will of the military could not be thwarted. The era of civilian government in Japan had come to an end.

Although both Germany and Japan were set on a path of foreign conquest by 1936, the most provocative act of aggression during this period came not from either of them, but rather from Italy. In 1933, 15 percent of the country's workforce was unemployed, and the regime was resorting to increasingly technocratic measures in pursuit of recovery. It oversaw the creation of a new public agency—the *Istituto per la Ricostruzione Industriale* (Institute for Industrial Reconstruction), which took over struggling banks and firms. The regime spent considerable sums on public works—including a much-heralded project to drain the Pontine Marshes just south of Rome—and in October it enacted a law limiting the workweek to forty hours in an effort to force businesses to hire more employees.

None of these measures, however, could solve the problem of Italy's declining export trade. Mussolini was determined that the lira would remain on the gold standard—at one point he swore to defend the lira "to the last breath, to the last drop of blood"[5]—making Italian products more expensive on world markets. But because Italy, like Japan, relied on imports for even the most basic industrial resources, the country's reserves of gold and foreign currency plummeted in 1933–1934. The government responded by announcing that autarky was now the official goal of Fascist foreign policy; there would be new regulations limiting the export of foreign currency, and licenses would be required for the import of materials such as copper, coffee, and wool. The regime also moved toward a barter-based approach to international trade, negotiating bilateral treaties with Bulgaria, Romania, and Germany and placing additional tariffs on goods from countries that refused to grant most-favored-nation treatment to Italian products. Still, the country's trade deficit grew—in 1934 the value of imports exceeded that of exports by nearly a third—and the Bank of Italy's reserves continued to drain away. That, in turn, meant deflation: in April the government decreed that retail prices for foodstuffs be reduced by 10 percent and rents by 12 percent, with salaries for state employees reduced accordingly.

Mussolini's boldest attempt to relieve Italy's economic distress was his invasion of Ethiopia, which after months of preparation was launched in October 1935. The regime's propaganda portrayed the impoverished African country as a treasure house of untapped resources that would help to free Italy from dependence on foreign imports. This assessment was not entirely inaccurate; indeed, Japanese, British, and US firms had all sent delegations to Ethiopia in recent years in search of trade relations and even oil concessions. What remained unclear was where Italy would find the capital to develop these resources, particularly after waging a costly war to bring them under control. Leading businessmen and politicians—even King Victor Emmanuel III—expressed misgivings about the campaign, but these were swept aside.

In fact, the very preparations for war helped to improve economic conditions in 1935. By that summer the number of unemployed had fallen 250,000 from the previous year's high, and per capita GDP had expanded by nearly 9 percent (see Figure 7.1). Industrial production soared, as did profits, as a result of mobilization. These trends accelerated once the war began, with unemployment returning to pre-Depression levels. However, all of this came at a high price. Ethiopian resistance was unexpectedly tenacious, and Emperor Haile Selassie's forces were even able to launch a counteroffensive in mid-December. Within days the country's gold reserves had fallen so low that the government called upon the women of Italy to turn over their wedding rings, with Queen Elena among the first to do so. By the time Ethiopian resistance ended the following May—thanks in large part to the use of poison gas by Italian troops—the state's budget deficit had tripled. Finally even Mussolini had to admit that the lira could no longer be tied to gold, and in October the Bank of Italy announced that henceforth it would be linked to the US dollar. Over the next six months the government managed to finance roughly a third of the public debt simply by printing money.

The war also changed Italy's patterns of trade. The League of Nations declared Italy an aggressor and imposed trade sanctions, cutting the country off temporarily from many of its traditional sources of strategic commodities. Italians would now, for a few months at least, get a small taste of autarky, and that meant widespread shortages—although the sanctions had no measurable impact on the war in Ethiopia. Nor was the sanctions regime complete: not only was oil exempted, but not all countries agreed to participate. Germany had left the League in 1933, so for Berlin the sanctions offered an opportunity to boost the nation's exports, as well as to draw Italy away from its traditional alignment with Britain and France. Italian imports from Germany increased rapidly in a trend that was to continue even after the sanctions were lifted in July, so that 27 percent of all of Italy's imports between 1936 and 1938 came from Germany.

In fact, Germany's interest in the Italian invasion of Ethiopia went far beyond trade. Up to this point Hitler's foreign policy had been cautious; he had, as mentioned previously, pulled Germany out of the League of Nations in 1933, and in March 1935 he had repudiated the disarmament clauses of the Versailles treaty and announced the reintroduction of conscription. Neither of these elicited a serious response from Britain and France; indeed, in June 1935 the Anglo-German Naval Agreement was a strong signal that London was no longer interested in upholding the terms of Versailles. Thus in March 1936, while much of the world's attention was focused on the war in Ethiopia, Hitler made his boldest move yet. He ordered his troops to reoccupy the Rhineland, German territory that under the Versailles treaty was supposed to remain demilitarized. [...] the Baldwin government made it clear that it did not regard the Rhineland as a vital national interest, while France, teetering on the brink of national bankruptcy, was unprepared to take on the Germans alone. The Führer's gamble paid off handsomely, and in the next few years he would raise the stakes repeatedly.

Notes

1 Quoted in Norman H. Baynes, ed., *The Speeches of Adolf Hitler* (New York: Howard Fertig, 1969), 111–112.

2 Gerhard L. Weinberg, ed., *Hitler's Second Book: The Unpublished Sequel to* Mein Kampf by *Adolf Hitler* (New York: Enigma, 2003), 158.

3 Quoted in Akira Iriye, "The Failure of Military Expansionism," in *Dilemmas of Growth in Prewar Japan*, ed. James William Morley (Princeton, NJ: Princeton University Press, 1971), 111.

4 Quoted in H. V. Hodson, *Slump and Recovery, 1929-1937: A Survey of World Economic Affairs* (London: Oxford University Press, 1938), 348–349.

5 Quoted in Franklin Hugh Adler, *Italian Industrialists from Liberalism to Fascism: The Political Development of the Industrial Bourgeoisie, 1906–1934* (Cambridge: Cambridge University Press, 1995), 353.

The Chinese Civil War and European Cold War, 1945–9

Mark Chi-Kwan

The Chinese Civil War of 1945–9 resulted in the establishment of the PRC and the transformation of East Asian international relations. While the conflict was domestic in origin, the outbreak of full-scale war in mid-1946 was significantly shaped by superpower politics. The final outcome was determined as much by the diplomacy of the two rival Chinese parties as by their military strategy and tactics. During 1949, Mao had to ponder on China's future relations with the Soviet Union and the United States, which remained in a state of constant flux.

Domestic Causes

By the time Japan accepted unconditional surrender in August 1945, the GMD under Chiang Kai-shek remained in power in China. Yet in the course of the Sino-Japanese War, Chiang had lost some of his best armed units, and his government became increasingly corrupt and incompetent. If President Franklin Roosevelt had regarded Nationalist China as one of the 'Big Four' in the defeat of Japan and the construction of a post-war international order, his successor, Harry Truman, harboured serious reservations about the ability of Jiang to maintain stability and unity in China.

In the post-war years, the Nationalist government faced serious domestic problems. It alienated many of the urban elites (businessmen, intellectuals, and local leaders) by imposing new taxes, monopolies, and levies on them to finance the civil war. Economic mismanagement proved to have fatal consequences. To cope with escalating inflation, Nationalist officials relied on money printing, thus creating a vicious circle for the

Chi-Kwan Mark, "The Chinese Civil War and European Cold War, 1945-9," *China and the World Since 1945: An International History,* pp. 9-18. Copyright © 2012 by Taylor & Francis Group. Reprinted with permission.

urban economy. By early 1949, the loss of legitimacy of the GMD state had reached crisis proportions. In January, Chiang announced his resignation from the presidency and his replacement by Li Zongren as 'acting president' (although Chiang remained the head of the GMD and was still influential in policy-making).

As a result of the Sino-Japanese War, the CCP became a viable political alternative to the GMD. The CCP transformed itself from a weak and disunited party into an efficient, highly disciplined, and mass-based organization, thanks to the leadership, charisma, and thinking of Mao. Through myth-making (such as the heroic myth of the Long March), theoretical writings (the 'Mao Zedong Thought'), and the rectification campaign of 1942–4 (in which Mao defeated his party rivals including Wang Ming), Mao established himself as the supreme leader of the CCP. Through moderate land reform and a de-emphasis on revolutionary ideology, Mao had attracted many peasants and other discontented elements to the Communist movement in the base areas.[1]

Nevertheless, by mid-1945 the balance of power between the GMD and the CCP was still very much in the former's favour. Militarily, the GMD forces were more numerous and better equipped, and controlled more territories, especially cities where the Communists were conspicuously absent. Diplomatically, Chiang's government was recognized by both the United States and the Soviet Union.

Cold War Impact

During the final stage of the Second World War in early February 1945, the three Allied Powers' leaders, Franklin D. Roosevelt, Joseph Stalin, and Winston Churchill, met at Yalta to discuss war strategy and the post-war order. To secure a Soviet invasion of Japan, Roosevelt and Churchill agreed to Stalin's demands that the Soviet Union would establish a predominant position in Manchuria in Northeast China. The secret Yalta Agreement on China was confirmed in the Sino-Soviet Treaty of Friendship and Mutual Assistance, signed between the Nationalist and the Soviet governments on 14 August 1945, the same day as Japanese Emperor Hirohito announced unconditional surrender. Accordingly, the Soviets used Port Arthur (Lushun) as a naval base and exercised joint control over Manchurian Railways (the Chinese Changchun Railroad) for a period of 30 years. China accepted the independence of Outer Mongolia. The Soviet Union recognized the GMD as the legitimate government of China, and would withdraw its troops from Manchuria within three months after Japan's surrender.[2]

Stalin approached China from a global perspective. In establishing Soviet prominence in Manchuria, he had an eye on the security threat posed by Japan to the Soviet border. By recognizing the legitimacy of Chiang's government, Stalin aimed to continue the wartime collaboration with the United States and prevent the resumption of civil war in China. On the other hand, Stalin had few illusions about the strength of the CCP in a military showdown with the GMD. For these reasons, the Soviets prevented the CCP forces from entering the main cities and communication routes in the Northeast.

Although believing that the GMD forces were far stronger than the CCP's, Chiang realized that he needed a period of peace to resolve China's economic and other problems. With Washington's and Moscow's diplomatic recognition, Chiang was confident that he could exploit superpower politics to force the CCP into a subordinate political position and eventually destroy it. On the same day as Japan's surrender, Chiang invited Mao to Chongqing to discuss the political future of China. The Chongqing talks, from 28 August to 10 October, resulted in the Double Ten Agreement, which recognized the equality of all parties and called for the unification of military forces and the democratization of the central government.

Mao agreed to participate in the peace talks on Stalin's advice. Realizing that the CCP forces were no match for the GMD's and the prospect of substantial Soviet assistance was remote, Mao indeed had little room for manoeuvre. By following Stalin's instructions, Mao hoped that the Soviets would restrain Chiang from launching a full-scale attack on the CCP. In short, in August and September, the situation in China stabilized due to US–Soviet cooperation and Chiang's restraint.

But US–Soviet cooperation in China was fragile. Although the Truman administration aimed to prevent the outbreak of civil war, it also wanted to contain Soviet influence in Manchuria. Thus, from the outset, the US policy of 'neutrality' in the GMD–CCP struggle was compromised. In September, the United States landed more than 50,000 marines in Tianjin and other northern ports pending the arrival of Chiang's forces; it also airlifted and transported half a million GMD troops to take over strategic locations in the North and the Northeast. Moscow became increasingly suspicious of Washington's policy in China—and in Japan. At the Foreign Ministers' Conference between the United States, Britain, and the Soviet Union in mid-September, it became clear that the Americans wanted to exercise exclusive control over the occupation of Japan. To indicate their displeasure at US policies, in early October the Soviets encouraged the CCP troops to enter the Northeast and provided substantial Soviet weapons. But after Chiang launched, in November, a large-scale assault on the then Communist-controlled Shanhaiguan (which was the gateway to Manchuria), together with Washington's diplomatic pressure, Moscow backed down.

The United States did not want the situation to deteriorate further. In late November, General George C. Marshall was appointed as the President's special representative to China with the objectives of securing a ceasefire and a coalition government. As a result of the Marshall Mission, the two rival Chinese parties reached a ceasefire agreement in early January 1946, and a military reorganization agreement in late February. But when it came to implementation, Mao was unwilling to give up his independent armed force in creating a unified national army, for it would leave the CCP at the mercy of the GMD.

What finally ended the fragile peace in China was the emergence of the Cold War in Europe. By March, US–Soviet relations deteriorated rapidly over Eastern Europe. In consequence, Moscow announced the withdrawal of Soviet forces from Manchuria, which meant that the CCP was now allowed to occupy the main cities and transport routes in the Northeast. From April onwards,

Mao sent CCP forces to replace the Soviet garrisons. By early May, the Soviets completed their withdrawal from Manchuria. In June/July, Chiang launched his large-scale assaults in Manchuria. The Chinese Civil War had erupted fully. Despite the fact that Marshall would stay on as mediator in China until early January 1947, it is clear that the United States could no longer exercise effective influence over the situation on the ground.

While planning his military campaigns, Mao, the Marxist theoretician, tried to clarify the relationship between the Chinese revolutionary movement and the growing US–Soviet conflict. One of the main issues to address was whether the Chinese Civil War would lead to a world war. In August, during an interview with visiting American journalist Anna Louise Strong, Mao talked of the concept of an 'intermediate zone'. To Mao, the 'main contradiction' in the world was that between 'the US reactionary clique' and the peoples of the 'intermediate zone'—capitalist, colonial, and semi-colonial countries of Europe, Asia, and Africa that separated the two superpowers. The United States would not unleash a third world war against the Soviet Union unless it controlled the 'intermediate zone'. As long as the peoples of the 'intermediate zone' persisted in their struggle against the American imperialists, Mao argued, a third world war could be avoided. As part of the 'intermediate zone', the CCP played an important role in the world-wide struggles of national liberation. Rather than causing a third world war, the Chinese Civil War thus contributed to world peace.[3]

Between mid-1946 and 1947, the Soviets provided more support to the CCP including weapons, military uniforms, and raw materials. Yet, the amount of aid was smaller than what Mao had expected and fell far below the level of US assistance to the GMD during this period. Although Marshall, who became Secretary of State upon his return from China in early 1947, ruled out direct US military intervention in China, the administration continued to provide military and economic aid to Chiang's government. As the Cold War in Europe gathered momentum in 1947, White House policy-makers and State Department officials had to mobilize support from Congress and the American public for the new grand strategy of containment. To secure congressional appropriations for the European Recovery Programme or the Marshall Plan, in 1947–8 the administration approved the China Aid Bill of 1948, which provided for $570 million worth of economic and military aid to the GMD government. In a word, the imperative of domestic mobilization for the European Cold War underscored the US involvement in the Chinese Civil War during 1947–8.[4]

US economic and military aid, however, was not enough to save Chiang's regime. From late 1947 onwards, the CCP forces began to seize the military initiative. In September Lin Biao launched an all-out offensive in Manchuria and basically conquered the entire region by November 1948. This decisive victory was followed by the capture of Beiping and Tianjin, the two major northern cities, and the battle of Huai-Hai, which involved more than a million men on each side fighting for the control of China north of the Yangzi River. By the end of January 1949, the Chinese Communists were in control of the northern half of China.

Establishing the Principles of Diplomacy

While planning his military operations south of the Yangzi, in early 1949 Mao contemplated the prospects for relations with the Soviet Union and the United States. Throughout the civil war, CCP–Soviet relations had been ambivalent and complicated, thanks to Stalin's global considerations and personal mistrust of Mao. In 1947 and 1948, Stalin had turned down Mao's requests for a visit to discuss Sino-Soviet cooperation. In 1948 Stalin fell out with Josip Tito, the leader of Yugoslavia, on the grounds of the latter's alleged deviations from Marxism-Leninism. Although the CCP quickly demonstrated its solidarity with Moscow, Stalin could not help but have doubts about Mao's credentials as a true Marxist, given the Chairman's emphasis on peasants rather than workers in the revolutionary struggle. It was feared that Mao would become a 'Chinese Tito' one day.[5]

Stalin's reservations about the CCP did not dissipate during 1949. In early January, Chiang, in his last-ditch attempt to prevent a total Communist victory, requested the Soviet Union to mediate the civil war. Historians have debated whether Stalin accordingly advised Mao not to cross the Yangzi River, but to seek a north–south division of China at the Yangzi. New research findings suggest that Stalin did consult with Mao about the prospect of a peaceful solution to the civil war through direct negotiation between the CCP and the GMD. His primary aim was to avoid a direct US–Soviet confrontation (especially at the time of the ongoing Berlin blockade), if not to keep the GMD in power. But when Mao indicated his strong objection to foreign interference in Chinese affairs, Stalin did not press the issue further.[6]

Mao, on the other hand, devised new principles and policies for dealing with the Western countries. Shortly after occupying Shenyang in Northeast China, in November 1948 the CCP's Military Control Commission in the city ordered all Western diplomats there to hand over their radio transmitters within 36 hours. The order was due partly to Moscow's advice and partly to the CCP's security concerns about American espionage activities in Shenyang. On Washington's instructions, the American Consul General in Shenyang, Angus Ward, refused to hand over the transmitter. On 20 November Ward was held under house-arrest by the PLA troops, and the consulate's offices and residential compound were confiscated. A year later, Ward and four of his colleagues were formally arrested on the grounds of espionage and finally expelled from China.

In handling the Ward case, Mao was simultaneously formulating the basic principles of New China's foreign policy, especially concerning diplomatic relations with the Western powers. Feeling strongly about the 'century of humiliation', Mao was determined to make a clean break with the old China. During the spring and summer of 1949, Mao developed the principles of 'making a fresh start' and 'cleaning the house before inviting the guests'. To Mao, the new Communist government would not recognize the legal status of any diplomatic establishments and personnel accredited to the former Nationalist regime as well as the treaties and agreements concluded or inherited by it. New China would establish diplomatic relations with all countries, including the Western ones, on the principle of 'equality'. But it would not be in a hurry to seek foreign recognition unless and until all vestiges of imperialist power and influence on the mainland were eliminated.[7]

In May/June the Chinese Communists established direct contact with American diplomats. After the fall of Nanjing in late April, on Washington's instructions, US Ambassador John Leighton Stuart was ordered to stay in order to protect American interests and remaining citizens in China and to maintain a channel of communication with the CCP authorities. A former missionary educator in China, Stuart felt that the United States could play a role in influencing the CCP's orientation and policy, for example, by offering US economic assistance to China after the civil war. Mao, for his part, wanted to explore the US attitude towards the CCP. In early May, Huang Hua, the director of the Bureau of Foreign Affairs in Nanjing, was asked to begin a series of secret talks with Stuart. (It was no coincidence that Huang was a graduate of Yenching University where Stuart had once served as president.) The talks touched upon the two governments' respective position and policy. In June, it was proposed that Stuart should visit Beiping to talk directly with Mao and other leaders.

In the summer of 1949, the Truman administration, preoccupied with European affairs, was pursuing an inconsistent and self-contradictory China policy. In view of the Communist occupation of Nanjing, in May the new Secretary of State, Dean Acheson, had laid down three basic conditions for US recognition of a new Chinese regime: the CCP's *de facto* control of territory, its willingness to discharge international obligations in full, and the general acquiescence of the Chinese people in its rule. The State Department ruled out the possibility of direct US intervention in China. But the Department of Defense was concerned about the impact of China's loss on Japan's security, while the Republicans in Congress and the China lobby warned against writing Chiang off. Consequently, Truman and Acheson decided on a strategy of continued military and economic assistance to the GMD to delay the inevitable for as long as possible. In other words, Acheson wanted to 'wait for the dust to settle': the United States would wait for the final collapse of the GMD and the emergence of a CCP government independent of Moscow before making the final decision on recognition.[8]

At the end of June, Truman vetoed Stuart's proposal for visiting Beiping. But this came as no great surprise to Mao, who used the Huang–Stuart talks mainly to explore Washington's real thinking and to prevent US intervention in China or subversion from within at the time of the Yangzi crossings. Now that both Nanjing and Shanghai had fallen into Communist hands, Mao concluded that New China would not establish diplomatic relations with any countries which maintained ties with the GMD. On 30 June, Mao proclaimed in a speech, 'On the People's Democratic Dictatorship', that China should 'lean to one side' in the bipolar Cold War, the side of the Soviet Union.

Mao's 'lean to one side' speech was meant to impress Stalin with his political loyalty and commitment to the socialist bloc headed by the Soviet Union. On 10 July, Liu Shaoqi, the Party's second in command, visited Moscow as a major step towards the formation of the Sino-Soviet alliance. Liu led a delegation comprising Wang Jiaxiang (a future ambassador to the Soviet Union) and Gao Gang (the Party head in Manchuria), both of whom were experienced in dealing with the Soviets. During their month-long stay, they held four formal meetings with Stalin and other Soviet leaders, covering important aspects of Sino-Soviet relations. Recognizing that Mao now represented the true leader of China, Stalin apologized for his insufficient assistance to the CCP during the civil war. Liu sought Moscow's and Eastern European governments' diplomatic recognition of the soon-to-be-established People's Republic, which Stalin promised. Liu and Stalin agreed on a 'division of labour' in the promotion of world proletarian revolution: China, due to geographical proximity and similar historical background, would focus on the colonial and semi-colonial countries in the East, while the Soviet Union would concentrate on Europe. They also discussed Sino-Soviet military cooperation. As a result of Liu's visit, the Soviets promised to help China to establish an air force, dispatch a team of Soviet experts to assist China's economic reconstruction and military build-up, and offer loans of $300 million.[9]

If a strategic Sino-Soviet alliance was in the making, by the summer of 1949 Mao's hostility towards the United States reached new heights, not least due to Washington's tacit support for the Nationalist blockade of China's eastern coast following Shanghai's fall. But the decisive battles of the civil war were all but over. Chiang retreated to Taiwan, bringing with him American weapons, gold reserves, and art treasures. The United States wanted to draw a political line with the failed GMD state on the mainland. In August, the State Department published the *China White Paper*, a huge volume of documents and analyses on pre-1949 US–China relations. In his open letter of transmittal of 30 July, Secretary Acheson defended the administration's opposition to full-scale intervention in the civil war, attributed the GMD's defeat to its misuse of US aid and its own inefficiency, and expressed the American hope that Chinese nationalism would eventually reassert itself against Soviet domination.[10] Unconvinced, Mao responded to the *China White Paper* by launching a nationwide anti-American propaganda campaign. In August the Xinhua News Agency published four consecutive articles written by Mao. In the article which appeared on 28 August, Mao denounced the White Paper as 'a counter-revolutionary document which openly demonstrates US imperialist intervention in China'.[11] Mao wanted to mobilize the Chinese people behind his anti-American policy.

On 1 October, Mao proclaimed on top of Tiananmen, or the Gate of Heavenly Peace, that the Chinese people had 'stood up'. Mao's China had formally joined the world.

Lost Chance or No Chance?

Was there a 'lost chance' for Sino-American accommodation in 1949? By using American documents and looking primarily from the American perspective, Warren Cohen and Nancy Tucker have put forward a 'lost chance' thesis on the basis of the troublesome CCP–Soviet relationship during the civil war, the Huang–Stuart talks, as well as the Department of State's 'hands-off' approach towards Taiwan. Given Stalin's reservations about the CCP on the one hand, Acheson's frustration with the GMD regime on the other, they argue, the Chinese Communist leadership was indeed flexible enough to reach a certain degree of accommodation with the United States, such as limited economic and political contact, if not full diplomatic recognition. But the Truman administration, under the influence of domestic and Cold War politics, was too inflexible to respond positively to the opportunities provided by, for example, Stuart's proposed visit to Beiping. The United States thus helped push Mao and the CCP to the side of the Soviet camp, thereby missing a 'chance' for Sino-American accommodation.[12]

By using Chinese archival sources, Chen Jian and Thomas Christensen found no evidence for any 'chance', highlighting instead the closeness of Sino-Soviet relations and the informal and exploratory nature of the Huang–Stuart contacts. Chen argues that Mao was determined to transform the Chinese state and society and to restore China's rightful position in the international system. For all the difficult moments in CCP–Soviet relations, Mao realized that Stalin's support was vital to the defeat of the Nationalists as well as his 'continuous revolution' after nationwide liberation. The Ward case reflected Mao's growing hostility towards the Americans, while hardening the Truman administration's attitude towards recognition of the CCP. Mao did not regard the informal Huang–Stuart talks as serious bridge-building for Sino-American accommodation. In 1949 he was not in a hurry to seek US recognition, given Washington's reluctance to cut all links with the GMD. The 'lost chance' thesis is therefore more myth than reality. Looking from the Chinese perspective and using Chinese archival sources, Chen and Christensen have avoided an America-centric approach that treated Mao or the CCP as a passive actor in the US–China relationship: China was not for the United States to 'gain' or 'lose'.[13]

In sum, in October 1949, Mao was in little doubt that China's new identity was to be a loyal ally of the socialist bloc headed by the Soviet Union.

Notes

1 See Suzanne Pepper, *Civil War in China: The Political Struggle, 1945–1949* (Berkeley: University of California Press, 1978); Odd Arne Westad, *Decisive Encounters: The Chinese Civil War, 1946–1950* (Stanford: Stanford University Press, 2003), 2–13.

2 My interpretation draws heavily on Odd Arne Westad, *Cold War and Revolution: Soviet–American Rivalry and the Origins of the Chinese Civil War, 1944–1946* (New York: Columbia University Press, 1993); Chen Jian, *Mao's China and the Cold War* (Chapel Hill: The University of North Carolina Press, 2001), 26–37.

3 Niu Jun, *From Yan'an to the World: The Origin and Development of Chinese Communist Foreign Policy* (1992), edited and translated by Steven I. Levine (Norwalk, Conn.: EastBridge, 2005), 288–9.

4 On this theme, see Thomas J. Christensen, *Useful Adversaries: Grand Strategy, Domestic Mobilization, and Sino-American Conflict, 1947–1958* (Princeton: Princeton University Press, 1996), 32–76.

5 On CCP–Soviet relations during the Chinese Civil War, see Niu Jun, 'The Origins of the Sino-Soviet Alliance', in Odd Arne Westad (ed.), *Brothers in Arms: The Rise and Fall of the Sino-Soviet Alliance, 1945–1963* (Stanford: Stanford University Press, 1998), 57–64.

6 Ibid., 64–5; Westad, *Decisive Encounters*, 216–19.

7 Chen Jian, *China's Road to the Korean War: The Making of the Sino-American Confrontation* (New York: Columbia University Press, 1994), 33–44.

8 See Nancy B. Tucker, *Patterns in the Dust: Chinese–American Relations and the Recognition Controversy, 1949–1950* (New York: Columbia University Press, 1983).

9 Chen, *China's Road to the Korean War*, 71–7; Sergei N. Goncharov, John W. Lewis, and Xue Litai, *Uncertain Partners: Stalin, Mao, and the Korean War* (Stanford: Stanford University Press, 1993), 61–75.

10 *The China White Paper, August 1949* (Stanford: Stanford University Press, 1967), iii–xvii.

11 *Selected Works of Mao Zedong*, vol. iv (Beijing: Foreign Language Press, 1969), 441–5.

12 Warren Cohen, 'Introduction' to 'Symposium: Rethinking the Lost Chance in China', *DH* 21 (Winter 1997): 71–5; Tucker, op. cit.

13 Chen Jian, 'The Myth of America's "Lost Chance" in China: A Chinese Perspective in Light of New Evidence', *DH* 21 (Winter 1997): 77–86; Thomas J. Christensen, 'A "Lost Chance" for What? Rethinking the Origins of US–PRC Confrontation', *Journal of American–East Asian Relations* (Fall 1995): 249–78.

The Cold War and Nationalism

Malcolm Anderson

The Cold War is conventionally regarded as commencing with Churchill's 1946 Fulton speech in which he coined the phrase 'the Cold War' and finishing with Gorbachev's appointment in 1985 as General Secretary of the Communist Party of the Soviet Union. The 'war' was not of uniform intensity or bellicosity and three, somewhat arbitrarily defined, phases are commonly identified.

First, an intense, Stalinist phase (1946–53) in which military confrontation between the West and Soviet Communism was possible and to many seemed imminent. Second, a phase of peaceful coexistence and détente which emerged after Stalin's death with Khruschev's speech to the twentieth congress of the Communist Party in 1956 condemning the crimes of Stalin and the difficult but peaceful resolution of the Cuban missile crisis in 1962. This phase culminated in a major strategic arms limitation agreement but merged gradually into the third phase—a revival of the Cold War in the 1970s and 1980s, with the failure to proceed with the ratification of the second strategic arms limitation agreement, the deployment of Soviet SS-20s in Eastern Europe, the stationing of US Pershing II nuclear missiles in Western Europe, Soviet intervention in Afghanistan, and finally the Reagan 'star wars' project for establishing a defensive laser-based shield in space against Russian nuclear attack. This third phase was also characterised by super-power rivalry in the less developed world with direct military intervention by Russia in Afghanistan and wars by proxy in Africa.

These phases were characterised as much by the mood and atmosphere of international relations as by these iconic events. Events were not tidily distributed into the three phases, since the major event of the second phase was the Vietnam war. But, at the rhetorical level, the language was different; in the third phase, Ronald

Malcolm Anderson, "The Cold War and Nationalism," *States and Nationalism in Europe Since 1945*, pp. 10-22, 99. Copyright © 2000 by Taylor & Francis Group. Reprinted with permission.

Reagan condemned the Soviet Union as 'the evil empire', a kind of phrase which no American President used in the second phase. No Soviet (or American) slogan emerged in the third phase to express the desire for mutual accommodation such as that of Khruschev in the second phase of 'peaceful coexistence'.

However interpreted, these phases were far from clear-cut and certain ideological themes persisted through the whole period. These themes seemed both to transcend and to marginalise nationalism. The political elites of the USA and the USSR affected to believe that the Cold War was a confrontation of two radically different political and social projects based on incompatible economic systems. There could be no compromise, at the level of ideas, because the two were mutually exclusive even though the other side could be accepted as a fact of life and practical arrangements could be agreed to avoid military confrontations. Famous dissidents such as Nobel prize winners Sakharov and Solzhenitsyn on one side, Bertrand Russell and Sartre on the other, as well as obscure human rights militants in the communist regimes and peace movements in the western countries, bitterly contested this analysis. But they recognised (and condemned) the dominance of Cold War ideas and slogans.

None of the orthodox accounts of the Cold War consider nationalism's importance. These accounts may be grouped under five broad headings:

- An ideological struggle between totalitarianism and liberalism
- A struggle between socialist and capitalist forms of economic organisation
- A traditional form of great power rivalry
- The need to expand the role of government in the West, to develop new mechanisms to avoid destructive economic competition, to minimise the role of communist parties and to continue the US domestic wartime consensus into the post-war world
- The expansionary nature of capitalism
- The determination of the Soviets to hold on to the territorial gains of World War II—military and ideological mobilisation for war was the only way of doing so

The neglect of nationalism is not because the super powers identified it with instability within their respective Cold War blocs. In the competition for influence in the nonaligned or less developed countries, a wholly pragmatic approach was adopted. Nationalism was designated as good or bad depending on whether the nationalists in question were prepared to accept the leadership of one or the other super power.

Nationalism and Universalism in the Cold War

Since Soviet control in central and Eastern Europe, compared with American in Western Europe, was much more direct, interventionist, and based on force, reactions to it were almost inevitable. Soviet domination was seriously challenged in Eastern Europe by the east Berlin disturbances of

1953, the Hungarian uprising of 1956, the Prague spring of 1968 and the Solidarity movement in Poland in the 1980s. A complex mixture of misjudgements in government policy, popular reaction against oppressive police and political surveillance, material shortages and grievances, as well as nationalist sentiments, were involved in these events.

In the West, the most serious challenge after the 1940s to the solidarity of the North Atlantic Treaty Organisation (NATO) and the American-led coalition did not come from the communist parties, who were effectively isolated by the Cold War. But de Gaulle, a creative and idiosyncratic nationalist, and certain 'neutralists' took a view of French interests that did not always coincide with those of America. The left-wing neutralists and, to a degree, de Gaulle, encouraged a cultural anti-Americanism which pre-dated the Second World War and took forms such as opposition to the marketing of Coca Cola and to the domination of American films in France.[1]

National sentiment and nationalism were clearly present in these major challenges to the hegemony of the two dominant powers. The struggle for freedom from perceived foreign domination as well as specific short-term issues fuelled both kinds of revolt. All of these countries had been occupied or dominated by the Nazis with the consequence that the nationalist sentiments against alien rule engendered by this experience were still very much alive in the 1950s and 1960s. Serious efforts were made by the East European satellite regimes to control and even suppress them. In the West, nationalist ideology was discredited in favour of the rhetoric (and reality) of collective security, international cooperation and European integration. But nationalist sensibilities were expressed whenever a country was involved in armed conflict, such as France in Algeria (1954–62), Britain and France in Suez (1956), and Britain in the Falkland Islands (1982). Moreover, the phenomenon that Michael Billig has called banal nationalism, the everyday flagging of national symbols, images and references to the nation, persisted and flourished.[2]

But the dominant ideas and ideologies of the Cold War seemed, in broad terms, to ignore nationalist principles in favour of universalist claims. They relegated the national idea to, at best, a secondary role and even consigned nationalism to the dustbin of history. The basic question is whether the universalist claims of the free world and of international communism were incompatible with nationalism or were a vehicle for expressing Russian and American national ideas. The intellectual origins of the universalist claims go back to the political ideas of Europe and America in the late eighteenth and the nineteenth centuries. On the American side, the inalienable Rights of Man which included the rights to freedom and self-determination contained in the Declaration of Independence of 1776 and the Preamble to the Constitution of 1787 were the basis of the American constitutional and political tradition.

These values, like those of the 1789 Declaration of the Rights of Man and the Citizen at the beginning of the French Revolution, were couched in universal terms and were, in that context, those which other nations ought to adopt. The liberalism, constitutionalism and rights-based American tradition rested on axioms considered valid throughout the world. They formed the basis of American propaganda and war aims in both World Wars and were a major impetus behind the Universal Declaration of Human Rights adopted in 1948 by the United Nations. The thrust of American anti-Soviet propaganda was that the Cold War was a struggle for freedom and human rights against those who wished to deny them by use of force and manipulation.

In the Russian case, there was an aggressive promotion of another universalism—scientific socialism. In the celebrated words of the Communist Manifesto of 1848 'all hitherto recorded history is the history of class struggle'; the class struggle would not end except through proletarian revolution and the triumph of socialism. The Soviet claim was based on the ideology of Marxism-Leninism which, it was claimed, had universal validity. Capitalist regimes, despite a veneer of constitutional democracy and legal protection of individual rights, were based on exploitation by the holders of capital of the mass of the population. They denied genuine social and economic rights to the workers; and they were inevitably aggressive because of the structural contradictions of capitalism and because they were bound to try to destroy genuinely socialist regimes. A proletarian revolution would complete the process started by the bourgeois French Revolution and install a peaceful, conflict-free, socialist society. The Soviets therefore claimed to be the camp of peace and the defenders of true human emancipation and liberty.

The Second World War produced a situation in which American liberalism and Soviet communism became the internationally dominant forms of discourse, which influenced all the major actors in the international system. The entry of first the Soviet Union and then the United States into the Second World War had the effect of changing the content of propaganda in the war of ideas to defeat Nazi Germany. Churchillian rhetoric in the early phase of the war, when Britain stood alone against the axis powers, was essentially defensive—a struggle to defend a way of life, an empire, particular institutions and political independence against aggression and against a general threat of barbarism. This rhetoric was broadened to defend the interests of the occupied countries of Europe against oppression and to promote the cause of democracy, in order to sustain resistance to the Nazis in occupied Europe. Also he particularly emphasised the cause of freedom and democracy to appeal to American public opinion and to draw the United States into the War. This rhetoric was important to show to the British Commonwealth countries that they were fighting not merely to defend the 'mother country' but to promote a common cause. There is little doubt that Churchill and other members of the British elite considered that they were fighting against nationalism and a particularly odious form of it.

The Components of Super-Power Nationalism

Only a minority of Americans would identify themselves as nationalists; like the English, a majority regard themselves as patriots and regard foreigners as nationalists, in any clash with US interests. One recent author, Zelinsky, has, however, persuasively argued that given the 'extraordinary nature of its inception' America can show more of the 'essential nature of nationalism than any other example'.[3] American nationalism (in the sense being used in this book) was forged in throwing off colonial rule and drawing up of a constitution based on general principles. It was consolidated by a civil war (1861–65), preventing the secession of the southern states, fostered by an extraordinary territorial expansion across the American continent (characterised as the 'manifest destiny' of the United States). Economic growth in the nineteenth century and an immense influx of people from Ireland and eastern and southern Europe who, far from being nostalgic for the old country, wanted fervently to become Americans consecrated the establishment of the United States as a great power.

This history has resulted in an exceptional self-confidence, the creation of a strong set of national sentiments among American citizens and adherence to national symbols by most Americans, even though some now see a fragmentation and undermining of this national solidarity by the assault from multiculturalism. The 'American way' became generally regarded as superior to that of other nations. The American federal government funded an Americanisation campaign in the 1920s characterised by a poster campaign in the inter-war period based on the slogan 'There's no way like the American way'; in this campaign, white Anglo-Saxon Protestants were represented as the best representatives of the American way. The 1997 Commission on Immigration Reform recommended that a renewed Americanisation campaign be initiated for immigrants, which triggered both negative and positive responses reflecting two strands in American nationalism.

These two strands both embody attitudes of superiority towards the rest of the world. Both have historical roots going back to the birth of the Republic, but have acquired particular importance in the twentieth century. Since the rejection by the US Senate of the League of Nations in 1920, the omnipresent isolationist strand of American nationalism becomes dominant from time to time. Isolationism is the view that American should, as far as possible, avoid involvement in matters outside the western hemisphere on the grounds that such involvement is against American interests, will lead to pointless expenditure, the loss of American lives and the possible contamination of Americans by 'un-American' ideas and philosophies. Isolationism is often associated with what Richard Hofstadter called 'the paranoid style in American politics',[4] that is to say the belief that foreign influences should be excluded from American life and that foreigners are constantly plotting to undermine the American way. This way of thinking, although often represented by the hyphenated Americans (Irish-, Polish-Americans, etc.), denounced by Presidents Theodore Roosevelt and Woodrow Wilson at the beginning of the twentieth century in favour of 'hundred per cent Americans', is often associated with an ethnic nationalism. This represents the American nation as derived from north European, particularly British stock, and the further removed from these roots, the less assilimable are immigrants. Legislation restricting immigration since the Chinese Exclusion Act of 1882 has been strongly influenced by this tradition.

The second strand is that it is America's destiny to be the first among nations, to show by example the superiority of the American way, and to assume a world leadership. This form of conventional wisdom held that free institutions, free enterprise, individualism, tolerance of diversity (often now called multiculturalism), separation of the churches and the state whilst adhering to Christian religious values, were the explanation of the rise of the greatest power and the most successful society ever known. The world therefore owes America respect and should follow American leadership. This situation is a burden for the United States because it involves the expenditure of energies, lives and money. Even adopted by successive American Presidents, it has often been difficult to mobilise a majority behind this view because large numbers of Americans have little interest in, or knowledge of, international affairs and indeed in matters outside their own state and locality.

In the post-1945 period, Senator Joseph McCarthy and President Kennedy can be regarded as emblematic figures of these two strands of American nationalism. The former led a notorious witch-hunt against communists and fellow travellers during the first period of the Cold War; he wielded great influence as chairman of two Senate subcommittees, which he used in his obsessive hunting down of communists and fellow travellers in American government and the media. His campaign was halted only when he accused the US Army, itself a powerful national symbol, of harbouring communists. By contrast, President Kennedy undertook, in his inaugural presidential address, to oppose any aggression by foreign (by implication communist) powers. He said that the United States would not permit the 'undoing' of human rights and, in a famous passage, that the nation would 'pay any price, bear any burden, meet any hardship, support any friend, oppose any foe' to ensure the survival of liberty. This way of thinking led to the beginning of the disastrous commitment in 1964 of American troops in Vietnam.

The dialectic between the isolationists and the 'globalists' is seen in the Congressional conflicts over international organisations, aid and solidarity; it also roughly coincides with the split between those who favour and those who oppose big government and heavy federal expenditure. The League of Nations and the United Nations were set up largely on American initiative but the weakness of the League of Nations was the direct result of American subsequent refusal to participate in it. The refusal of a hostile Congress, influenced by isolationist assumptions, to pay the dues owed by the United States to the United Nations in the 1980s and 1990s has undermined the organisation. The reduction, in the case of sub-Saharan Africa to almost zero, of US foreign and military aid, except in the cases of Israel and Egypt, has contributed to instability in the world's poorest countries.

The burden of the world role was borne more willingly during the Cold War when the Soviet Union was perceived as a direct military threat, and increased arms expenditure under Reagan (1980–8) was tolerated when Marxist insurrection threatened in Guatemala and Nicaragua (traditionally 'America's backyard'). There was also a marked tendency in Reagan to view the world as a struggle between good and evil: the former was represented by all that is best in America; the latter by secret conspiratorial meetings planning world domination, terrorism, drugs, alien contamination and massive influx of Latin immigrants.[5] The obsessive search for an enemy since the end of the Cold War is partly a result of the necessity of finding a threat, credible to broad sections of the American public, to sustain a willingness to pay for supporting a world role. When such a threat is not present, there is marked reluctance to support the use of US troops abroad, as shown by the precipitate 1993 withdrawal from Somalia after the death of eighteen US soldiers shocked American opinion.

Both the isolationist and global role tendencies contain within them strong pressures towards requiring conformity on the part of American citizens. These pressures are normal features of the politics of nationalism. The unique mission of America is supported by a simple, banal, beliefs in the virtues of saluting the flag, 'hailing the chief' (the President and Commander-in-Chief), and in the self-evident superiority of American values. Presidents who took the responsibility for a global role during the Cold War, from Truman through Kennedy to Reagan, unquestionably regarded America as the leader of the 'free world'. This rhetoric has continued, in a modified form, after the end of the Cold War with President Bush referring, on being elected, to America as 'the world's greatest nation' and President Clinton to 'the greatest nation in human history'. This continuing hymn to the glory and universal mission of America is designed to reinforce already existing beliefs and mobilise support for military action overseas such as the (very limited) interventions under both Bush, in the Middle East, and Clinton, in Kosovo. The rhetoric of sacrifice and valour in the service of the nation is necessary to underpin the global role of the USA.

The Russian trajectory has contrasted, in most respects, with the American. The expansion of Russia, from the modest beginnings of the late medieval Duchy of Muscovy, was greater than the American expansion. At its greatest extent in the nineteenth century, it stretched halfway round the world. But it was an empire built by war and conquest, and governed by autocratic tsars. Representative democracy did not take root in Russia until the 1990s and its future remains uncertain. The cement, which held the Russian people together before 1917, was not a democratic project but an autocratic administration and the Russian Orthodox Church. The tsarist autocracy was destroyed by the Bolshevik Revolution of 1917, and the Soviet Communist Party persecuted orthodoxy, but both have had a lasting effect on Russian nationalism.

The Orthodox Church cultivated and propagated the belief in the superiority of Russian spiritual values. This belief encouraged the view that Russia should stand apart from the rest of Europe and, with the idea of Moscow as the 'Third Rome', that it was the home of values which were both universal and true. The tsars helped to embed beliefs that Russia was destined to be a great power and yet was vulnerable because it was socially and, above all, technologically backward. The most celebrated of all the Russian tsars, Peter the Great, is an emblematic figure in that he established Russia as a Baltic and European power but, at the same time, was concerned to introduce Western ideas and technologies into Russia. From his reign (1682–1725) there has been a tension between 'westernisers' and 'slavophiles' which persists today. For westernisers, the salvation of Russia lay in adopting Western ideas and methods in order to become a great power. For slavophiles, the West had to be rejected because it would corrupt what was best and most virtuous in Russia.[6]

The Bolshevik Revolution, however, marked an apparently sharp discontinuity in the development of the Russian sense of nationhood. The official communist ideology, as noted above, was both a rejection of the Russian past and a claim to represent certain new universal truths. But there is a parallel, drawn by Leo Trotsky and others, between the French Revolution and the Russian Revolution. Both commenced with an appeal to universal truths but were soon transformed into projects to advance the interests of their respective states and ruling groups. The French revolutionary armies in the 1790s saw themselves not as conquerors but as liberators in the service of the universal principles, Liberty, Equality, Fraternity, and the Rights of Man.

They were on a crusade to rescue oppressed peoples from oppression, religious bigotry and aristocratic privilege. In the case of the Soviet Union, the internationalist rhetoric was as strong as with the French revolutionaries, but this time in the cause of the working class, which would overturn capitalism and install a conflict-free, property-less socialist society. This creed accorded well with a certain messianic strand in Russian religious thinking which had contributed much to the sense of Russian nationhood.

Tsarist Russia and the USSR were, however, multinational states dominated by ethnic Russians. After the revolution, the treatment of the non-Russian peoples was justified in Marxist terms but the policy was nonetheless an expression of Russian nationalism. Self-determination for the subject peoples of Tsarist Russia, proclaimed by Lenin in 1917, was quickly abandoned. Priority was given to a defence of the revolutionary homeland against intervention by the Western powers and against the internal threat of the White Russian armies. Russian nationalism (expressions of superiority over other peoples of the USSR and nationalist objectives in foreign policy) reappeared. With the victory of the Red armies over the White armies, securing and spreading socialism by armed force to the old territories of the Russian Empire became the prime objective. The failure of attempts at revolution in West Europe led to the Stalinist programme of 'socialism in one country'. Accompanied by the setting up of the third international of communist parties (the Comintern), internationalist ideology became an instrument of Soviet foreign policy. Russians dominated the Communist Party and the state institutions of the USSR, and the international communist movement.

The official ideology of the USSR also allowed a temporarily successful synthesis between two strands of Russian nationalism, the westernising and the slavophile. The Bolsheviks had adopted from the West both a philosophy and industrial technologies but the Soviet Russian way was presented as at the vanguard of progress and on the path to the future salvation of mankind. As external threats grew more menacing in the 1930s, openly nationalist themes became more evident. Internally, a symbolic change occurred with the dissolution in 1937 of the committee charged with latinising the Russian alphabet. At the same time, the Russian language was designated as the 'international language of socialist culture' together with the adoption of the patriotic teaching of Russian history in schools.

Stalin, having decided that it was prudent to come to an arrangement with Hitler in the Nazi–Soviet Pact of 1939, was surprised by the German attack in 1941 and ill-prepared for it. He had the difficult task of rallying a people, some of whom regarded the Nazis as liberators, to a desperate defence of the Soviet Union. He notoriously changed official propaganda from the building of socialism to the patriotism of 'eternal' Russia. The themes of revolutionary Marxism were downgraded in favour of the defence of the homeland and with this strategy went the abandonment of religious persecution and the mobilisation of religious sentiment in the cause of the defence of Holy Russia.

The superiority of the Soviet system, particularly its capacity to produce tanks, aeroplanes and subsequently missiles, was also constantly vaunted. It was claimed that Russian economic organisation was more just and equitable in that workers were not exploited by private capitalists. These two later became the major themes of Soviet propaganda at the end of the war (and were fervently believed by many Western intellectuals, communists and fellow travellers). They formed the basis of the legitimation of Soviet rule in Eastern Europe in the post-war period. Russian nationalism, the state nationalism of the USSR and the rhetoric of international communism became indissolubly linked in a powerful and threatening combination. There was little doubt in the vast majority of Western political elites believed that communism was an instrument in Soviet foreign policy to promote the domination of Russians over other peoples.

Russian and American Nationalism Compared

Russian and American convictions that their nation has unique virtues which should be propagated to the rest of the world have parallels. During the high tide of nationalism, from 1880 to 1914, many German, French and British intellectuals, as well as broad sections of public opinion thought similarly. This conviction disappeared in Germany, at least for a time, with the catastrophe of the Second World War but lingered in France and in Britain, especially in terms of belief in the benefits to other countries of the export of their institutional practices. French universalist rhetoric derived from the Revolution, fully displayed in the bicentenary celebrations of the French Revolution in 1989, and pride in the French cultural tradition made belief in the universal benefits of French civilisation seem more enduring than the British. The British believed in the superiority of their institutions which, they thought, embodied certain political virtues — moderation, tolerance, fair play, integrity, acceptance of the rules of the game. Such a belief contributed to the view that if British virtues and British practices spread to the rest of the world, it would be in everybody's interest.

As already noted, the British (now perhaps only the English) were of the opinion that the British were patriotic whilst other peoples were nationalistic. This is to regard nationalism as a sort of political pathology, or at least an undesirable political outlook, which provokes tensions and conflicts. This outlook was undoubtedly shared by the Americans and the Russians, who scarcely recognised their own nationalist assumptions, during the Cold War period. The Russians described their struggle during World War II as 'the Great Patriotic War' which inevitably seemed to them a defensive struggle against a virulently nationalist and aggressive power. In the aftermath of the war, they felt menaced by hostile capitalist powers, which possessed superior weapons technologies. Hence they engaged in propaganda campaigns, assisted by Western communist parties, in favour of peace and disarmament. However, they engaged in apparently aggressive acts such as the Berlin Blockade, backed communist-led wars in Korea and Indo-China and ruthlessly suppressed dissent in the East European satellite states. Governments in Western Europe therefore considered that the USSR was pursuing a policy of national aggrandisement under the cover of an internationalist ideology.

The Russians took a similar view of the United States. The rhetoric of the free world, human rights and collective security which was the ordinary currency of American discourse about international relations was usually regarded by the Russians as a blatantly hypocritical cover for American imperialism. The other countries in the American sphere of influence were regarded as being governed by cliques, either dupes or with an interest in the maintenance of the capitalist order. American support for democracy was regarded as a sham because of the American willingness to support dictatorial regimes in Latin America, Asia and Africa as long as they were anticommunist. The Americans gave this view credence by their willingness to collude in the overturning of regimes, whether elected or not, if they were at risk of take-over by left-wing and potentially pro-Soviet groups.

The effect of super-power hegemony on other countries in the two blocs was to turn nationalism into a diet mainly for domestic consumption. The system of blocs suppressed neither the sovereign nation-state nor nationalism but they more or less successfully subordinated them to a wider purpose. Throughout the Cold War politicians and the newspaper press as well as television journalism never ceased to address their audience as members of a nation. This was as true in the Eastern bloc as in the Western. Overt nationalism was encouraged in certain restricted and non-disruptive domains such as sporting competition. The dominance of the hegemonic powers within the blocs was never successfully challenged, except perhaps by de Gaulle in 1966 leaving the military structures, although not the alliance, of NATO. The main difficulties the super powers had with nationalism during the Cold War was in the non-aligned world. Third-World nationalists tended to play one super power off against the other to increase the supply of aid and armaments.

Conclusion

The outcome of the Cold War was, in the rhetoric of American presidents and in some academic writings such as those of Jeanne Kirkpatrick, a vindication of America. What happened, according to this school of thought, was an American victory of a particularly comprehensive kind—political, military, moral, foreign policy and economic. This assumption of no particular American responsibility for aggressive actions, except where legitimated by the actions of the other, no major errors in conducting the 'war', and a wholly benign outcome, is the epitome of nationalist discourse. This 'vindicationist' school of thought is not unique and limited to America—it characterised much of the governmental response and early accounts in the United Kingdom to the events of the Second World War.

Super-power confrontation during the Cold War also shows that universalist ideologies are not incompatible with promoting their national interest, sustaining national identity and espousing forms of nationalist ideology. The French revolutionaries of 1789–94, whose role in creating modern nationalism is central, had already shown this to be possible. The compatibility of nationalism and universalism has also been demonstrated in other contexts. The dominance in a population of a universalist religion—Catholicism, Orthodoxy or Islam—has not been a barrier to the success of nationalism and nationalist politicians in a wide variety of countries. A particular country can be represented as the vanguard or the purest form of the religion (France as the 'eldest daughter of the Church', Iran as representing the purest form of Islam, etc.).

One difficulty in understanding of American and Russian nationalism is that they do not conform to any model of the nation-state based on West European experience. The United States is the modern world's first 'new nation' in the sense that it is built on immigration. Others have followed—Canada, Australia, New Zealand—and all have been concerned with the integration of new arrivals and have also been self-conscious about their identity. They have been extraordinarily successful in creating stable political systems, which owed much to favourable material circumstances but also to the cultural process of creating founding myths, images and symbols. This continuing process is best illustrated in the way in which the foundation of their states is commemorated.[7]

Unlike the Americans and the Australians, the Russians did not decimate and marginalise the peoples who stood in their way during their great eastward expansion from the seventeenth to the nineteenth century. But they had an exalted vision of their country and people as 'Holy Russia' which crystallised around three poles—the imperial court, the bureaucracy and the peasant community. The idea of Russia was the bringing together of an unusual combination of elements in a quasi-mystical union. The communist experience transformed these elements but, in a denatured form, they can still be identified in contemporary Russia. Russia and America both demonstrate that the content of nationalisms can take very different, and almost diametrically opposed, forms and that these forms change over time.

Notes

1 See Kuisel, R. F. (1993) *Seducing the French: The Dilemma of Americanization*, Berkeley: University of California Press.

2 Billig, M. (1995) *Banal Nationalism*, London: Sage.

3 Zelinsky, W. (1988) *Nation into State: The Shifting Symbolic Functions of American Nationalism*, Chapel Hill: University of North Carolina Press, p. 6.

4 Hofstadter, R. (1979) *The Paranoid Style in American Politics*, Chicago: Chicago University Press.

5 Rogin, M. P. (1988) *Ronald Reagan, the Movie, and other Episodes in Political Demonology*, Chicago: University of Chicago Press.

6 See Walicki, A. (1975) *The Slavophile Controversy*, Oxford: Oxford University Press.

7 For a study of centennial and bicentennial celebrations see Spillman, L. (1997) *Nation and Commemoration: Creating National Identities in the United States and Australia*, Cambridge: Cambridge University Press.

Africa, Europe, and Asia in the Making of the 20th-Century Caribbean

Aisha Khan

The Caribbean of today began to form half a millennium ago, impelled by European colonial expansion harnessed to nascent capitalism and centered on resource extraction and sugar plantations producing for a global market. Within 50 years of Columbus's landing, indigenous Caribbean populations had been dramatically reduced, largely due to disease and the harsh conditions of labor imposed by the Spanish colonizers. This diminution of indigenous peoples was accompanied by the addition of foreigners from the "Old World" of Europe, Africa, and later Asia—a socially engineered assemblage of disparate ethnolinguistic groups under conditions of coerced labor and massive wealth accumulation. The imported groups included indentured Europeans, enslaved Africans, and, later, indentured Africans and Asians.

The transformations of the plantation system had various effects on the racial and demographic composition of different colonial territories. For example, the Hispanophone Caribbean, particularly Cuba and Puerto Rico, was not significantly developed for the global sugar market until the 19th century (although by mid-century Cuba and Puerto Rico had emerged as the first and third largest producers of sugar in the hemisphere), and the proportion of European populations compared to non-European populations was far greater there than in the Francophone and Anglophone colonies.

Over the 19th century, slavery was gradually abolished in the Caribbean. Newly independent Haiti (formerly Saint-Domingue) abolished slavery in 1804, followed by the British West Indies in 1838, the French possessions in 1848, all Dutch territories by 1863, and Cuba in 1886. Emancipation presented plantation owners with a dilemma:

Aisha Khan, "Africa, Europe, and Asia in the Making of the 20th-Century Caribbean," *The Caribbean: A History of the Region and Its Peoples*, pp. 399-413. Copyright © 2011 by University of Chicago Press. Reprinted with permission.

ensuring sugar and other production at high levels without the benefit of enslaved labor, or with diminishing numbers of freed workers willing to engage in plantation labor under the conditions offered by the plantocracy. One strategy implemented by Britain and France was that of freeing Africans from the slave trade of other European colonizers (Dutch, Spanish, Portuguese) and then sending them to British and French Caribbean colonies as indentured laborers. Almost 40,000 Africans were thus sent to the British West Indies and approximately 16,000 to the French West Indies (Schuler 1980).

Another form of 19th-century indenture brought immigrant laborers from Asia into the region. Organized as either state projects or private enterprises, indenture schemes evolved over eight decades and changed the demographic, cultural, and social terrain of the Caribbean as irrevocably as African slavery had done earlier. Between 1890 and 1939, for example, the Dutch recruited almost 33,000 Javanese, primarily from Central Java and Batavia, for their Caribbean colony of Suriname. The two principal source regions of indentured labor, however, were India and China. Itself a British colony, India experienced indenture as a government-regulated industry, with laborers recruited primarily from the regions of Oudh, Bihar, and Uttar Pradesh and shipped out from the ports of Calcutta and Madras. Between 1838 and 1917, almost 400,000 Indians arrived in the British Caribbean, the majority in Guyana and Trinidad. Although China was never colonized, its political vulnerability allowed private interests to orchestrate indenture schemes, largely from Canton. Between 1840 and 1875, approximately 142,000 indentured Chinese arrived in Cuba (Helly 1993, 20); from 1853 until 1866 and in trickles thereafter, about 18,000 Chinese were indentured in the British West Indies (Look Lai 1993, 18). Later—beginning around 1890, and concentrated between 1910 and 1940—a second wave of Chinese immigrants, this time not under indenture, arrived in the Caribbean.

The relationships of Asian indentured laborers with the local populations they encountered have influenced the values, identities, and cultural practices of their respective societies. To one extent or another, all the Asian immigrants were initially viewed by the locals as labor competition. Particularly where they constitute a large percentage of the population, Indians have been represented by local anti-indenture interests as "scab" labor, yet historically they also have been pitted against Afro-Caribbean workers. The tensions arising from perceived and actual labor conflicts have left a monumental legacy of racial politics in such contemporary societies as Guyana and Trinidad, where Indians represent more than 40% of the population. Perhaps because of their relatively smaller numbers, Chinese and Javanese laborers have had less fraught relationships with established populations, especially with those in similar occupational and class positions. In Cuba, for example, Chinese indentured laborers worked side by side with enslaved Africans. Enmity between these two groups was encouraged by colonial authorities as a divide-and-rule strategy, but tensions expressed in racial terms did not significantly persist into the present, either in Cuba or in other parts of the region. Once the Chinese found their economic niche primarily in the retail trades and shopkeeping, they no longer represented labor competition to other populations.

Figure 15.1 Newly arrived Indian laborers in Trinidad. Photograph (1897).

Migrants to the Caribbean from the Levant—known as "Syrians," "Syrian-Lebanese," or *árabes*—also began to arrive in the 1860s, increasing their numbers significantly by the 1890s. Most were Maronite Christians leaving Ottoman-occupied regions. Lebanese immigrants came first, followed by Syrians and Palestinians. Although they spread out across the Caribbean (and into Latin America, where they are also called *turcos*), certain communities predominated in particular countries. For example, of the three groups from the Levant, Lebanese comprise the largest population in Jamaica and the Dominican Republic, and Palestinians in Haiti (Nicholls 1980). These immigrants came as individuals, or sometimes in families, rather than in an organized migration arrangement; over the years, other family members followed. Although a few went into agricultural production, others became itinerant peddlers. Within a few generations these communities branched out into import-export trading, and today they comprise a large population of affluent and politically active citizens.

In addition to the transcontinental migrations, intraregional population movements have been crucial in contributing to the character of today's Caribbean. Although interisland labor migrations commenced soon after emancipation in the British West Indies, the late 19th century and first decades of the 20th saw the most dramatic population movements within the Caribbean basin. For example, between 1900 and 1914, some 60,000 Barbadians labored on the Panama Canal. Likewise, between 1917 and 1931, some 300,000 Jamaicans, Haitians, and other labor migrants from the region worked in Cuba on sugar plantations and in factories (De la Fuente 2001, 102), and several thousand more left the Leeward Islands to work in the US-owned sugar industry in the Dominican Republic (Conway 2003, 339). From the 1880s, Haitians crossed into the Dominican Republic to work on foreign-owned plantations as well as to farm smallholdings along the border. By 1935, Haitians in the Dominican Republic numbered perhaps 200,000—more than 10% of the national population (Andrews 2004, 140). Aside from the economic dimension of these population displacements, the resulting cultural and linguistic exchanges contributed significantly to the continuous formation of new social fabrics.

Interpreting "Creole" Societies

Four major languages are spoken in the Caribbean: Spanish, English, French, and Dutch. The 17 Caribbean countries that are predominantly Anglophone comprise more than 17% of the region's population, yet the total English-speaking population of the Caribbean is less than that of the Dominican Republic alone. These statistics clarify the demographic predominance of the Spanish-speaking countries of Cuba, Puerto Rico, and the Dominican Republic, which represent 61% of the Caribbean population. Of the 20% of Caribbean peoples who speak French or variations of French, three-quarters live in Haiti. The Dutch speakers of Suriname and the Netherlands Antilles represent another 2% (Knight 1995, 34). Other languages, spoken by fewer numbers of people, include Hindi and Javanese.

The languages of the European colonizers remain the official languages of formal Caribbean education and legal systems, but numerous African languages brought by the slaves fused with European, Asian, and Amerindian languages to create numerous "creole" languages, which are the spoken vernaculars of everyday life in a number of Caribbean countries. Most Caribbean creole languages are young as languages go, having existed for not more than two or three centuries. Today, however, there are growing written literatures in creole languages, and movements to promote the languages to equal standing as vehicles of formal instruction and communication. Among the most familiar examples is Haitian Kreyol, the spoken language of approximately 12 million insular and diasporic Haitians, which along with French has been an official language in Haiti since 1961. Other widely spoken creoles include Jamaican patois, which is spoken by about four million people in and outside Jamaica, and the patois of Trinidad and Tobago, a historical legacy primarily of French on Trinidadian English, which has been in decline since about the mid-20th century. In Suriname, Sranan Tongo is the language of approximately 300,000 people; in Aruba, Bonaire, and Curaçao, Papiamento is spoken by more than 350,000. And although the varieties of Spanish spoken in Cuba, Puerto Rico, and the Dominican Republic share a number of linguistic properties, they also have discernable differences based on geographic location and local histories.

As a region whose very foundations lie in multiple origins—assorted languages, varied religions, diverse worldviews, contrasting cultural traditions—the Caribbean has long been represented by observers, local and international alike, as the epitome of heterogeneity (Trouillot 1992; Glissant 1995). For more than a century, the region has been the object of attempts to explain cultural change over time as phenotypically and culturally heterogeneous peoples come into what is commonly known as "culture contact" and undergo the cultural transformations that such contact engenders. The questions about how cultures retain or lose continuity across vast geographical spaces (for example, after transatlantic migrations) and over extended periods of time (from the colonial period to the present), how the dynamics of unequal power relations foster or challenge cultural assimilation in new environments, and how identities and worldviews are forged in the process remain central to the study of Caribbean cultures. And certain concepts that have emerged from this study—creole, creolization, *creolité*, survivals, retentions, transculturation, and syncretism—have achieved much broader usage.

From its colonization, the Caribbean has represented newness, which Europeans captured in the term "creole." When applied to the region, the Spanish word *criollo* and the Portuguese word *crioulo* (derived from the verb *criar*, "to raise or bring up") signified something or someone originating in Europe (or Africa) and reproducing itself in the New World. Thus animals, plants, and people could all be designated as creole. Creole people were the descendants of Europeans or Africans born in the Caribbean, as well as the offspring of African and European parents. Inherent in the idea of creole identity was an assumption that being born in the Caribbean or being the "mixed" descendant of two racially differentiated parents meant losing one's ancestral cultural heritage.

Many of the earliest and most important social science studies of creole identity in the Caribbean were concerned specifically with Afro-Caribbean populations. They framed the question of cultural change over time in terms of the search for cultural heritage through "survivals" (or "retentions") and reinterpretations. Heralded in North America by anthropologists Melville and Frances Herskovits, this approach emphasized empirical evidence: the prevalence and intensity of survivals—as perceived by the Herskovitses in, for example, art forms, cuisine, technology, language, and religion—could prove cultural continuity between Africa and the Americas. As debates about African survivals progressed, however, the emphasis shifted from observable traits in the identification and study of cultural forms toward values, style, and systems of relationships.

While retaining an assumption that creole identity involves the loss of former cultural heritage in the process of forging new cultural adaptations, this shift brought greater interest in the variations of cultural forms and identities produced from dissimilar types. Thus the question of how new, creole types were produced became as much a focus of study as the types themselves. The creation of models to explain these processes emerged from different thinkers throughout the Hispanophone, Anglophone, and Francophone Caribbean. Among the most influential of these were Fernando Ortiz's early 20th-century model of *transculturación* based on Cuba, Edward Kamau Brathwaite's mid-20th-century model of creolization derived from Jamaica, and Jean Bernabe, Patrick Chamoiseau, and Raphael Confiant's (1993) late 20th-century model of *creolité* based on Martinique.

Ortiz coined the term "transculturation" as a way to interpret the multiplicity of histories, cultures, languages, religions, and worldviews that collectively form the Caribbean, and to express the various phases of the processes of transition from one culture to another. Ortiz saw these processes as entailing more than the simple and passive acquisition of, or submission to, other cultures, which he equated with "acculturation." Instead, transculturation involved the simultaneous loss or displacement of a preceding culture ("deculturation") as well as the resultant creation of new cultural phenomena ("neoculturation") (Ortiz 1995, 102– 3). Parsing the concept into processes, or active elements, allows a highlighting of the ways in which subjugated peoples create their own versions of the dominant culture.

In the Anglophone Caribbean, Brathwaite's analysis of what he called the "creole society" of Jamaica emphasized the creation of new forms through the synthesis of existing ones. Arguing against understanding black and white populations as "separate nuclear units," Brathwaite saw them as being "contributory parts of a whole" that produce a uniquely Caribbean culture. Creolization here represents the potential for social integration and unity, where the "mixed" population serves "as a bridge, a kind of social cement" that integrates society (Brathwaite 1971, 307, 305). In calling for a renewed emphasis on creole identity and the literary value of the creole language, the most recent Francophone *creoliste* writers and activists celebrate the heterogeneous dimensions that together comprise the Caribbean or, in the words of Martinican poet and writer Edouard Glissant, constitute *Antillanité* (Caribbeanness). The *creoliste* position, along with those of other thinkers, points to the abiding debates about how to characterize and give meaning to the forms of diversity so apparent in the region.

Ideologies of Race, Color, and Class

From the earliest days of colonial rule, the Caribbean social and moral order was based on ranked gradations of "races" and "colors" represented by such physical attributes as skin color, hair texture, and facial features. These criteria were treated as literal descriptions of appearance, and their presumed fixed qualities formed a hierarchy of identities—from "white" at the top to "black" at the bottom, with various mixtures and gradations in between—supported by legal structures as well as social values and mores. Consequently, for much of Caribbean history, race and color also have connoted social position and class status. Yet the recognition of a vertical color continuum separates the Caribbean from the rigid binary racial logic of the United States.

Given the legacies of colonial rule and ideology, color and race are still commonly used in daily conversation as idioms for social organization. In Jamaica, for example, the color term "brown" (or "colored") serves as a category of racial identity but also connotes middle-class status. Color terms are necessarily relational; being "white" or "brown" or "black" necessarily means not being something else. In Haiti, *mulâtre* is an in-between term connoting a mixture of "black" and "white," flexible in its interpretation yet typically positioned above "black" and below "white." In the Dominican Republic, *indio* literally translates as "Indian," suggesting indigenous heritage, but its contemporary application signifies a lighter skin color (and perhaps straight hair)—someone not "black," yet also not "white." In Martinique, *beke* refers to French "white" slave owners and their descendants. "Trinidad white" and "French creole" have served as categories of racial identity in Trinidad, specifically distinguished from British, French, and Spanish "whites," who, in this racial accounting system, historically could claim to be "pure" white and, concomitantly, members of the upper classes. In Trinidad, the term "red" generally refers to a light-skinned individual of mixed "black" and "white" parentage (positioned toward the upper-status end), while in Barbados it is also a historical reference to "red legs" communities—poor whites who, from the days of the slave plantation, labored outdoors and hence were likely to get sunburned.

Mixedness can also refer to multiple combinations, not simply the amalgamation of "black" and "white." Thus, in the Francophone Caribbean, the term *marabou* refers to a black-white-Amerindian combination. In Trinidad the term "Spanish" should be interpreted as if in quotation marks, indicating a particular and fluctuating combination of local criteria, including area of origin (Venezuela, or certain locations in Trinidad with historical concentrations of Spaniards, Amerindians, and Venezuelan immigrant labor), skin color (some variation of "brown" or "red"), hair texture (not curly), and self-ascription (Khan 1993).

Notably, these terminologies are based on an African-European axis: the hierarchical color continuum does not lexically include South Asians or Chinese, or the mixed offspring of South Asian or Chinese and European parents. Though the term *achinado* is used in Cuba to index Chinese phenotypical features (as, for example, in *mulato achinado*), there is only one term, *dougla*—common in Guyana and Trinidad—indicating individuals of mixed South Asian and African descent. *Indio* (Amerindian) in the Hispanophone Caribbean and "Spanish" or "French creole" in Trinidad are not color terms per se, but are measured along the continuum of black and white ancestry. "Indian" (South Asian), "Chinese," and "Syrian-Lebanese" in the Anglophone Caribbean, "Hindustani" in the Dutch Caribbean, and *Hindou* in the Francophone Caribbean are common categories not amalgamated into the black-white lexicon.

Twentieth-century anticolonial movements encouraged Caribbean societies to project themselves as modern, sovereign democracies. Race and color were thus applied by political leaders to nationalist projects, with local perceptions of cultural, racial, and color heterogeneity representing the ideal of "unity in diversity": multicultural tolerance and harmony. In this mid-century nationalist narrative, evident throughout the region, evoking creolization became tantamount to celebrating the strengths of cultural heterogeneity. The claimed character of such "creole" societies as Trinidad, Guyana, Suriname, Jamaica, Belize, Cuba, Martinique, Curaçao, and French Guiana is a national identity in which culturally and racially distinct groups cooperatively coexist as united, independent nations. Claims about the strengths of diversity are deliberated across the region, and the discussion largely reflects debate about representation—that is, which constituent cultural-racial groups will be at the forefront of defining national identity and, by implication, national interests. The lack of any uniform local understanding of what constitutes "diversity" across the region complicates these claims and the narrative of harmony; each nation-state's self-perception is configured somewhat differently in terms of its cultural, religious, racial, and ethnic composition. Thus nationalist projects tackle the broad Caribbean theme of multiplicity in historically and ideologically particularistic ways. Whatever direction these discussions take, however, they show no indication of muting the salience of racial accounting and color categories in the region.

Gender and Kinship

Caribbean kinship forms have been shaped by the different governing structures and sociocultural character of European colonizers. In the British-influenced Commonwealth West Indies, for example, social welfare policy played a significant role in shaping family life, particularly during the period of high social unrest between the two world wars. Throughout the wider Caribbean, however, kinship is understood to have certain common patterns that transcend specific colonial identities. These patterns derive largely from two contexts that share certain region-wide similarities: slave plantation society, and class stratification systems that arose after emancipation. Because all the populations associated with slavery are African in origin, for example, kinship practices among Afro-Caribbeans have generally been distinguished in terms of social class positions rather than in terms of the ethnic, cultural, or racial differences that exist among these populations. Such differences come into play only when kinship practices are compared across the ethnoracially, culturally heterogeneous groups of the region, usually based on divisions among "African," "European," and "Asian" (or "East Indian") peoples.

In slave plantation societies, West African kinship forms met the constraints and agendas of European colonial rule. Although each colony had legal structures to control slaves' cultural practices, patterns of conjugality and religious worship largely remained outside the purview of the master's control. Over time, many forms of mating and cohabitation—from legal marriage to extra-residential unions, with a range of arrangements in between—became part of the social landscape. Such flexible diversity in domestic forms contributed significantly to the idea that the Caribbean consisted of, at best, fluidly adaptive social institutions and, at worst, unstable ones—in alleged contrast to European and North American society. Until the late 20th century many policy makers, scholars, and other observers assumed that among Afro-Caribbean peoples, corporate kinship groups were less important than dyadic ties between individuals. Today these assumptions are under more careful scrutiny, and the gender dynamics of Caribbean kinship are primarily understood as constructive responses to such shifting forces as migration, educational opportunity, and labor conditions.

In the context of post-emancipation society, the values and behaviors associated with different classes reflect a status hierarchy. According to a model first elaborated by anthropologist Peter Wilson (1973), Afro-Caribbean women are judged on their "respectability," which reflects bourgeois European colonial values, while Afro-Caribbean working-class men are judged on their "reputation," which reflects local or creole values and a disinclination to emulate European values and standards of behavior (nuclear families, wage employment, formal education, obedience to social and legal norms, self-control). Reputation is meant to convey an alternative system of status and prestige, one that emphasizes verbal dexterity, ease and mobility in the public sphere, sexual prowess, and lack of restraint in engaging in these behaviors. Although this model has been critiqued for its oversimplified binary opposition of gender roles—for example, Caribbean women engage in their own practices of "reputation"—it remains useful for understanding the ways in which gender in the Caribbean is culturally expressed and ideologically linked to class divisions.

Along with class differences, ethnocultural distinctions are significant in the formation and representation of Caribbean kinship practices. Like Afro-Caribbean peoples, Indo-Caribbeans who settled in the region were a diverse population. They came from various parts of the Indian subcontinent, spoke several languages (notably Hindi, Urdu, and a dialect called Bhojpuri), belonged to different religions (primarily Hinduism and Islam), and had a number of family and household arrangements. But Indo-Caribbean populations differed from their Afro-Caribbean and other neighbors in some key respects. Whereas plantocracies throughout the region discouraged enslaved Africans from practicing their cultural traditions, colonial authorities in the age of the indentured labor system were more flexible regarding Indian immigrants' activities. Practices and observances that were thought to hinder plantation production were curtailed, but cultural life was far freer than under slavery. Yet Hindu and Muslim marriages were not legalized in the Caribbean until the mid-20th century, presenting challenges for Indo-Caribbeans not faced by their neighbors who practiced Christianity or Afro-European religions. Moreover, marriages between Indo-Caribbeans reflected cultural traditions brought from the subcontinent—that is, they were often arranged, with families seeking potential mates for their children through the services of matchmakers from the community. This practice continues today, though less formally and much less frequently.

Cosmologies and Belief Systems

The basic distinction made between religions local to the Caribbean and those derived from outside the region raises an interesting question about the meaning of "indigenous." Because the first peoples to inhabit the region, Amerindians, succumbed very early to European conquest, there are no indigenous religions in the Caribbean, in the sense that the term is used to describe religions of native peoples in Latin and North America. Rather, all Caribbean religions have undergone transformation over time and derive from predecessor religions that were variegated in their belief and practice. Yet because of the legacy of cultural creolization, the Caribbean represents a major crucible of creole, or syncretic, religions.

As in other parts of the world, religion has offered the peoples of the Caribbean a way to interpret and engage past and present social conditions and forms of inequality. Among the most well known examples is the role of vodou priests and priestesses in slave revolts, such as

Boukman's 1791 insurgency, which is thought to have initiated the Haitian Revolution. Similarly, in 1884, in response to British colonial curtailments, the insistence of Trinidadian Muslims and Hindus on carrying on Hosay (the Caribbean version of Muharram, the Shi'a Muslim ritual mourning the martyrdom of the Prophet Mohammed's grandson, Imam Hussain) resulted in Trinidad's "Hosay Riots."

At the same time, Caribbean religions offer alleviation of natural and supernatural distress, notably problems of health, success, and fidelity. For example, brujería in Puerto Rico—a blend of popular Catholicism, Afro-Latin religions, French spiritism, and folk Protestantism—engages in healing, advocacy, and solving both metaphysical and practical problems among populations who have few alternatives or who avail themselves of a number of religious options (Romberg 2003). Although they possess their own distinctive histories, characteristics, and modes of practice, vernacular religions such as Haitian vodou, Cuban Santería, and Trinidadian orisha also serve such needs. And institutionalized forms of religious practice such as Christianity, Islam, Judaism, and Hinduism have found fertile ground in the region. Associated with European colonizers, the Catholic and Protestant churches have worked to conserve their formal traditions and doctrines even under the forces of transformation and syncretism. Hindu and Muslim communities in the region have sponsored missionaries and educators from India since the mid-19th century and from Pakistan in the 20th.

Caribbean religions are among the most complex examples of the emergence and transformation of cultural lifeworlds in the Americas. Given their numerous sources and formations, and their tendency to eschew orthodox axioms in favor of heterodox practices guided by a few broad principles, religions emerging from the Caribbean are characterized by amalgamation and recombination. Added to syncretic or creole religions deriving from the Caribbean context are religions whose doctrines and belief systems, themselves varied and changing over time, derive from "Old World" origins. Thus, today even a cursory list of religions in the region would be long—Catholicism, Protestantism, evangelical and Pentecostal movements, Judaism, Hinduism, vodou, Santería, Islam, espiritismo, Rastafari, and orisha—made even longer by a number of demographically smaller but socially significant traditions such as Kali worship in Guyana, brujería and Mita worship in Puerto Rico, Quimbois in Martinique, and Winti in Suriname.

Equally important are historical and contemporary magical practices (often subsumed under the term "obeah") that involve supernatural powers, deriving largely from West African divination and healing practices and, to a lesser extent, Hindu and Christian cosmologies. The meaning of obeah has changed over the centuries. Among 17th-to 19th-century Africans and Afro-Caribbeans it was associated with salutary objectives, such as alleviating illness, protecting against harm, and avenging wrongs. Euro-colonial and local bourgeois ideologies emphasized the dangerous aspects of obeah, often equating it with Judeo-Christian interpretations of evil forces. Often, positive and negative assessments existed simultaneously, making local opinion about obeah ambiguous. Today, as in earlier eras, its practice represents tensions between the ways in which practitioners interpret obeah's methods and objectives, and the ways in which those methods and objectives are perceived by outsiders.

Caribbean religions are expressions of traditions of creativity, resistance, and flexibility that continuously build on as well as disassemble older and current forms of knowledge, heritage, and custom. The challenge in understanding them is to grasp that difference and similarity exist at the same time. Hinduism, as practiced by the progeny of indentured laborers, reflects both the remembered traditions that early immigrants brought with them from India and a contemporary global Hinduism that travels across the Hindu diaspora. While Caribbean Hindus may interpret their forms of worship as replicating those in India, they also recognize that certain transformations and syncretisms have occurred for almost 170 years in the Caribbean.

In contrast, Rastafari's origins are in Jamaica, where religious movements based in Afro-Caribbean folk Christianity, the pan-Africanism of Marcus Garvey, grassroots reinterpretations of the Old Testament, and the veneration of Haile Selassie of Ethiopia coalesced in the 1930s, giving rise to the religious, philosophical, and political worldview of today's Rastafari movement. In it, Africa plays a great symbolic role as a place of desired return and the antithesis of "Babylon"—all places and forms of consciousness in which predatory relationships and "mental slavery" abound. Yet although thus memorialized, Africa is not literally remembered by many Rastafari, the vast majority of whom have never had direct experience with societies and cultures in Africa or Ethiopia (two terms often used synonymously). Nonetheless, Africa/Ethiopia represents for them an indispensable emblem of unity, self-determination, authenticity, and morality.

Figure 15.2 A tadja at Hosay in St. James, Trinidad. Photograph by Dr. Ted Hill (1950s).

Islam, meanwhile, first came to the Caribbean as the religion of some African slaves. With the advent of indentured laborers from India, Islam gained an increased presence in the region. Notable today are the numerous *masjids* (mosques) that dot the landscape of many countries, from Trinidad to Guyana, Puerto Rico, and Suriname. Some masjids are humble, built to serve small communities and local villages; others are grand, built as centers of learning as well as centers of worship for larger populations in the towns and cities. In these places of worship that serve *jamaats* (congregations) large and small, imams (religious leaders) work to preserve the *Sunnah* (Muslim way of life). At the same time, Islam in the Caribbean encapsulates the simultaneous inclusiveness and exclusions of a religion claimed by different ethnic groups, practiced according to divergent interpretations of doctrine, and, in certain contexts, participated in by non-Muslims. This is perhaps best seen in the ritual of Hosay, the Caribbean version of Shi'a Islam's commemoration, Muharram.

Historically spread throughout the Anglophone Caribbean, today Hosay is practiced on a major scale only in Trinidad, where it is simultaneously an important religious event, a freighted political statement, an embattled heritage claim, and a multicultural symbol. Mourners of Hussain march with enormous, elaborate representations of the *tadjas* (*tazzias*, or representations of the martyrs' tombs; see Figure 15.2). This procession has been treated by some local participants less like a sacred commemoration than like a parade, where music and general revelry may occur on the sidelines. Despite its Muslim origins, Hosay in Trinidad also has always involved Hindus and Afro-Trinidadians. Hindus have long been key participants in the building of the tadjas, and Afro-Trinidadians traditionally have played a significant role as drummers as well as bearers (along with Hindu and Muslim Indo-Trinidadians) of the tadjas in procession. Moreover, Hindus sometimes make their own vows and offerings during Hosay. This ritual was the only significant element in the Indian cultural repertoire that provided a social bridge to the rest of 19th-century Trinidadian society (Singh 1988, 4). Given its multiple interpretations and diverse participants, Hosay lends a distinctive religious and cultural tenor to Trinidad's national culture. The combination of participants and their varied forms of involvement has given rise to debates among Muslims and non-Muslims about the authenticity of Hosay and its appropriateness in Islam. Other observers argue that this ceremony's heterogeneity and cooperation counters the divide-and-rule antagonism among subordinate groups (notably Afro-and Indo-Caribbeans) encouraged by British colonizers, offering a natural space for a creole unity.

Religion is just one of innumerable examples of the ways in which Africa, Europe, and Asia have together produced the 20th-century Caribbean. In the organization of labor, language, group identities, and kinship as well as religion, these Old World continents inspired the creation of many multidimensional New World cultures and societies. The productive relationship between "old" (existing) and "new" (emerging) that gave rise to the Caribbean of today must be understood as a consequence of the protracted and often painful tension between domination (initiated by the articulation of colonialism and capitalism, which significantly defined the region) and resistance (local forms of accommodation and challenge) to that domination. The 20th-century Caribbean represents one of the most diverse places on earth; this diversity is richly symbolic of the workings of the human imagination in both felicitous and forbidding circumstances.

Works Cited

Andrews, George Reid. 2004. *Afro-Latin America, 1800–2000*. New York: Oxford University Press.

Bernabe, Jean, Patrick Chamoiseau, and Raphael Confiant. 1989. *Eloge de la creolite*. Paris: Gallimard.

Brathwaite, Edward Kamau. 1971. *The Development of Creole Society in Jamaica, 1770–1820*. Oxford: Clarendon Press.

Conway, Dennis. 2003. "The Caribbean Diaspora." In *Understanding the Contemporary Caribbean*, edited by Richard S. Hillman and Thomas J. D'Agostino, 333–53. Boulder, CO: Lynne Rienner.

De la Fuente, Alejandro. 2001. *A Nation for All: Race, Inequality, and Politics in Twentieth-Century Cuba*. Chapel Hill: University of North Carolina Press.

Glissant, Edouard. 1995. "Creolization in the Making of the Americas." In *Race, Discourse, and the Origin of the Americas*, edited by V. L. Hyatt and R. Nettleford, 268–75. Washington, DC: Smithsonian Institution Press.

Helly, Dorothy, ed. 1993. *The Cuba Commission Report: A Hidden History of the Chinese in Cuba*. Baltimore: Johns Hopkins University Press.

Khan, Aisha. 1993. "What is 'a Spanish'? Ambiguity and Mixed Ethnicity in Trinidad." In *Trinidad Ethnicity*, edited by Kevin Yelvington, 180–207. Knoxville: University of Tennessee Press.

Knight, Franklin. 1995. *Race, Ethnicity, and Class: Forging the Plural Society in Latin America and the Caribbean*. Waco, TX: Markham Press Fund.

Look Lai, Walton. 1993. *Indentured Labor, Caribbean Sugar*. Baltimore: Johns Hopkins University Press.

Nicholls, David. 1980. *Arabs of the Greater Antilles*. New York: Research Institute for the Study of Man.

Ortiz, Fernando. 1995. *Cuban Counterpoint: Tobacco and Sugar*. Durham, NC: Duke University Press.

Romberg, Raquel. 2003. *Witchcraft and Welfare: Spiritual Capital and the Business of Magic in Modern Puerto Rico*. Austin: University of Texas Press.

Schuler, Monica. 1980. *"Alas, Alas, Kongo": A Social History of Indentured African Immigration into Jamaica, 1841–1865*. Baltimore: Johns Hopkins University Press.

Singh, Kelvin. 1988. *Bloodstained Tombs: The Muharram Massacre 1884*. London: Macmillan Caribbean.

Trouillot, Michel-Rolph. 1992. "The Caribbean Region: An Open Frontier in Anthropological Theory." *Annual Review of Anthropology* 21:19–42.

Wilson, Peter. 1973. *Crab Antics: A Caribbean Case Study of the Conflict between Reputation and Respectability*. New Haven: Yale University Press.

Credit

- Fig. 15.2: Copyright © Ted Hill (CC BY-SA 3.0) at https://kids.kiddle.co/Image:A_tadjah_at_Hosay.jpg.

Africa

Decolonization and Independence, 1945–2007

Antony Best, Jussi M. Hanhimäki, and Joseph A. Maiolo

Introduction

In most accounts of the history of the twentieth century it is fair to say that references to Africa are often few and far between. Arguably this is because the prevailing image in the West of the continent is that it is one locked in an endless cycle of corruption, poverty and political violence, which brings misery to Africans but has little impact on international politics as a whole. However, it is wrong to see Africa in this simplistic way, for the history of the continent involves some of the key themes of the second half of the twentieth century, such as the end of European imperialism, the debate about underdevelopment and the degree to which the Cold War paradigm dominated international politics. Indeed, few areas of the world have changed so drastically in a political sense since 1945. When the Second World War came to an end, Africa remained very largely under the control of European imperial Powers and with no prospect of independence being offered in the immediate future. Yet within the space of twenty years most of the continent had thrown off the shackles of direct colonial rule, and by 1994 the last vestiges of white minority rule had disappeared completely with the collapse of **apartheid**. In addition, Africa is important because it is seen so often in the West as a prime example of how **Third World** poverty perpetuates itself. This naturally raises the question of why this should be so. Has Africa simply been singularly unfortunate in its rulers since independence? Or are its problems the result of the global Cold War and the machinations of international capitalism? Or is it that the factors that have led to endemic corruption and instability are inextricably linked to its colonial past?

Antony Best, Jussi M. Hanhimäki, and Joseph A. Maiolo, "Africa: Decolonization and Independence, 1945-2007," *International History of the Twentieth Century and Beyond*, pp. 404-428. Copyright © 2008 by Taylor & Francis Group. Reprinted with permission.

The End of Empire

Apart from the campaigns in East and North Africa, Africa largely escaped the fighting that ravaged the world between 1939 and 1945. The continent was not, however, by any means isolated from the war, for the Allied need to mobilize colonial resources to defeat the Tripartite Powers led to a number of significant developments. The most obvious was that the loss of the raw materials of South-East Asia in 1941–42 necessitated the rapid expansion of production of resources such as rubber and tin in the African colonies. In addition, the war was important because it saw an even more extensive mobilization of the population than had occurred in 1914–18, some 374,000 Africans being recruited into the British armed forces alone. Those who served overseas were often changed by the experience, returning home more politically conscious than before and keen to achieve European standards of living.

Recognizing that the continent was changing, some of the colonial Powers, most notably Britain and France, saw the necessity during and immediately after the war for a degree of constitutional reform that, by increasing local representation, would legitimize the drive towards economic development. In 1944 the French held a conference at Brazzaville in Equatorial Africa, at which it was agreed to end forced labour, to expand African involvement in local politics and to establish a constituent assembly in Paris that would draw up a constitution for a new French Union. Meanwhile in West Africa, Britain decided in 1946 to establish an African majority in the legislative councils of Nigeria and the Gold Coast (Ghana) and to extend the powers of these bodies.

It would, however, be a mistake to see these reforms as part of a programme that was intended to lead to independence in the near future. The French at Brazzaville made it clear that independence was not on their agenda, while in 1943 the British colonial secretary, Oliver Stanley, ruled out a transfer of power in Africa for generations to come. Instead these political reforms were designed to perpetuate imperial control, for the colonies, both during and after the war, were seen as vital for the future prosperity and security of the metropole. Indeed, once the Second World War came to an end, the European colonial Powers diverted more resources than ever to develop their African possessions. In 1945 the Labour government in Britain passed the second Colonial Development and Welfare Act, which provided £120 million for its colonies in Africa, the Caribbean and South-East Asia, while in 1947 the French established the *Fonds d'Investissement et de Développement Economique et Social des Territoires d'Outre-Mer* (FIDES). Between 1943 and 1957 FIDES invested $542 million in French West Africa alone, far outstripping the British effort to develop its colonies. This push for development came about because it was believed in Britain and France that an expansion of raw material production would increase the ability of their empires to earn dollars, thus assisting the post-war recovery of their metropolitan economies. In addition, it was hoped that greater mobilization of African resources would help to maintain Britain and France as world Powers able to operate independently of the United States and the Soviet Union.

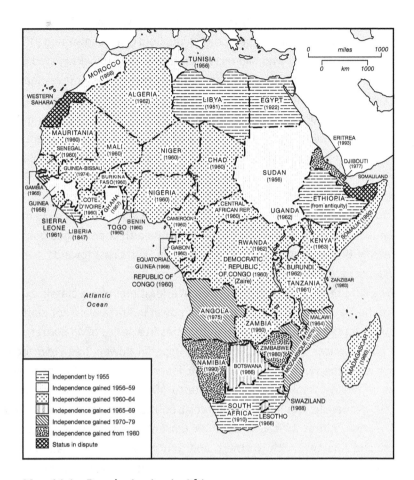

Map 16.1 Decolonization in Africa

Source: After Brown and Louis (1999)

APARTHEID

The Afrikaans word for racial segregation. Between 1948 and 1990 'apartheid' was the ideology of the Nationalist Party in South Africa

THIRD WORLD

A collective term of French origin for those states that are part of neither the developed capitalist world nor the communist bloc. It includes the states of Latin America, Africa, the Middle East, South Asia and South-East Asia. Also referred to as 'the South' in contrast to the developed 'North'.

DECOLONIZATION

The process whereby an imperial power gives up its formal authority over its colonies.
see Map 16.1

The hope that Africa would contribute to a return to prosperity and power turned out to be a chimera, not least because the very act of encouraging development led, as in the case of India before, to increasing political, economic and social unrest. Indeed, the drive for development proved to be one of the main causes of the rapid shift towards **decolonization** in Africa in the 1950s, for the social and economic discontent that it generated meant that those who preached the cause of liberation from colonial rule began to find a ready audience for their rhetoric.

This first became evident in February 1948 when riots broke out in Accra in the Gold Coast. The roots of this urban unrest lay in a number of factors arising out of the push for development, such as high inflation and discontent about employment prospects, particularly among recently demobilized soldiers, and the virtual monopoly that British companies exercised over imports. The

COMMONWEALTH, THE

An organization of independent self-governing states linked by their common ties to the former British Empire.

initial British reaction was to use the mailed fist and to arrest the leaders of the newly established nationalist party, the United Gold Coast Convention (UGCC), including an organizer who had recently returned from university studies in the United States and Britain, Kwame Nkrumah. However, after investigating the causes of the rioting, the British government decided that only further constitutional reform could bring about a return to stability. Accordingly, in 1949 the British introduced a new parliamentary system of government, believing that this would quieten discontent. This hope proved to be misplaced, for in 1951 Nkrumah's new political party, the Convention People's Party, which took a far more radical stance on self-government than the UGCC, won the first legislative elections. Aware that the choice lay between a rapid move towards self-government within the **Commonwealth** or prolonged political instability, Britain chose the former, setting the Gold Coast towards its path to independence as Ghana in 1957.

The case of the Gold Coast is instructive, for it provides a classic example of the way in which many transfers of power in Africa were not planned but were forced upon the colonial authorities in a series of *ad hoc* retreats and compromises. In many colonies the imperial Powers had clear ideas about what they wanted to achieve, but found that circumstances forced them to make compromises acceptable to African opinion. For example, Britain desired to establish a multiracial political system both in Kenya and in the Central African Federation (an entity that brought together Nyasaland [Malawi] with Northern and Southern Rhodesia [Zambia and Zimbabwe]), but was eventually forced to abandon these plans in the early 1960s and agree to independence under African majority rule. France, meanwhile, declared in 1958 its intention to turn its empire into a French Community which would allow the Equatorial and West African colonies to become states that controlled their own domestic affairs but co-operated with Paris over foreign affairs, security issues and overall economic policy. This bold initiative was, however, fatally undermined when Guinea voted against joining the Community and soon after Senegal and French Sudan (Mali) opted for full independence, leading to a general exodus which France had little choice but to accept. The Belgian Congo too was affected by this pattern of events. In January 1959, following riots in Leopoldville (Kinshasa), Belgium announced its intention to transfer power in four years' time, but the mounting pressures in the colony forced it to truncate this to a period of eighteen months, granting independence in June 1960.

Reinforcing this trend was the fact that where the colonial Powers did attempt to resist nationalism through the use of force, the results were often disastrous. The most obvious example of this was the French effort to defeat the challenge posed by the *Front de Libération National* (FLN) in Algeria between 1954 and 1962. The fact that Algeria contained a large number of European settlers and that it was constitutionally part of France meant that, as far as the government in Paris was concerned, its status was not negotiable. It therefore reacted to the FLN's war of national liberation with a savage campaign of repression. However, while France was able to stem the tide militarily, the political costs of the conflict proved very damaging and gradually sapped its spirit of defiance. A key element in this was that the FLN was very effective in presenting its cause to international opinion as symbolic of the Third World's struggle against colonialism. Accordingly, France's effort to force the Algerians into submission generated much international criticism, for it was made to appear as though it was attempting to hold back an irresistible moral force. French efforts to win back its esteem and to isolate the FLN, such as its decision in 1956 to grant independence to Morocco and Tunisia, proved to be in vain, for in the end there was no alternative to full Algerian independence. Eventually, realizing the damage that had been caused to French prestige and unity, in 1962 President de Gaulle consented in the Évian agreement to a transfer of power.

In the light of its agony in Algeria, it is not surprising that France largely avoided resisting African nationalism elsewhere. Indeed, Algeria generally heightened European sensitivities to the costs of 'holding on', for no state wished to find itself in the same morass. For example, the hard-line policy that the Conservative government of Harold Macmillan followed over Kenya and the Central African Federation was dealt a fatal blow in 1959 when there was public outcry over the revelation that the police in both colonies had acted with unnecessary brutality. In addition, Algeria was important because the FLN's ties with the leading Third World states and its occasional flirtations with the communist bloc confirmed to both the colonial Powers and the United States that it was better to make concessions over self-government in the short term than to risk radical or pro-Soviet national liberation movements taking power in the long term. The other side of the coin was that, for their part, nationalist governments and movements in the Third World played on the fears of the colonial Powers and their American patron by lauding the FLN, seeking ties with the Afro-Asian movement and hinting at the possibility of finding a sympathetic voice in Moscow or Beijing. They were therefore able to manipulate the Cold War for their own benefit.

Apart from the costs of resistance, one other factor played a key role in African decolonization, namely that as the capitalist world economy flourished under the umbrella of the **Bretton Woods** system, the imperial Powers found themselves less reliant on trade with their colonial possessions. Not surprisingly, this sapped their will to spend precious resources on areas that were now a drain on rather than a benefit to the metropolitan economy. Moreover, there remained the broad hope that the granting of independence in good time would involve a political transfer of power but not necessarily a change in economic ties, and that the large European trading concerns, such as Britain's United Africa Company, would therefore continue to flourish.

The result of the above pressures was that by 1966, when Botswana became independent, the majority of the territories that made up Africa had become sovereign states, the only significant

BRETTON WOODS

The site of an inter-Allied conference held in 1944 to discuss the post-war international economic order. The conference led to the establishment of the IMF and the World Bank. In the postwar era the links between these two institutions, the establishment of GATT and the convertibility of the dollar into gold were known as the Bretton Woods system. After the dollar's devaluation in 1971 the world moved to a system of floating exchange rates.

SELF-DETERMINATION

The idea that each national group has the right to establish its own national state. It is most often associated with the tenets of Wilsonian internationalism and became a key driving force in the struggle to end imperialism.

PAN-AFRICANISM

The belief that Africans wherever they live share common cultural and spiritual values. Pan-Africanism was an important influence on the rise of nationalist movements in Africa in the first half of the twentieth century, but after decolonization its impact waned as the new states were reluctant to compromise their independence.

exceptions being those colonies controlled by Portugal, the anomaly of Southern Rhodesia and South-West Africa (Namibia), which remained under the rule of South Africa. However, while this was a victory for the cause of **self-determination**, it came at a price, for now the new states faced the difficult task of plotting both their individual and collective fortunes. This involved a vast array of issues, including not just economic development and constitutional reform, but also whether there should be a move towards regional federations and perhaps eventually a united government of Africa.

The Rise and Fall of Pan-Africanism

One of the most important strands in the nationalist movements that developed in Africa from the early twentieth century onwards was the influence of pan-Africanist thought. **Pan-Africanism**, which stresses the cultural and spiritual unity of people of African descent, had its roots not in Africa itself but in the African diaspora, its leading lights being such figures as the American academic and writer W. E. B. Dubois and the Jamaican activist Marcus Garvey. However, in the 1930s and 1940s a number of African students from the British colonies, such as Nkrumah, Jomo Kenyatta from Kenya and Julius Nyerere from Tanganyika (Tanzania), became interested in pan-African thinking, and used its tenets in their respective struggles for liberation. Meanwhile, in the French Empire, figures such as the Senegalese poet Léopold Senghor developed their own *négritude* movement, which also stressed the cultural affinity of African peoples.

When the process of independence began in the mid-1950s, one important question was that of what influence pan-Africanism would have on the new Africa. As its fundamental belief was that all African peoples shared common social and cultural ties, the logic of pan-Africanism suggested that the continent should cast aside the artificial state boundaries established by the Europeans and move towards a federal form of government. This was certainly the view of Nkrumah who, as the leader of the first major Sub-Saharan state to achieve independence, was in a strong position to further this agenda. In April 1958 he convened a conference of the independent African states in Accra, and in December followed it with an All-African People's Conference which included delegates from countries still under colonial subjugation. In these gatherings he preached the cause of African unification, and added weight to his words by deeds, such as agreeing in November 1958 to form a loose union between Ghana and Guinea, to which Mali was added in 1961.

Nkrumah's ideas proved, however, to be extremely divisive. On one side, Ghana's stance won support from its fellow radical states in the Casablanca Group, such as Guinea, Mali, Morocco and the United Arab Republic. On the other, Nkrumah was opposed by the more numerous Monrovia Group—the traditionally independent states of Ethiopia and Liberia, as well as Nigeria, Sierra Leone and the majority of the former French colonies. Their opposition to Nkrumah's ideas rested on two factors. The first and most obvious was that the leaders who made up the Monrovia Group saw little benefit to themselves in merging their states into a larger political entity. Indeed, Nkrumah's vision only exacerbated disputes that had already appeared at a regional level. One of the reasons why the French Community had collapsed between 1958 and 1960 was the fact that tensions had grown up over the question of whether French West Africa should continue as a federation or become a series of sovereign independent states. In the end, the latter solution had been chosen, largely as a result of the vehement opposition to federalism of one of the most influential figures in Francophone Africa, Félix Houphouët-Boigny of the Ivory Coast. Having won the battle once, Houphouët-Boigny had no intention of losing the second round of this struggle against Nkrumah and became his bitter enemy.

The second reason for opposition to Nkrumah was that the policies which he pursued as Ghana's leader provoked resentment among his neighbours. The defining issue here was his stance towards the major international issue affecting Africa in the early 1960s, the **Congo Crisis**. This began in July 1960 when, shortly after the granting of independence, Belgian troops unleashed a unilateral military intervention to suppress a mutiny by the Congolese army, while almost simultaneously the copper-rich southern province of Katanga announced its secession. In order to defend itself against this double-pronged attack, the Congo government of Patrice Lumumba appealed to the **United Nations (UN)** for assistance. This was granted and the Belgians were persuaded to withdraw, but the UN then proved reluctant to assist with the defeat of Katanga. Exasperated by this attitude, Lumumba made overtures to the Soviet Union for support, but in doing so he signed his own death warrant, for in January 1961, as the Congo slid into full-scale civil war, he was assassinated by a coalition of both domestic and international conservative forces. The Congo Crisis then dragged on for a further two years until the Katangan secession was ended.

CONGO CRISIS

The civil war that took place in the Congo (the former Belgian Congo) from 1960 to 1963. The crisis was caused largely by the attempt of the copper-rich province of Katanga to secede from Congo. The secession was defeated eventually by a UN force, but in the process there were scares that the dilatory UN response would lead the Congolese government to turn to the Soviet Union for support.

UNITED NATIONS (UN)

An international organization established after the Second World War to replace the League of Nations. Since its establishment in 1945, its membership has grown to 192 countries.

ORGANIZATION OF AFRICAN UNITY (OAU)

The organization of African states founded in Addis Ababa in 1963. It has upheld the territorial status quo in Africa and acted in the 1960s and 1970s as an important forum for attacks on colonialism. At the July 2002 Durban Summit the OAU was formally disbanded and became the African Union (AU).

The significance of the Congo Crisis for African international politics was not so much that it brought the Cold War into the continent, for in 1960 the Soviet Union clearly lacked the capability to intervene effectively, but that it further radicalized those regimes that were appalled by the West's connivance in the ousting of Lumumba. Chief among these was Nkrumah, who had strongly backed Lumumba on the basis that they shared a common pan-African, socialist vision. Following Lumumba's assassination, Nkrumah's rhetoric became increasingly radical and confrontational, while reports circulated that Ghana was creating links with disaffected groups in other countries in order to promote the overthrow of their 'bourgeois governments'. For example, in January 1963 Ghana was implicated in the assassination of President Olympio of Togo. This naturally did little to widen the appeal of Nkrumah's pan-African vision, and even those, such as Nyerere, who sympathized with his agenda, advised him to adopt a more gradualist approach.

The final defeat for Nkrumah's pan-African schemes came in May 1963 with the holding of a conference of the independent African states in Addis Ababa, which agreed that rather than moving towards continental federation, the African states should become members of an **Organization of African Unity (OAU)**. While the name paid due respect to the ideals of pan-Africanism, the reality was that the OAU's main function was to uphold the status quo. Indeed, in 1964 the OAU passed a resolution pledging member states 'to respect the frontiers existing on their achievement of national liberation'. From this point on the pan-African dream faded, a process that was accelerated by Nkrumah's losing power in a coup in 1966.

Imperialism and 'White Rule' in Southern Africa

While the OAU supported the territorial status quo in Africa, it naturally took a more radical line in regard to the perpetuation of imperialism on the continent and the existence of white minority governments. Accordingly, it offered its support to the national liberation movements in these countries. By the early 1960s the areas concerned were mainly in southern Africa, consisting of two Portuguese colonies, Angola and Mozambique, South Africa and its satellite, South-West Africa, and Rhodesia. The only important exception was Portuguese Guinea (Guinea-Bissau) in West Africa.

The strongest and most significant of these states was South Africa. The Union of South Africa had become an independent state within the

British Empire in 1910. Its political life was, ironically, dominated by the very people whom Britain had defeated in the Boer War, the **Afrikaners**. Imbued with racist ideas of white supremacy and the desire to concentrate South Africa's mineral wealth in white hands, the Afrikaners had long supported the idea of racial segregation and of using the black population as nothing more than a cheap migrant labour force in the mines and factories. For example, in 1913 the Native Land Act forbade the purchase or lease of land by Africans outside certain reserved areas, while in 1923 municipalities were given the right to segregate Africans from Europeans. In 1948, in the wake of the wartime expansion of black labour in urban areas, a rise in worker militancy and black political agitation for equal rights, a more radical government took power under the leadership of D. F. Malan. The National Party, which Malan headed, won the 1948 elections on a programme of introducing apartheid (the separate development of the races). The idea behind apartheid was to safeguard white control of the country by vastly increasing the degree of segregation in South Africa. This was accomplished in the following years by banning mixed marriages and sexual relationships, introducing separate residential districts and amenities, controlling the movements of all blacks, Indians and coloureds, and giving limited autonomy to black rural homelands, dubbed 'Bantustans'.

At first, apartheid won the support of only a minority of the white population, mainly Afrikaners, but over time it widened its appeal. One reason for this was that apartheid all too predictably provoked resistance by the black population, which under the leadership of the African National Congress (ANC) became increasingly militant. In 1961, following the killing of sixty-seven black demonstrators at Sharpeville near Johannesburg, the ANC adopted a policy of armed struggle, which led to a number of acts of sabotage. The government reacted by introducing a security clampdown, and by 1964 a number of senior ANC figures, including Nelson Mandela, the head of the movement's armed wing, had been imprisoned. The rise in political violence, along with the fact that much of Africa was either already, or in the process of coming, under black majority rule, created a sense that the state was under siege. Accordingly, those of British descent now came to accept apartheid as the only guarantee of their security and continued social privilege. In addition, apartheid won support because it delivered sustained economic prosperity for the whole of the white population. During the 1960s the South African economy grew at 5 per cent per annum as it rapidly developed **import substitution** industries. Assisting this process was a rich flow of capital investment from Britain and the United States, which was in itself a sign

AFRIKANERS

The white population in South Africa who are of Dutch descent, also known as Boers.

IMPORT SUBSTITUTION

The process whereby a state attempts to achieve economic growth by raising protective tariffs to keep out imports and replacing them with indigenously produced goods.

AUTARKY

A policy that aims at achieving national economic self-sufficiency. It is commonly associated with the economic programmes espoused by Germany, Italy and Japan in the 1930s and 1940s.

NORTH ATLANTIC TREATY ORGANIZATION (NATO)

Established by the North Atlantic Treaty (4 April 1949) signed by Belgium, Canada, Denmark, France, Great Britain, Iceland, Italy, Luxembourg, the Netherlands, Norway, Portugal and the United States. Greece and Turkey entered the alliance in 1952 and the Federal Republic of Germany in 1955. Spain became a full member in 1982. In 1999 the Czech Republic, Hungary and Poland joined in the first post-Cold War expansion, increasing the membership to nineteen countries.

of confidence in South Africa's future. Thus by the 1960s apartheid was no longer the policy of a militant Afrikaner minority, but had the support of a broad white coalition.

North of South Africa was another state—Rhodesia—that had much to lose from any shift towards black majority rule; indeed it unilaterally declared its independence from Britain in 1965 over exactly this issue. Faced with pressure from London to introduce a more equitable electoral system before independence could be granted, the government of Ian Smith decided that the only way to preserve white privilege was by going it alone. This was a risky policy, but the Smith regime survived, in part because the Labour government in Britain was loath to implement a military intervention against people of British descent, but also because the international sanctions introduced by the United Nations in 1966 were undermined by the support it received from South Africa and Portugal.

The last element in the white redoubt in southern Africa was the Portuguese Empire. That Portugal was able to survive as a colonial Power in Africa longer than Britain, France and Belgium might seem surprising. This, however, was based on the fact that, unlike the other imperial Powers, Portugal was an autocracy which, under the leadership of António de Oliveira Salazar, had developed an **autarkic** economy that was largely based on trade with its colonies. The Salazar regime thus relied on continued control over its African possessions and was willing to pay the necessary blood-price to hold on to them.

That the states still under white domination were neighbours was clearly a vital element in their ability to resist the 'wind of change' sweeping across the continent, but, in addition, they were bolstered by the fact that they could take advantage of their value to the West. Portugal was a member of **NATO** and, moreover, controlled the Azores in the mid-Atlantic, where the United States maintained extremely valuable air and naval bases. Salazar was therefore able to blunt American criticism by threatening to withdraw access to these facilities. South Africa was not a member of any Cold War alliance, but its virulent anticommunism, its gold, diamond and uranium deposits, and its strategic position as the power that dominated the Cape route from Europe to Asia, meant that it too was in a good position to manipulate Western governments. Rhodesia was in a much weaker position, but even it was able to find some room for manoeuvre as a result of its position as one of the world's largest producers of chrome. Apart from the very practical ways in which these states used their assets to their own advantage, it has to be said that there also existed in the West some residual sympathy for these regimes, particularly among Republicans in the United States and the Conservative Party in Britain.

Convinced that there was no need to compromise with the forces of African nationalism and with the tacit support of the West protecting them from world opinion, the white governments in southern Africa resisted all calls for change. The result, not surprisingly, was that resistance manifested itself in the shape of armed struggle. This was very different from what had transpired in other regions of the continent, where, apart from Algeria and Kenya, the decolonization process had been remarkably peaceful. The need to resort to violence in the confrontation with imperialism in southern Africa was to have very important consequences, because the national liberation movements that emerged sought international sponsors for their wars of resistance. Unable to broker support from the West, some of them naturally inclined towards the Soviet bloc, thus helping to bring the Cold War into Africa.

The Cold War in Africa

In the wake of the transfer of power some of the new African states, including Ghana, Guinea, Mali, Congo (Brazzaville) and Tanzania, had adopted an overtly left-wing stance. Although this had caused some concern among the Western states, the international impact of the phenomenon was in the end fairly limited. One reason for this was that the new African leaders, having won independence, were determined not to replace one imperial master with another, and were therefore wary of becoming too close to Moscow. Underlining this point is the case of Guinea, whose leader, Sékou Touré, accepted Soviet technical aid in 1960, but then ordered the withdrawal of Soviet diplomatic personnel in 1961 after learning that they were in contact with his domestic opponents. Another important factor was that, although leaders such as Nkrumah and Nyerere were keen to introduce socialist-style planning for economic development, they were far from being orthodox Marxist-Leninists. Their ideas reflected instead what was loosely described as 'African socialism', which held little appeal to the ideologues in the Kremlin. Doubting the revolutionary potential of Africa and seeing it as a low global priority, the Soviet Union therefore diverted few of its resources to the continent, concentrating its efforts instead on winning over India and the radical Arab states. The main exception was the close relationship that developed between the Soviet Union and Somalia, which was prized for its naval facilities at Berbera. At the same time the United States saw Africa as being of little significance within the Cold War and felt that the former colonial Powers should take the primary responsibility for the continent's security.

The extension to southern Africa of the struggle against imperialism began to change this picture and force the superpowers to pay greater attention to Africa. This tendency began in the early 1960s, when national liberation struggles started in the Portuguese colonies with the appearance of the Liberation Front of Mozambique (FRELIMO) as the main party in Mozambique and of the National Front of Liberation of Angola (FNLA), the Popular Movement for the Liberation

PEOPLE'S REPUBLIC OF CHINA (PRC)

The official name of communist or mainland China. The PRC came into existence in 1949 under the leadership of Mao Zedong.

of Angola (MPLA) and the National Union for the Total Independence of Angola (UNITA) as contending voices of nationalism in Angola. From relatively early on both FRELIMO and the MPLA relied for much of their support on the communist bloc, and this pattern was mirrored in the case of South Africa, where the exiled ANC developed links with the Soviet Union, and in Rhodesia, where Joshua Nkomo's Zimbabwe African People's Union (ZAPU) followed the ANC's example, while Robert Mugabe's Zimbabwe African National Union (ZANU) was closer to the **People's Republic of China (PRC)**. Naturally the association of these parties with communist regimes alienated them from the political mainstream in the West, who saw them as nothing more than Soviet puppets. In reality, however, communist support did not initially bring these parties significant advantages, for the degree of military and political assistance provided by the Soviet Union, the PRC and Cuba was too insubstantial to make any serious impact.

This situation changed drastically in April 1974 when Salazar's successor, Marcello Caetano, was overthrown by a military coup. One of the major factors behind his ousting was that elements in the Portuguese army were determined to withdraw from the debilitating colonial wars in Africa. Consequently the new regime in Lisbon rapidly negotiated transfers of power in Guinea-Bissau, Mozambique and Angola. This in turn provoked a chain of events that led to increasing superpower intervention in Africa and the erosion of white rule in the south of the continent.

The most important of these events was the civil war that erupted in Angola. Under the January 1975 Alvor Agreement Angola was due to become independent in November of that year, while in the interim elections were to be held to determine the character of the new government. The problem was that the three leading political parties were unwilling to work together. Their mutual contempt in part reflected ideological differences, but was also shaped by tribal and ethnic animosities and by a simple hunger for power. The result of this inability to cooperate was that each party sought to strengthen its position by appealing to outside forces, the FNLA to Zaire and the United States, UNITA to South Africa and the United States, and the MPLA to Cuba and the Soviet Union.

Once the Angolan parties had generated foreign interest in their civil war, the fighting in the country quickly escalated. The first major foreign intervention came in October 1975 when South African forces invaded in order to prevent an MPLA victory. The danger that South Africa might assist the recently formed FNLA–UNITA coalition to seize Luanda led in turn to Cuba sending its own troops to support the MPLA. The United States interpreted the arrival of Cuban forces, which numbered 12,000 by early

1976, as a Soviet attempt to establish Angola as a client state, but it was not able to respond in kind as Congress refused to supply the appropriate funds. The result was that the Cuban troops, well equipped with Soviet weaponry, were able to assist the MPLA to defeat the South African and the FNLA–UNITA forces. Angola thus emerged on independence as a state with strong links to the communist bloc. Moreover, it threatened the wider security of southern Africa by offering support to SWAPO, the leading force fighting for the liberation of Namibia.

At the same time the regional balance of power was also being transformed by the appearance of a FRELIMO government in Mozambique, for this meant that Rhodesia was now bordered on three sides by hostile states. In particular ZANU, which was able to operate from Mozambique with the open support of FRELIMO, greatly benefited from this new environment. The subsequent escalation of the guerrilla war within Rhodesia and the possible encroachment of Cold War tensions transformed the situation in that country, and made the Smith government more susceptible to pressure from Britain and the United States for a political settlement that would deliver majority rule. Smith tried at first to avoid having to deal with the ZANU/ZAPU Patriotic Front by seeking an internal solution, by which in 1979 a moderate black political figure, Bishop Abel Muzorewa, formed a government. However, this solution, which retained many white privileges, was not acceptable to the Patriotic Front or to world opinion. Faced with a worsening security position, Rhodesia was finally forced at the Lancaster House talks in London in 1979 to agree to majority rule and in April 1980, after elections won by Robert Mugabe's ZANU, Zimbabwe came into being.

The spread of the Cold War was not limited to the southern part of the continent, for it also affected East Africa. In 1974 a coup in Ethiopia dethroned Emperor Haile Selassie. The new republic was controlled by a military council, the Dergue. This body espoused vaguely socialist ideas, but it came to rely increasingly on Marxist advisers as it introduced policies designed to modernize what was still a largely feudal country. This transformation was completed in 1977 with the emergence of Mengistu Haile Mariam as the key political figure. Ethiopia's shift to the left alienated the country's former patron, the United States, but attracted the interest of the Soviet Union, which believed that at last a truly Marxist-Leninist regime was emerging in Africa. Accordingly in 1977, when Somalia launched a war against Ethiopia to seize the province of Ogaden, whose population was ethnically Somali, the Soviet Union cut its ties with the Siad Barre regime in Mogadishu and began shipping large quantities of arms to Mengistu's government instead. In addition, in a repeat of events in Angola, some 10,000 Cuban troops arrived to assist in warding off the Somali challenge. Ethiopia thus became another Soviet client state. This in turn created the impression that communism was on the march in the continent, and raised the danger that the application of Marxist-Leninist ideas might be perceived within the continent as the best way for African states to achieve rapid economic development.

While the events of the middle to late 1970s suggested that Africa could be on the verge of being divided along Cold War lines, in the end the impact was less substantial. In part, this was because the Marxist regimes in Africa faced such severe domestic problems that it was impossible for them to export their beliefs to their neighbours. In the case of Ethiopia, the

COMECON

The Council for Mutual Economic Assistance, a Soviet-dominated economic organization founded in 1949 to co-ordinate economic strategy and trade within the communist world.

EUROPEAN ECONOMIC COMMUNITY (EEC)

Established by the Treaty of Rome 1957, the EEC became effective on 1 January 1958. Its initial members were Belgium, France, Italy, Luxembourg, the Netherlands and West Germany (now Germany); it was known informally as the Common Market. The EEC's aim was the eventual economic union of its member nations, ultimately leading to political union. It changed its name to the European Union in 1992.

radical land reform policy launched by the Mengistu government and its refusal to make any concessions to the secessionist movements in Eritrea and Tigre helped to spark a debilitating civil war, while Angola was beset by the continued resistance offered by UNITA, which was able to draw on support from the United States and South Africa. Another important constraint on the spread of communism was the fact that the West could still massively outbid the Soviet bloc in the provision of economic aid. The relative weakness of the Soviet position in Africa was graphically illustrated in 1980, when Mozambique's application to join **COMECON** was rejected on the grounds that it would prove too great a strain on that organization's resources. Desperate to find trading partners, Mozambique was forced to turn instead to the **EEC**, and negotiated its entry into the Lomé Convention agreement that regulated trade between the Community and African, Caribbean and Pacific countries.

The End of Apartheid in South Africa

The collapse of the Portuguese Empire not only heightened Africa's profile within the Cold War, but also had profound implications for the future of the apartheid regime in South Africa, which became more isolated than ever. With the buffer between it and Black Africa now removed, the South African government felt that its country was under siege by hostile forces linked to the Soviet Union. South African self-confidence was thus replaced by a restless sense of insecurity, which led it to introduce greater repression at home and to try to browbeat its neighbours into denying sanctuary to the ANC. Thus, South Africa steadily isolated itself even further from the international community, while turning its domestic politics into a powder keg.

In retrospect it can be said that the end of apartheid began in June 1976, when an uprising erupted in the black township of Soweto, outside Johannesburg, which was rapidly followed by protests, strikes and riots across the country. The primary causes of this upsurge in unrest were domestic factors, such as the rise of the Black Consciousness movement, the deteriorating economic conditions after the oil price hike of 1973 and anger at the attempt to introduce the compulsory learning of Afrikaans in black schools. It was therefore a largely spontaneous, indigenous phenomenon that had few direct links with the Soviet-backed ANC. However, the government in Pretoria saw these events through a Cold War prism, and thus believed that, rather than a sudden explosion of fury, it was the premeditated work of ANC agitators encouraged by news of the MPLA victory in Angola. Accordingly, the initial conclusion drawn from the Soweto uprising was that South Africa needed to toughen both its external and internal security policies. It was within this context that in 1977 the Black Consciousness leader Steve Biko was murdered while in police custody. South Africa's claim that its new campaign of repression was justified by the threat from communism did not, however, win much sympathy abroad, and in October 1977 the UN General Assembly introduced a mandatory embargo on arms sales with which even the United States and Britain complied.

Faced with international condemnation and a deteriorating security situation, the government of P. W. Botha, which took office in 1978, introduced limited reform of the apartheid system, removing some of its more objectionable, ideologically derived features in an attempt to appease its domestic and foreign critics. Thus labour laws were relaxed and the law banning mixed marriages was repealed. In addition, in the late 1970s and early 1980s a number of the Bantustan homelands were given nominal independence and in 1983 a new constitution was introduced which gave limited rights to coloureds and Indians. However, these steps were not enough to pacify black opinion or critics within the international community. From the mid-1980s the pressure on the Botha government escalated both at home and overseas. In 1985 a new wave of political mass action began, including outbreaks of violence, which soon forced the government to introduce a formal state of emergency over much of the country. Reflecting broad international distaste with the South African government, the US Congress in 1986 passed the Comprehensive Anti-Apartheid Act, overriding President Reagan's veto. The Act introduced sanctions against a wide range of South African goods and banned the export of oil products. Botha's government had no answer to its mounting problems, a point that was underlined when the prime minister's much touted 'Rubicon' speech of August 1985 emphatically rejected the idea of 'one man, one vote'.

The effect of the National Party's paralysis in the face of this worsening situation was that the white coalition which had sustained apartheid since its heyday in the 1950s and 1960s began to break up. In particular, faced with the fact that apartheid could no longer deliver economic prosperity or social order, the business community signalled its dissatisfaction by holding private talks with the ANC leadership. This change in attitude was reflected in the elections that took place in September 1989, shortly after Botha had passed the reins of power to F. W. de Klerk. In this election, for the first time since 1958, the National Party won less than half of the total votes cast, losing support both to liberals and to right-wing Afrikaner parties whose supporters felt that too much had already been conceded. Influenced by this disarray in white ranks and the unceasing violence in the black townships, de Klerk staggered his country and the world on 2 February 1990 by announcing the end of apartheid and the lifting of the ban on the ANC. Ten days later Mandela was freed from custody and South Africa began the tortuous road to its first democratic elections in 1994, which culminated in a sweeping ANC victory.

These dramatic changes in South Africa were rooted in domestic factors, which boiled down to the fear that apartheid was unsustainable and that if it collapsed involuntarily, it could lead to economic chaos and political violence on an unprecedented scale. However, the Cold War also had some influence on events, for it was arguably the Soviet Union's withdrawal from the Third World in the Gorbachev period that made the ANC acceptable as a potential government of South Africa. This was important for two constituencies that played a crucial role in the collapse of apartheid, namely the business community within South Africa and the countries, such as the United States, that tightened the sanctions noose from 1986 onwards. Thus, the de-escalation of the Cold War was important, because it created a new situation in which a shift towards black majority rule was not as terrifying a prospect for the white community and for America and its allies as it had once been.

The African State and the Legacy of Empire

While southern Africa moved towards decolonization and the end of white minority rule, the history of much of the rest of the continent from the early 1960s onwards was defined by the tasks of stimulating economic development and creating new nation-states from the colonial legacy that they had inherited from the Europeans. However, these proved not to be easy undertakings, and the euphoria generated by the granting of independence soon dissipated as the new states became mired in an apparently unending cycle of corruption and factionalism at best, and at worst descent into coups and civil wars.

To a considerable degree the problems that the new states faced were the result of the legacy of colonial rule, which created a number of obstacles to the establishment of effective government. One important factor that hindered development and the practice of good governance was the shortage of qualified professionals capable of providing key services. For example, on independence in 1961 Tanzania had two trained engineers and nine doctors for a population of nine million people, of whom 85 per cent were illiterate. The situation was similar in the Congo, which in 1960 contained only sixteen university graduates. While these shortcomings could be overcome by expanding university education and sending young men and women to study abroad, this solution took time to produce results, causing frustration among a population who had come to expect that independence meant the rapid extension of social provision.

More significant still was the very nature of the struggle for independence, which arguably had come too early for the good of the successor states. The independence movements that developed in Africa in the 1940s and 1950s tended to consist mainly of the educated classes from the urban population and the leaders of organized labour movements. Once it was clear that the drive for independence could not be suppressed, the colonial Powers came to collaborate with the nationalist elites in the belief that figures such as Nkrumah and Houphouët-Boigny could deliver a peaceful transition of power. In many ways these leaders appeared to offer a better prospect for the future than the traditionally minded tribal chiefs who had been dominant in the years of indirect rule, for men such as Nkrumah had been educated in the West and were seen as aspiring to create modern states based on constitutional government, the rule of law and a rational approach to economic planning.

The problem with this approach was that it was unduly optimistic. The newly independent states had no tradition of pluralist political institutions upon which to draw and were therefore all grossly ill prepared to act as parliamentary democracies. Indeed, the reality of the situation was that the political figures who took power on independence did not rely on well-organized political parties based on the Western model with roots in class identification. Rather they looked to support from regional, tribal and familial groups linked to them by ties of patronage that had developed under colonial rule. Patron–client relations had been vital in the colonial era, because in this period the best way to get access to jobs and other privileges and to avoid tasks such as forced labour was to find a patron using one's tribal or family ties. However, there was naturally a cost involved for the client in this relationship, for the patron expected to be rewarded for his services with political support.

On independence, with the resources of the state now open to them, the irresistible temptation for the new leaders was to cement their rule by building on the patronage system. Thus, the members of their political parties and other supporters were rewarded with access to appointments in state-run organizations and to state funds and contracts as a means of ensuring their loyalty. This drift towards a position where 'clientelism' became the political norm was reinforced by the fact that the new leaders inherited the autocratic state apparatus that had underpinned colonial rule. This provided them with an all-too-effective means of silencing their opponents, meaning that effective peaceful opposition to the government became virtually impossible. The result was a steady drift towards the establishment of one-party states in which the civil service and party more or less merged and in which the state itself became the supreme patron. Accordingly, corruption became a normal part of political and bureaucratic activity; it was the price that had to be paid for loyalty. In some cases, such as Zaire (as the Congo was renamed in the early 1970s) under Mobutu Sese Seko, the looting of the state's resources became so huge that the regimes were described as 'kleptocracies'.

The rapid move away from parliamentary democracy towards a one-party state did not, however, mean that governments became all-powerful, for other obstacles inherited from the colonial era acted to frustrate their ambitions. One of the most important was that a key feature of the colonial period in Africa had been the propensity, particularly in British colonies, towards '**indirect rule**' as a form of governance. Indirect rule had been attractive because, by finding collaborators among tribal chiefs and allowing them to raise taxes and administer customary law, the colonial

INDIRECT RULE

The system whereby a colonial power delegates limited powers to indigenous institutions.

Powers did not have to direct scarce resources towards developing an administrative network to cover the sparsely populated rural peripheries of their territories. What proved convenient for the colonial Powers was less so for their successors, for the consequence of indirect rule was that the leaders of the newly independent states discovered that they had only tentative control over much of their respective countries, as the state apparatus tended to be underdeveloped in rural areas.

This had a number of dangerous ramifications. One of the most important was that the tribal chiefs who had benefited from indirect rule were loath to give up their privileges and, being able to draw on the tendency towards tribalism that had been cultivated in the colonial period, often set themselves up as alternative centres of power to the government. The position of such tribal groupings was a challenge for many African states. In some countries, such as Tanzania and Guinea, where a large number of tribes existed without any one predominating, the one-party state was able to take rapid action on independence to break tribal power, seeing this as a prerequisite for the creation of national unity. However, where large and powerful tribes existed, they could lead to perpetual instability.

One example of this phenomenon is Uganda, where before transferring power the British decided in the face of pressure from the kingdom of Buganda to establish a federal constitution that would allow the latter considerable autonomy. However, this arrangement proved to be a serious obstacle to nation-building and political stability. Accordingly, in 1967 President Milton Obote declared the existing situation to be unsustainable and introduced a new centralized constitution that gave the presidency sweeping powers. The result was a wave of Bagandan agitation, which culminated in 1971 with the tribal elders supporting the successful coup against Obote launched by Idi Amin. Amin then promptly followed his predecessor's centralizing policies, recognizing that this was the only way to maintain power. Uganda only escaped from this cycle of violence in 1986 when, following Amin's fall and Obote's disastrous second term, Bagandan peasants led by Yoweri Museveni launched their own rebellion against both their own elite and Obote's state. Meanwhile in Nigeria, the existence of three powerful tribal groupings, the Hausa, the Yoruba and the Ibo, rapidly led to problems that culminated in 1967 with the secession of the Ibo-dominated south-east of the country, which named itself Biafra. The Biafran War lasted for three bloody years until eventually the rebellion was broken.

Another important problem that was in part inherited from the colonial era was the urban–rural divide which appeared in many of the newly independent African states. The key difficulty here was that the European colonial states had tended to raise revenue through taxing trade rather than land. Accordingly, when the Europeans sought to encourage economic development in their colonies from the 1940s they had concentrated on the expansion of agricultural exports as a way of generating wealth. In particular, they had developed the use of marketing boards, which bought goods cheaply from farmers and then sold them on the world market for a considerable profit, which could be invested in development. This model had great appeal to the largely urban elites that took office on the transfer of power, for they saw the profits from cash crops as a way of creating capital for investment in import substitution industries.

Debating the African State

One of the key issues for historians of Africa when dealing with the period since the transfer of power is why so many African states have found it difficult to achieve political stability and sustained economic development. One school of thought that was particularly prevalent in conservative circles in the West in the 1970s was that the fault lay with the political elites in African states, who abused power and squandered development aid in order to enrich themselves and the cliques that had gathered around them. Accordingly, it was argued that the answer to Africa's problems was to reduce the state sector in the economy and let future development be shaped by market forces. While accepting that the exercise of power has been seriously flawed, other observers have noted that this tendency was not an arbitrary development, but rather one rooted in the legacy of colonial rule and the continuation of neo-colonialism. For example, David Fieldhouse has argued, in his *Black Africa 1945–80: Economic Decolonization and Arrested Development* (London, 1986), that one of the key errors committed by the new leaders was to continue the colonial policy of regulating the export of cash crops through marketing boards.

Other writers have gone even further in their analysis of the colonial state and the way in which it shaped the policies and politics of the new states. Crawford Young, in *The African Colonial State in Comparative Perspective* (New Haven, CT, 1994), has outlined the importance of the autocratic nature of the colonial state, arguing that this has played a crucial role in encouraging the centrality of the bureaucracy and intolerance of opposition. Conversely, Mahmood Mamdani, in *Citizen and Subject: Contemporary Africa and the Legacy of Late Colonialism* (Princeton, NJ, 1996), has argued that the legacy of colonialism was a weak rather than a strong state. Mamdani has pointed to the problems caused by indirect rule, which has helped to exacerbate the tendency towards tribalism in Africa and thus widened the urban–rural divide. Jeffrey Herbst, in *States and Power in Africa: Comparative Lessons in Authority and Control* (Princeton, NJ, 2000), has taken this idea even further, noting that state formation in Africa has been blighted by the problems caused by the difficulty of extending control over countries with relatively low population densities. This, in turn, has meant that the attempt to construct states in line with the traditional European model has been enormously problematical.

This proved to be a dangerous path to follow for, as both Ghana and Senegal discovered in the 1960s with their exports of cocoa and groundnuts respectively, one could not rely on a single cash crop to generate sufficient revenue to fund import substitution. In addition, the concentration of taxation on cash crops for export led to few funds being allocated to diversifying agricultural production for the domestic market and to general neglect of rural areas. The result was that governments lacked any political or economic incentive to develop such regions, and therefore areas of low population density saw little state activity. This reached its apogee in Zaire under Mobutu, where the state was reduced to the capital, Kinshasa, and the mineral-rich region of Katanga, whose population relied ironically on food imports rather than on domestically produced crops. It is thus not surprising that, in the 1990s, the country disintegrated into civil war.

Another unfortunate colonial legacy was that the state boundaries did not respect religious divisions. For example, a swath of countries bordering on the Sahara inherited states that contained both Muslims and Christians, and the different attitudes of these religions towards social and political questions only helped to exacerbate tribal and ethnic confrontations. This was one of the issues that caused problems in Nigeria, where the Hausa are followers of Islam. However, the difficulties were even greater in Sudan, where the religious divide led to a cycle of violence that has plagued the country ever since independence.

Other factors blighted the quest for stability and development. One important point to remember is that the promises made on independence were always unrealistic, for African states faced serious natural obstacles to any increase in agricultural production. These included poor soil quality and the inability to use draught animals because of the tsetse fly. Most serious of all, however, was the unreliability of the climate. In the 1970s the countries bordering on the Sahara saw food production hit by a series of drought years that set back some of the progress that had been made in the 1960s. African states were also, of course, prey to the problems that afflicted developing countries more broadly, including fluctuations in the world economy and the frequent changes in thinking among economists about development issues. For example, African states suffered badly from the debt crisis and the collapse of commodity prices in the 1980s, and were poorly placed to benefit from the **structural adjustment programmes** urged on them by the World Bank. They were also in many cases trapped in **neo-colonial** relationships with their former imperial masters, this particularly being the case for the former French colonies. This had some advantages in terms of ensured access to markets, but also perpetuated a relationship of dependency.

Even those states that possessed great mineral wealth did not necessarily do well. For example, oil-rich Nigeria, which saw its overseas earnings soar in the 1970s as a consequence of the **OPEC** oil price hike, did not use its new prosperity to fund a breakthrough in development. Instead, much of Nigeria's oil wealth was dissipated on the financing of imports for the urban population. Moreover, imagining that oil prices would remain high, in the late 1970s the government sought vast loans from Western banks in order to finance its plans for import substitution. This proved, however, to be a costly error of judgement, for when oil prices fell in the early 1980s, Nigeria found itself weighed down by its debt burden. However, it is worth noting that some resource-rich states did prosper: for example, Botswana with its vast diamond deposits has been able to ensure political stability and a rising standard of living. That these states have prospered while others with rich reserves of raw materials have not implies that the colonial inheritance cannot be used as a blanket excuse for Africa's current state, and that the quality of African leadership needs also to be studied. In addition, the fact that those African states with a long tradition of independence, such as Liberia and Ethiopia, have also suffered from severe political and economic problems suggests that the colonial legacy cannot explain everything.

Poverty, Resources and the Troubled Road to Democracy

The sense of increasing pessimism that had replaced the immediate post-independence euphoria did, however, begin to lift in the late 1980s and early 1990s. The victory of liberal democracy over socialist autocracy in the Cold War quickly emboldened opposition groups in Africa into demanding a shift away from the one-party state towards a more pluralistic political system. For example, in 1990 the first freely contested local elections were held in Algeria and in 1992 democracy returned to Ghana after a prolonged absence. Meanwhile, the end of the Cold War also helped to bring about the termination of the civil wars that had racked Angola and Mozambique since independence and sealed the fate of Mengistu's regime in Ethiopia. Above all, however, the new spirit of optimism in the continent was symbolized by South Africa's unexpectedly smooth transformation into a fully democratic state and by the statesmanship displayed by Nelson Mandela.

However, in a number of countries the shift towards democracy proved to be a false dawn. All too often the new leaders turned out to be just as corrupt as those who had been voted out of office. Another problem was that some opposition parties proved to be unacceptable to the established elite. For example, in Algeria in January 1992 the army stepped in to re-establish martial law in an effort to prevent the *Front Islamique du Salut* from winning the country's first free national election. This in turn sparked a savage civil war that lasted for the rest of the decade.

The most tragic case, and the one with the greatest consequences for those bordering upon it, was that of Rwanda. Ever since 1959, shortly before independence from Belgium in 1962, politics in Rwanda had been

STRUCTURAL ADJUSTMENT PROGRAMME

The idea propagated by the World Bank from the end of the 1970s which linked the provision of development aid to Third World states to the latter committing themselves to balanced budgets, austerity programmes and the sale of nationalized industries and property.

NEO-COLONIALISM

The process whereby a colonial power grants juridical independence to a colony, but nevertheless maintains *de facto* political and economic control.

ORGANIZATION OF PETROLEUM EXPORTING COUNTRIES (OPEC)

The organization founded in 1960 to represent the interests of the leading oil-producing states in the Third World.

dominated by the Hutu majority, with the Tutsi elite who had traditionally controlled the country being forced into either submission or exile. In the late 1980s economic problems caused by a rapidly increasing population, land pressure, declining commodity prices and anger at government corruption led to calls for the authoritarian Hutu government of President Juvenal Habyarimana to agree to multi-party elections. The apparent weakness of the Habyarimana regime, in turn, led the Rwandese Patriotic Front (RPF), a group of Tutsi exiles in Uganda, to launch an abortive invasion of the country in October 1990. While this invasion did not succeed, it did spur on the democracy movement, consisting of both Hutus and Tutsis, to increase its pressure on Habyarimana. Consequently, in 1992 Habyarimana was forced to form a coalition government and then in 1993 to sign the Aruya peace agreement with the RPF, which would allow the latter to become part of a transitional administration that would steer the country towards free elections.

At this point radicals within the Hutu elite decided to take violent action in order to ward off the threat of democracy and overcome the economic crisis by seizing Tutsi land and property. Utilizing the government propaganda machine and their own client networks, they inculcated among poor and unemployed Hutus a fervent hatred of the Tutsis, drawing on the memory of what was perceived as the latter's gratuitous repression prior to the breaking of their hold on power in 1959. The trigger for genocide came in April 1994, when following the assassination of Habyarimana, the Hutu extremists proceeded to carry out genocide against the Tutsi population and against Hutu moderates who supported the trend towards democracy. Over the next two months some 800,000 Tutsis, about 11 per cent of the total population of the country, were slaughtered.

The potential for genocidal violence in Rwanda was clear to anyone willing to observe the situation, but both before and during the events of the spring of 1994 the international community showed little interest or willingness to act. Indeed, such was the level of international inaction that the genocide in Rwanda soon spread to infect much of southern central Africa. To a substantial degree this occurred because the action taken by the Hutu extremists provoked the RPF into launching a new and this time successful invasion of Rwanda. Fearing Tutsi retribution, more than two million Hutu refugees fled into Tanzania, Burundi and Zaire, bringing disaster to the latter two countries. In Zaire the ensuing crisis was particularly serious, for the influx of refugees led to increasingly serious outbursts of inter-communal violence, particularly against Tutsis living in the eastern province of Kivu. Citing concern for this community, but also motivated by an interest in gaining access to Zaire's abundant raw materials, the Rwandan and Ugandan governments intervened by providing assistance to anti-Mobutu rebels led by Laurent Kabila.

The ensuing civil war brought about Mobutu's fall from power in 1997, but the nightmare was not yet over, for, soon after he gained power in Kinshasa, Kabila broke with his Rwandan and Ugandan backers. As a result the newly renamed Democratic Republic of Congo (DRC) became immersed in a prolonged and bitter conflict, in which rebels in the east of the country received armed support from Rwanda and Uganda, while Kabila himself turned to Angola, Zimbabwe and Namibia for military assistance. This escalation of the fighting into an international war once again arose largely out of the desire of the DRC's neighbours to gain access to its vast mineral wealth, which included coltan, a mineral vital in the production of mobile phones. The result was the bloodiest African conflict of the post-colonial period in which it is reckoned that more than three million people died. Eventually in January 2001 Laurent Kabila was assassinated. He was succeeded by his son, Joseph, who quickly acted to start talks with his father's political enemies. The result in July 2002 was a negotiated settlement that brought a measure of peace to the country, although violence continued to erupt periodically, particularly in the areas bordering on Uganda and Rwanda.

Competition for control over mineral wealth also led to conflict elsewhere in Africa. The worst case came in Sierra Leone. From 1991 rebels against the government in Freetown started to receive support from the warlord Charles Taylor, whose fiefdom in neighbouring Liberia bordered on the diamond-rich eastern provinces of Sierra Leone. This sparked a nine-year war that brought misery to both Liberia and Sierra Leone. At first, the international community distanced itself from this chaos, leaving the restoration of order to the neighbouring states in the region in the form of the Economic Community of West African States Monitoring Group (ECOMOG). ECOMOG, which in reality was a vehicle for Nigerian claims to be the regional hegemon, proved, however, to be incapable of bringing peace and found its forces dragged into the morass. In the end the hopeless anarchy in Sierra Leone and the inability of ECOMOG to restore order led in 2000 to a British intervention followed by the arrival of a large UN peacekeeping force, and soon after the rebels were defeated. Following on from this reverse of his fortunes, Taylor, who had prospered enormously from the diamond trade, was forced in 2003 to stand down as president of Liberia and peace finally returned to the two war-torn countries.

While some countries in Africa leaned towards becoming failed states, in other areas notable progress was achieved. For example, Botswana continued to act as a beacon of democracy, while Mozambique and Tanzania made rapid economic progress, achieving annual growth rates of 8 per cent and 5 per cent respectively. However, even in these areas of relative stability, problems still existed. The most serious was the rapid spread of AIDS/HIV. According to UN calculations, by 2000 there were 24.5 million people infected with the virus in Sub-Saharan Africa, with the rate of infection being particularly serious in the southern half of the continent. For example, in Botswana, 35 per cent of the population were believed to be infected. Another serious issue was that many of the African states still suffered from the high level of indebtedness inherited from the 1970s. This debt burden was hard to shake off, for the continuing fluctuations in commodity prices and the refusal of the West to accept free trade in agricultural production restricted the ability of African states to earn sufficient revenue from exports. What Africa needed therefore was for the West to agree both to a coherent programme of debt relief and to the reduction of subsidies to agriculture, particularly in the United States, Japan and the **European Union (EU)**.

However, in order to persuade the West that Africa was worth supporting, it was necessary for the continent's leading political figures to demonstrate that they were willing to act responsibly in the cause of development, thus banishing the image of corruption and ineptitude. An important move in this direction was made in 2001 with the launching of the New Partnership for African Development (NEPAD), which was the brainchild of the South African president, Thabo Mbeki. The

EUROPEAN UNION (EU)

A political and economic community of nations formed in 1992 in Maastricht by the signing of the Treaty on European Union (TEU). In addition to the agreements of the European Community, the EU incorporated two intergovernmental—or supranational—'pillars' that tie the member states of the EU together: one dealing with common foreign and security policy, and the other with legal affairs. The number of member states of the EU has expanded from twelve in 1992 to twenty-seven in 2007.

fifteen governments that signed the NEPAD agreement committed themselves to the pursuit of good governance, democracy and sound economic management and in return sought better terms of trade with the West allied to debt relief. To a degree, NEPAD met with a positive response in the West, but the rhetoric and promises made by leaders such as the US president, George W. Bush, and the UK prime minister, Tony Blair, at events such as the G-8 summit at Gleneagles in 2005 were frequently not matched by actions. In part, this was because Africa remained a low political priority but it also reflected the ingrained belief that many governments in Africa were simply not deserving of support. In particular, Mbeki himself was tarnished in Western eyes by his blindness to the causes of the AIDS epidemic in South Africa and by his unwillingness to criticize the increasingly harsh and inept government of Robert Mugabe in Zimbabwe.

Africa therefore continues to be plagued by the colonial legacy and its poor terms of trade with the West. While some success has been achieved in terms of the spread of democracy and higher economic growth, and while the continent has largely benefited from the emergence of South Africa as a significant voice within the international community, old and new problems ensure that progress remains fitful. Moreover, all too often Western governments and institutions either ignore or misunderstand Africa's problems.

Conclusion

In the second half of the twentieth century, Africa was shaped to a considerable degree by events and trends in international politics. Above all else, the most important was decolonization, in which, of course, Africans themselves played a vital role. However, the winning of independence was a long-drawn-out struggle, and as anti-colonialism failed to make headway into southern Africa in the 1960s it increasingly dragged the Cold War into the continent as well, as some of the national liberation movements in Angola, Mozambique, Zimbabwe and South Africa turned to Moscow and Beijing for support. During the 1970s and 1980s the Cold War shaped the struggle against both imperialism and white minority rule, in some cases hastening victory and in other areas, such as South Africa, acting to delay the end-game.

In the long run though, the effects of the Cold War were not as significant for the future of the continent as those of the colonial inheritance. It was the latter, above all, in the form of the inadequate preparations for transferring power, the consequences of indirect rule and the colonial approaches towards taxation and development, that shaped the problems which African leaders faced and unfortunately in many cases influenced the way in which they responded to these challenges. Moreover, at the international level it was the state boundaries that the imperial Powers had left behind which lay at the basis of the African states system, the short-lived attempt by Nkrumah and others to shake off this legacy failing miserably. Africa therefore may have freed itself from direct colonial rule, but it has still not shaken off the effects of what in most cases had only been a half-century of European domination.

Cold War and Globalization

Unintended Consequences

Bruce Mazlish

Present-day globalization is the result of many factors interacting with one another. Some observers look upon this result as foreordained, a teleological outcome. Others, and I number myself among them, see globalization as an unintended, yet logical, consequence of powerful forces all pushing in a discernible direction toward greatly increased interconnection and interdependence of peoples and societies.

In seeking to date the coming of globalization—or, really, new globalization, for, as we have seen, there have been previous episodes that could claim the name—much depends on the weight one gives to the various factors. Thus, a case can be made for new globalization starting in the 1950s, or the 1980s, or even the 1990s. What I think is incontestable is that while consciousness of globalization arose with the term, which appeared to emerge first in the 1960s, there are strong grounds for believing that the process itself must be viewed as arising initially during and post-World War II. With that granted, what I want to argue here is that the forcing house of globalization is to be found not only in the 1939–45 war, but also in the Cold War that succeeded it.

(1)

World War II, coming after World War I, was even more global in its nature than its predecessor. Its operations covered almost all parts of the world, even if in unequal fashion. The philosopher Karl Jaspers perceived this fact presciently in 1955, when he wrote: "It was the Second World War which first accorded full weight to the

Bruce Mazlish, "Cold War and Globalization: Unintended Consequences," *The New Global History,* pp. 25-33, 116-118. Copyright © 2006 by Taylor & Francis Group. Reprinted with permission.

contribution from everywhere, to the globe as a whole. The war in the Far East was just as serious as that in Europe. It was in point of fact the first real world war."[1] Thus the conflict of 1939 to 1945 served as an anticipation of some of what was to come under the later heading of globalization; it is a forerunner in military dress of the mobilization of the entire globe in a singular struggle.

There were many other important implications for globalization emerging from WW II. As a result of the Nazi horrors, the judicial road to international justice was broadened via the Nuremberg trials. Here the momentous shift from war crimes to crimes against humanity was made. Genocide was declared the defining feature. Genocide, however, was a limited operation. More important for the emerging globalization was the reification of people into Humanity, a transcending concept befitting the new world being created. People live in territories. Humanity is an abstraction whose abode is necessarily global. Henceforth, a constituency existed in ideal form—Humanity—whose coincidence with the globalization process was self-evident, and in whose name "local" decisions could be judged.[2]

The war also meant the destruction of Germany and Japan as great military powers, paving the way for the emergence of a bi-polar world made up of the two superpowers, the Soviet Union and the USA. None of this would have been possible, of course, if the world had still been divided up into areas dominated by the Axis and Allied powers. But with the field of competing states simplified, a major step could be taken toward a more unified world—once the Cold War ended with the removal of one of the superpowers. Needless to say, this was a long-drawn-out process, and was not really settled until 1991. But at that point, in principle, there was only "One World," with different countries having different weights to place in the scale of power, but that power exercised in a world that was global in nature.

First, however, there had to be the Cold War, to settle which of the superpowers would prevail. Their visions of the coming one world were very different. The Soviet version was construed in old-fashioned international terms—after all, Marxism was modeled on an International of the workers. Its success was presumably foreordained, as communism would spread by virtue of its superiority to a dying bourgeois order. Eventually, it would penetrate to all parts of the globe. There was no "plot" of expansionism, though the Soviet Union was not loath to push where it could. It could, however, or so it believed, afford to be patient, for History was on its side. In fact, the vision of the future unified world held by communists was vague. In the meantime, there were competing contestants—China as well as Russia, for example—as to who would lead the way to that utopia.

On the other side, the US pursued a strategy of containing the Soviets worldwide, while seeking to establish in the areas under its control a "free world" built on a "free market" and democratic institutions. The idea specifically was to rebuild Western Europe, which was done by means of the Marshall Plan, and thus to pin it on the side of the free world. Japan was to be so included by other means. Both were then to function, democratically, in an economic system, operating in terms of the Bretton Woods agreement and a number of international organizations, such as the World Bank, the International Monetary Fund (IMF), and the World

Trade Organization. Nominally free, a closer look shows that this entire system was largely dominated by the USA.[3]

Whatever America's intentions, however, the world began to spin out of its control. Favored by the economic aspects of globalization, pioneered and led by the United States, the glimmerings of a global civil society emerged during the 1960s and 1970s. Once the US perceived this emergence, it began to throw its weight against it, leading to the later rejection of Kyoto, the land mines treaty, the International Criminal Court, and other such initiatives.[4]

Nevertheless, as we can now see, it was the Cold War struggle between two superpowers in the midst of a process of globalization that became the *sine qua non* for the continuation of that process. In 1940, at the beginning of World War II, Wendell Wilkie ran for president on the Republican ticket, on a platform of "One World," the name of his book. He was unexpectedly prescient. Though it took a number of decades during which the world was semi-globalized, i.e., split over the competing visions of the Soviet Union and the USA, the end result was indeed a one world of sorts, created in the image of the American dream. As it turned out, however, little recognition was given by American administrations to the fact that the world had changed and become global. Or, when dimly aware that the ideological pursuit of the free market had helped create something new and different, resort was to be had to an American Empire rather than a global society.

(2)

We need now to go into greater detail and to retreat a bit in our thinking, going back to World War II and then the Cold War as the cradle of globalization. During World War II itself, two new technologies were developed with major implications for the transcending of national boundaries. One, of course, was the development of nuclear weapons. With the bombing of Nagasaki and Hiroshima, a force was introduced into the world with the potential to destroy all or most of humanity. Clearly, its use overstepped traditional boundaries and left the nation-state in the position of being unable to defend itself against this threat. Even a "local" use of nuclear in the form of energy could erupt past lines on the map, as was illustrated by Chernobyl, and "invade" its neighbors. Nuclear technology, in short, was by nature a global force.

Equally significant was the development of rockets during the war, especially at first by Germany. After hostilities ceased, these quickly led to the development of missiles (which, of course, could carry nuclear warheads) and to the exploration of outer space. When "Mankind" launched itself beyond the planetary atmosphere, it embarked upon a revolutionary step that had both philosophical and practical consequences of enormous importance. In terms of philosophy, it meant that, at the most extreme, *Homo sapiens* had become, so to speak, a new species. If a lion acquired wings, would we not classify it as a new species? With human beings, of course, we don't think in this way; yet it is not clear why we should not. The main reason we do not in fact do so is that human beings, unlike the mythical lion we have conjured up, can take off their "wings" and put them on again. Evolving into a prosthetic god, the human remains the same at the same time as "it" evolves.[5]

More easily graspable is that the step into space has fostered a new consciousness. As we look back from the space craft in which we are speeding to the moon, we see the blue planet behind us as "spaceship earth," as R. Buckminster Fuller put it. Airplanes before this had allowed us to see portions of the earth from on high. Only out in space, however, can we actually see the full earth, spinning in its orbit, as we orbit far above it. This is a global vision, and enhances the consciousness we have of how globalization requires a changed mentality. Like the implied species change spoken of earlier, this philosophical development is a late product of what had happened during the war of 1939–45.

With the mutation of that war into the Cold War of the succeeding years, both nuclear and ballistic missile development proceeded apace. The coming of the hydrogen bomb, the launch of Sputnik, the US response, and the leapfrogging that took place subsequently in these areas meant a weapons race that increasingly was fought out in terms of space—outer space. Such space transcended the national sovereignties involved and has to be thought of more and more as global. In this view, "World" War II recedes into a local happening that is largely a preliminary to the spatial expansion of conflict that we call the Cold War.[6]

Two other technical developments are central to the emergence of the present-day globalization process. One is the lofting into the sky of satellites, foreshadowed by Sputnik. These made possible an enormous compression of space-time, so that real-time exchanges became possible, superseding anything previously accomplished by telegraph, telephone, or radio. Again, the impact on consciousness was deep and pervasive even when unconsciously so. More immediately, the satellites, allowing for instantaneous communication, greatly facilitated the growth of MNCs and NGOs. Both exhibit a lift-off after World War II that takes the shape of a J curve, as we will see in more detail in later chapters. Both, of course, are defining agents in the globalization process with which we are concerned.

Add to this the development of computers, the so-called computer revolution. Although already foreshadowed in the nineteenth-century work of Charles Babbage and his difference engine, the development took a quantum jump in the course of the world war (for example, in terms of encryption devices) and especially in the immediate aftermath. Financed by the US Defense Department, under the heading of ARPANET, which went on-line in 1969, this development became the seedbed for the establishment of the World Wide Web and the global network it makes possible. ARPANET, in fact, was an accident, in the sense that the military felt it had to have decentralized computer facilities, with the unexpected result that the computer networks were "free."[7]

(3)

Much of what I have just spoken about concerns technology or technology-related developments that made possible greater globalization. Other factors are more political. One of great importance is anti-colonialism. World War II made the assertion of independence by former European colonies feasible in a new way. Quick to take advantage of the situation was, for example, India, followed rapidly by Indo-China, and then Algeria, to name just a few. This breakdown of empire was called by General George S. Marshall a "world revolution," and so it was.[8]

The end of colonial status for many peoples was requisite for a global world of juridical equals. (In reality, of course, some nations were more equal than others.) It allowed for a United Nations that grew from 60 or so nations to around 190 at the turn of the millennium. Before going on further about that development, let us stick with decolonization. This last must be linked to the emergence of what was called the Third World. Though I have been speaking about a bi-polar world preceding a One World, during the Cold War of the superpowers an intermediate space seemed to open between them. The result, of course, was fierce competition between the Soviet Union and the USA for their allegiance. Each decolonized country was seen as a military base to be denied to the rivals in the superpower conflict, or as a source of raw materials, such as oil. Only with the end of the Cold War and the US triumph has the notion of a Third World faded away. In the resultant globalized world it has been replaced by a North–South divide. Such a divide, however, takes place in a One World or facsimile thereof.

Before leaving this aspect of our subject, we need to recognize that the war taking place during the 1950s to 1980s was "cold" only in regard to the two superpowers. In fact, a "hot" war raged on non-US or Soviet soil consisting of about 149 localized wars, resulting in about 23 million deaths. It is these wars that led some, including the Mexican Subcomandante Marcos, to argue that the Cold War should be renamed the "Third World War," fought out by the superpowers in that third part of the globe.[9]

Yet another part of the Cold War struggle saw the projection of military power in terms of American bases in Germany, Japan, and South Korea, to be matched by the Soviets in Eastern Europe, Cuba, Angola, and other places. Another piece of the puzzle wherein we discern the dismantling of a bi-polar into a single world has to be the impact of this competition on the Soviet Union, contributing to its demise. A case can be made that the Soviet Union, geared as it was to an industrialized world, could not make the transition to an information society.[10] This failure contributed to the move to a greater globalized world than the one that had helped undo the Soviet empire.

The markers on that decline and fall can be seen in the Helsinki Accord of 1975, and the subsequent proliferation of NGOs in Eastern Europe, the rise of Solidarity, and so forth, all features of the expanding globalization process. Or at least aided by it. While clearly so momentous a development as the collapse of communism in the Soviet Union cannot be explained in terms of single-factor causality, the pressure of globalization must be recognized as an essential element.

(4)

In history's strange movements we can also glimpse how the Soviets' invasion of Afghanistan in 1979 was both part of its Cold War rivalry with the USA and a major contributing factor to the rise of a post-Cold War version of globalization: Global (or Globalizing) Islam. As can be seen, particular decisions have general consequences. The Soviet move to expand its presence and power evoked an American response. The US decided to support and arm radical Islamists as they waged a jihad against the spread of Soviet communism in their country. The American move was part of its containment policy, with momentous and paradoxical results.

First, the Soviet side of the matter. Between 1979 and 1989, when the Soviets withdrew in a debacle that undermined its strength at home as much as abroad, hundreds of thousands of Afghans were killed and many millions displaced. Vietnam had been a similar disaster for the USA, but did not effectively call into question the legitimacy of the governmental regime (not the same as the administration) that was behind the debacle. In Russia the case was more extreme; the failed invasion and humiliating retreat were factors in the collapse of empire in Eastern Europe and within two years of the Soviet empire itself. The Cold War was over, the USA the winner.

Paradoxically, however, the victory was pregnant with future battles and threats. With the Soviets gone from Afghanistan, the Taliban took over. The jihadists now became America's Frankenstein, picking up where the Soviets had left off in their opposition to globalization in the form of "Western" values, power, and influence. Fundamentalist Islam now asserted itself as a global contender. Its jihad fighters, having honed their skills in Afghanistan, turned their attentions more and more not just to the Middle East but to the whole world. In fact, as globalization fostered migrations of Muslims into the Western countries, they were perceived by some as an internal threat, a kind of Trojan horse. The US, drawn into Afghanistan, but now with its own forces as well as its Afghan alliances, has become responsible for providing security to over 25 million people—and to nation-building (that it has been doing this badly and irresponsibly does not alter the fact).[11]

Meanwhile, local jihad has turned into global jihad. Osama bin Laden's Al-Qaeda has morphed into other shapes and with other leaders. Its followers' destruction of the World Trade Center in New York in 2001 carries great symbolic meaning, as well as wide-ranging security and economic costs, not to mention the way in which the death and destruction gave new life to the otherwise declining fortunes of the George W. Bush administration. The consequences of 9/11 are far-ranging and only briefly glimpsed at the moment. We must settle here for a simple pointer to what must be studied carefully and in detail [...]. What can be seen clearly is how the Cold War helped spawn a new variant of globalization, Global Islam, one that now interacts with all the other factors of the new globalization being produced after World War II.

(5)

Having been diverted, via decolonization, the appearance of a Third World, the impact of globalization on the Soviet Union, and, finally, the Soviet invasion of Afghanistan leading to the unexpected fostering of Global Islam, we can now return to the UN as it emerges from World War II and into the period of the Cold War. As I have remarked, from the beginning the organization has had a split personality. It was the creature of sovereign nations, whose sovereignty it was to protect from aggression, and thus ensure a peaceful world. In this aspect of its being it was a continuation of post-World War I's dedication to inviolable nation-states, all theoretically gathered in a League.[12] As such the UN is an international organization, not a global one. It has another side, however, manifest in the Declaration of Human Rights. Its preamble speaks of peoples, not states. Its mandate to protect humanity encourages the UN when necessary to "violate" national sovereignty. Thus, the Declaration points the organization in a global direction.

The UN, of course, also became the site of the Cold War contestation. The Soviet Union and the US both tried to control the votes of the so-called nonaligned states, most of them newly decolonized, and to influence "world opinion" by incessant maneuvering over votes and positions increasingly oriented to globalizing tendencies. Neither was prepared to give up its veto in the Security Council (nor were the other three members), nor any erosion of what it took to be its sovereign national rights. Yet, inexorably it seems, the pressures involved in the Declaration of Human Rights and in various agencies of the UN pushed the globalization process forward.

Thus, the UN, a product of World War II and a site of contestation in the Cold War, must be numbered among the numerous factors we have been noting as fostering the globalization process. It almost seems as if everything—technological and economic developments, national and international decisions, movements of consciousness—was moving, in to and fro fashion, toward a single end. This is misleading in many ways—little or none of this was intentional—but it does add up as if to a predetermined pathway. As I remarked earlier, one must be careful and not mistake tendencies for teleologies, nor a present development for an assured one. One must be equally careful, however, not to miss the drift of events.

In earlier centuries, appeal was had to God, or Providence, or an invisible hand to explain what I am calling the drift of events. It is worth detouring for a moment to give depth to this idea. Thus, in his *Natural Theology* (1802), the Reverend William Paley wrote: "Those actions of animals which we refer to instinct, are not gone about with any view to their consequences ... but are pursued for the sake of gratification alone; what does all this prove, but that the prospection [that is, knowledge of ultimate benefit], which must be somewhere, is not in the animal, but in the Creator?"[13] Elsewhere, Paley uses the phrase "invisible hand."

We can take this quotation in two directions. One is to Darwin, who read Paley carefully, and who substituted the theory of evolution by natural selection for the Creator, thus leaving us with a secular explanation of how things unfold. In Darwin's story, there is no intention, no teleology, in nature, only the mechanism of survival of the fittest. What direction, if any, this leads in is a matter of much contestation, with some biologists alleging a movement toward greater diversity and complexity of creatures and others denying any such thing. I myself believe that evolutionary theory must be the backdrop for any explanation regarding human behavior, but cannot be directly applied to humans and their historical journey because humans do have conscious intentions.

We must go back before Paley and Darwin for other inspirations as we attempt to understand human evolution. The phrase "invisible hand" takes us to Adam Smith, of course, for his transmutation of this idea into that of market mechanisms—laws of supply and demand—and to the less precise idea of what he calls the "silent revolution," which brought about the shift in Europe from feudal society to commercial society. It is, as he tells us, the result of peddlers wishing to turn a penny profit, and noblemen bartering away their landed strength in order to purchase baubles and trinkets. Thus an event of the greatest importance was a result of what Smith recognized as the working of the mechanism of unintended consequences.

Even before Smith, a fellow Scotsman, Adam Ferguson, had grasped the idea clearly and forcefully. In his *Essay on the History of Civil Society* (1767), we find a passage such as the following: "Like the winds that come we know not whence, and blow whithersoever they list, the forms of society are derived from an obscure and distant origin; they arise ... from the instincts, not from the speculations, of men. ... Every step and every movement of the multitude, even in what are termed enlightened ages, are made with equal blindness to the future; and nations stumble upon establishments, which are indeed the result of human action, but not the execution of any human design."[14]

One such "establishment," I am arguing, is globalization. It has come about, and is coming about, from human actions, only a small number of which are intentional about global society as an end, but most of which are rooted in other human designs. My argument, therefore, is that globalization is an unintended consequence, which is nevertheless to be understood as the consequence of numerous factors, such as those I have tried to outline above.

One of these factors has been World War II and the Cold War that followed upon it. For many historians war is such an unpleasant fact of life that they prefer to ignore its role in history. Ferguson would have none of this view. In fact, his theory of civil society is predicated on the belief that conflict among nations, including war, is requisite for social bonding and civic well-being. It is animosity that brings about national cohesion.[15] There is much evidence in support of this view, especially in an age of nation-states and more recently the ethnic and religious struggles that swirl around them.

For better and worse, war has been a mother of invention, and of unintended consequences. It is this view that I have been applying to my analysis of the Cold War and globalization. One of the "inventions" emerging from that war has been an intense drift toward globalization, which has as one of its aims the abolition of war as such, with ironically the Cold War as one factor in this drift. If humanity does not destroy itself in the process of pursuing its instinctual ends, one of the paradoxical consequences may well be a profound change in the conditions of human social bonding. In a possible global civil society, other ties than those created by enmity and war with "others" may be in the process of being created. In place of the Creator spoken about in previous epochs we have unintended consequences converging in a particular direction and acting as the *deus ex machina* of the global epoch.

Notes

1 Karl Jaspers, *Vom Ursprung und Ziel der Geschichte*, quoted in Martin Albrow, *The Global Age* (Stanford: Stanford University Press, 1997), 75.

2 A project seeking to deepen our understanding of Humanity as a concept emerging operationally out of WW II (philosophically, of course, there were predecessors) and as a tradition to be found in pre-WW II societies such as China, India, etc. is now underway. It is under the guidance of Zhong Longxi (City University of Hong Kong), Jorn Rusen (University of Bielefeld) and Bruce Mazlish (MIT).

3 For an interesting and provocative treatment of this development see Peter Gowan, *The Global Gamble: Washington's Faustian Bid for World Dominance* (London: Verso, 1999).

4 Cf. Chapter 6, "The Hijacking of Global Society."

5 For an extensive treatment of this aspect of *Homo sapiens*, see my book *The Fourth Discontinuity: The Co-evolution of Humans and Machines* (New Haven: Yale University Press, 1993). The thinking in that book stands in back of much of what I am saying here, although in a different vein.

6 An early and classic treatment of this space race is Walter A. McDougall, *The Heavens and the Earth: A Political History of the Space Age* (New York: Basic Books, 1985). It must be noted that nationalism did not fully retreat from outer space. When the American flag was planted on the moon, it was an anachronism, recalling the placing of flags on earth sites such as the New World in the fifteenth century and the South Sea islands in the eighteenth century. More ominous today are the plans, especially by the USA, to "militarize" space.

7 Extremely useful in understanding these developments is Manuel Castells, *The Rise of the Network Society*, op. cit.

8 Quoted in Matthew Connelly, *A Diplomatic Revolution: Algeria's Fight for Independence and the Origins of the Post-Cold War Era* (Oxford: Oxford University Press, 2002), 27.

9 Quoted in the very interesting article by Fernando Coronil, "Towards a Critique of Globalcentrism: Speculations on Capitalism's Nature," *Public Culture* vol. 12, no. 2, (2000), 359. His argument, as he explains, is that "dominant discourses of globalization constitute a circuitous modality of Occidentalism that operates through the occlusion rather than the affirmation of the radical difference between the West and its Others," p. 354. For anyone interested in the question of whether globalization is simply a new form of imperialism, Coronil's article is essential reading; it also offers an astute qualification to my analysis of globalization. In the end, however, he softens his criticism and declares

that: "A critique that demystifies globalization's universalistic claims but recognizes its liberatory potential may make less tolerable capitalism's destruction of nature and degradation of human lives and, in the same breath, expand the spaces where alternative visions of humanity are imagined." (370) Another article by Coronil, "Beyond Occidentalism: Toward Nonimperial Geohistorical Categories," *Cultural Anthropology*, vol. 11, no. 1 (Feb. 1996), offers an important reading of the effects of globalization on the self. His is a voice that needs very much to be heard in the debates over globalization. A relevant article is my own "Edward Said: The Colonial Spirit in a Globalizing World," *The Discourse of Sociological Practice*, vol. 7, nos. 1 and 2 (Spring/Fall 2005).

10 Cf. Charles S. Maier, "The Collapse of Communism: Approaches for a Future History," *History Workshop Journal*, vol. 31 (1991), 34–59.

11 An interesting account is given in Pankaj Mishra, "The Real Afghanistan," *New York Review of Books*, March 10, 2005, 44–8.

12 Such a dedication is generally attributed to Woodrow Wilson. As Erez Manela of Harvard University points out, however, Wilson's own initial draft of Article III "diluted the concept of inviolable sovereignty to the point of irrelevance." In the final text, as incorporated in Article X, the "preservation, even freezing, of the international status-quo" was reinstated by other hands. I owe this illumination of Wilson's actual position, and the quotes supporting it, to a personal communication from Professor Manela as well as to his article "A Man ahead of His Time?," *International Journal* (Autumn 2005).

13 Quoted in Stephen Jay Gould, "Darwin and Paley Meet the Invisible Hand," *Natural History*, vol. 11 (1990), p. 8.

14 Quoted in Fania Oz-Salzberger, "Civil Society in the Scottish Enlightenment," in *Civil Society: History and Possibilities*, ed. Sudipta Kaviraj and Sunil Khilnani (Cambridge: Cambridge University Press, 2001), 69–70.

15 Cf. Kaviraj and Khilnani, 72–3.

Discussion Questions

Recovery Through Nationalism: The "Have-Nots," 1933–1936

1. How did the National Socialist ideology of Adolf Hitler and his party differ from Marxist socialism?

2. How did Nazism differ from other reformist movements in the US and Britain during the 1930s? Give some specific examples of these differences.

3. What was needed to achieve Hitler's goal of self-sufficiency? Why did he want to achieve this for Germany?

4. How did economic recovery during the global Great Depression play into Hitler's plans for German resurgence? Did it work? Why or why not?

5. What similarities does the author highlight between German National Socialism and Japanese ultranationalist ideology? Discuss at least two similarities in some detail.

6. What role did economic recovery play in Japan's post-Great Depression expansion plans? How did other world powers in the West respond?

7. How did Japan's trade policy relate to its expansion policy in the 1930s?

8. How did Fascist Italy respond to the Great Depression? Was their response similar to or different from the responses of Japan and Germany? Explain.

The Chinese Civil War and European Cold War, 1945–9

1. In what shape was the Chinese Nationalist government by the end of World War II? Why?

2. In what shape was the Chinese Communist Party by the end of World War II? Why?

3. What was the state of relations between the Chinese Nationalists and the Communist Party as of mid-1945?

4. Explain the onset of the Chinese Civil War in the mid-1940s. Provide details.

5. What role did the United States play in the Chinese Civil War? Why? What do you think of the role the Americans played? Was it appropriate given the global situation in the late 1940s?

6. What role did the Soviet Union play in the Chinese Civil War? Why? What do you think of the role the Soviets played? Was it appropriate, given the global situation in the late 1940s?

7. How did the relationships between the United States and the Chinese Communist Party, and between the Soviet Union and the Chinese Communists, change after Mao's forces were victorious in 1949?

8. What do you think of the "lost chance" theory of a better relationship between Mao's China and the United States, as described by the author? Does it have merit? Why or why not?

9. What do you think of the "no chance" theory, that nothing would have improved the relationship between Mao's China and the US as described by the author? Does it have merit? Why or why not?

10. Which theory is more believable? How so? Use specific evidence for your answer.

The Cold War and Nationalism

1. According to the author, what were the three phases of the Cold War?

2. Why do "none of the orthodox accounts of the Cold War consider nationalism's importance"? Given what you know about nationalism's effects on world history in the century or so before 1946, does this lack of focus on nationalism make sense to you? Why or why not?

3. Explain the complicated state of post-World War II nationalism in the West that included some adherence to nationalist ideas but also some movement away from them.

4. How did universalism come to compete with nationalism during the Cold War? Explain.

5. Briefly summarize the history of universalism claims up to the start of the Cold War.

6. What does the author mean by "Super-Power Nationalism"?

7. How did the US, the Soviet Union, and Britain try to frame their lack of nationalism? How does the author argue against those claims? Do you agree? Why or why not?

Africa, Europe, and Asia in the Making of the Twentieth-Century Caribbean

1. What was one of the main ways Europeans made up for the loss of slave labor when emancipation occurred over the course of the 1800s?

2. How did the new indentured laborers brought to the Caribbean in the 1800s interact with local populations?

3. Briefly explain the linguistic situation in the modern Caribbean. How do *creole* languages fit into that picture?

4. Define the concepts of "survivals" (or "retentions") and "transculturation" discussed by the author.

5. According to the author, how do "races" and "colors" factor into Caribbean societies, both historically and more recently? What are some examples of the latter?

6. How do gender and kinship factor into Caribbean societies? How do they relate to each other in modern Caribbean societies?

7. How has religion historically developed in the Caribbean? What are some important elements of that development?

8. How is religion "one of the innumerable examples of the ways in which Africa, Europe, and Asia have together produced the twentieth-century Caribbean"? What are some other examples?

Africa: Decolonization and Independence, 1945–2007

1. How do the authors describe what they term the West's "prevailing image" of the African continent during the twentieth century? Why do they say that simplistic view is wrong?

2. What questions do the authors highlight as to why there have been persistent problems of poverty in Africa? Which questions seem most important to you? Why?

3. How did development lead to decolonization in the post-World War II era? Be specific.

4. How and why do the authors describe the "case of the Gold Coast [as] instructive"?

5. What are some examples of disastrous resistance to African nationalism by European colonial powers?

6. How do the authors define "Pan-Africanism"? How was it successful? How was it a failure?

7. What role did the global Cold War have in post-World War II Africa? Explain.

8. How did the Cold War relate to South African apartheid?

9. What are some notable legacies of Western imperialism in Africa?

10   How do the authors define "neocolonialism," and in what ways did it exist in Africa in the 1980s and beyond?

11   How have shifts toward democracy throughout Africa proved to be what the authors call "false dawn[s]"? How does the Rwandan genocide show this?

12   Do you agree with the authors' contention that colonialism's legacy has had a significantly bigger impact on Africa's development than the global Cold War? Why or why not?

Cold War and Globalization: Unintended Consequences

1   Where does the author chronologically situate the foundations of modern, or *new*, globalization? Do you agree? Why or why not?

2   How did World War II and its immediate aftermath set the stage for increased globalization?

3   How did the largely bipolar nature of the Cold War continue and strengthen globalization, but in a *semiglobalized* way?

4   In arguing for a globalizing world by the middle of the twentieth century, what technological and scientific elements does the author highlight? Is this argument convincing? Why or why not?

5   What political elements of the Cold War were important in bringing on greater globalization from the 1950s through the 1980s?

6   In what ways has what the author calls "Global (or Globalizing) Islam" factored into recent globalization? Does that argument make sense to you? Why or why not?

7   How has the United Nations fostered the process of globalization?

8   Do you agree with the author's ultimate contention that globalization is largely an "unintended consequence" of several human factors over the last seventy-five years or so? Why or why not?

CONCLUSION

The world we live in today has obviously been shaped by the last five-plus centuries, but the story of how we got from then to now is, without a doubt, complex. This anthology attempts to chart that progression from several angles, some likely very recognizable to many readers, others less so. While political and economic factors tend to dominate any discussion of world history—for perfectly defensible reasons—this book has blended those more commonly focused-upon themes with other themes such as of culture, society, and intellectual development.

In particular, the traditional religions of Africa and the disease environments of the early modern world are highlighted alongside the rise of Venice, Genoa, Spain, and the Ottoman Empire. Furthermore, from the European Scientific Revolution and Enlightenment to the Industrial Revolution and modern nationalism, various forms of progress have defined the transition to our modern world. On the other hand, much less positive aspects of modernity, such as new Western imperialism, global depression, world wars, and the Cold War, have similarly guided the development of the world we inhabit today.

It should come as little surprise, then, that modern globalization has proven to be so controversial. For all the good scientific and sociological progress have undoubtedly done, catastrophes of war, disease, economic depression, and nuclear proliferation have mostly if not completely countered those developments. But, lucky for us, our story is far from over. Where we go from here is up to us, and if the last half millennia has proven anything, it is that humans have the capacity for great things as much as (and hopefully more than) we have the capacity for destruction and evil.

CPSIA information can be obtained
at www.ICGtesting.com
Printed in the USA
LVHW021410201218
601100LV00001B/4